WOMEN
AND
JUDAISM

WOMEN
AND
JUDAISM

Myth, History, and Struggle

— ✿ —

Roslyn Lacks

Doubleday & Company, Inc.
GARDEN CITY, NEW YORK
1980

ISBN: 0-385-02313-8
Library of Congress Catalog Card Number 74-25113

To Jennifer, Daniel, and Julia—who are the future.

Contents

Author's Note

"Women in Judaism?" hooted Semitics scholar Theodore H. Gaster. "There aren't any!"

Here I was in the lounge of the nation's leading Reform rabbinical seminary, trying to come clean with the professor whose class I had illicitly attended all semester long. I had been invited to an early session by someone who knew how impressed I was with his work and simply kept coming back. The class was composed of eight male rabbinical students, one female rabbinical student in her senior year—Laura Geller, who went on to become a Hillel rabbi at the University of Southern California, one of more than twenty women rabbis serving in pulpits and college campuses across the United States; one female graduate student in Jewish education; and one female stowaway —me.

The term was nearly over, the professor was planning a final exam for each of us, and it was time for me to come clean—to admit that I was only a journalist who had been working on a book about the images of women in Judaism and beyond, and the impact of those images on the lives of men and women today.

What had impressed me about Gaster's work was his elegance of language, combined with genuine scholarship, and the capacity for original thought, laced with an iconoclastic streak. As a lecturer, he was a dramatic and volatile figure, a kind of elongated Charles Laughton, but with a delivery far more Cambridge than cockney, and a distinct flair for playing the *provocateur*.

"Aren't any," chuckled the eminent professor, sipping his late-morning tea.

"Not *in* Judaism," explained the stowaway journalist, "women *and* Judaism."

So much, at least, seemed possible.

Yet if anyone had suggested to me ten years ago that I would be here today, following so elusive and dense a trail, immersed in an area with which I had had little contact for more than twenty years, I would have judged him mad.

What curious conspiracy of temperament and circumstance had led me, then, to this?

To begin with, my grandparents, with whom as a first grandchild, I spent a good deal of time. My mother's parents, Zayde Yakov and Bubbe Jenny, were Orthodox Jews from Russia; my father's, Zayde Yisrael and Bubbe Gittel, were Hassidic Jews from Poland. Distant cousins, Zayde Yisrael and Bubbe Gittel married when he was sixteen and she was fifteen, and he went to live with her family in Lembourg, where Bubbe Gittel's father was *dayyan* (judge) in the Beit Din (Jewish Court of Law). My father was born the following year.

When Zayde Yisrael was eighteen, he and his father made a pilgrimage to the Belzer *rebbe* to ask his advice about emigrating to America. The Belzer *rebbe* advised against it. Zayde Yisrael evidently—and fortunately, as it later turned out—didn't listen. He emigrated to New York, via Montreal, with plans to send for my grandmother and father as soon as he had gotten his bearings and could make arrangements for them.

Meanwhile, World War I ravaged Lembourg, and Bubbe Gittel and my father had to flee to relatives in Warsaw. My father thus spent a good part of his childhood barricaded in the Warsaw ghetto during the last years of the war, the street fighting between Ukrainians and Poles that erupted shortly after, and the series of *pogroms* that followed. Yet nothing frightened him so much, my father once told me, as the thought of getting on a boat to come to America.

They arrived ten years after my grandfather. "It was strange," my father commented. Yet, of course, it was a pattern typical for immigrants of that era.

My mother and father met and married in New York. It was considered a kind of endogamous intermarriage destined for disaster. "A marriage between a Litvak and a Galizianer," neighbors warned, "impossible." But they didn't listen, either.

I was born the following year. "An accident," my mother explained. "Your father was still at City College and I was working as a bookkeeper. We didn't plan on having children for five years." When I periodically confronted her about endowing me with such peculiar status (an accident, indeed!), she was quick to take umbrage. "Who knew?" she would shrug. "We were just fooling around. . . ."

At any rate, my brother was born three years later, and we moved around a great deal until I was five when we settled—or so I thought—in an apartment in the Bronx in the same building as my mother's parents, Zayde Yakov and Bubbe Jenny, my Aunts Ida and Mollie, and my Uncle Leon. Since neither set of grandparents spoke English, I quickly learned to alternate between the Galician lilt of my father's parents, who now lived in Brooklyn, and the crisper Litvak intonations of my grandparents in the Bronx.

I spent a good deal of time in my grandparents' apartment, highlighted weekly by preparations for the Sabbath—Friday afternoon cleaning and scouring, food simmering on the stove, a special cloth for the Sabbath table, my grandmother reciting the prayer over the lighting of Sabbath candles, the blessings and the breaking of the braided challah, and the sharing of the meal.

Zayde Yakov enjoyed taking me to the synagogue with him, and I loved going—every Sabbath and all the holidays of the year. As a five- or six-year-old, I was permitted to sit downstairs with him and all the men. Occasionally, I would deliver messages from him to my grandmother seated above with the women in the balcony. They seemed worlds apart. Downstairs, bright with prayer and laughter, and the sacramental sipping of wine; upstairs dark, remote, and silent.

On weekday evenings, my grandfather taught me Yiddish from copies of the *Daily Forward* and a book called *Yingele Ringele,* detailing the adventures of a little boy, while my grandmother padded about in worn slippers serving us tea. My father provided my brother and me with more formal Hebrew lessons. My mother at that time found herself sufficiently occupied with caring for our newly born sister.

But all of this was after dark. Before dark and after school, we children were out in the street, playing ringolevio, stickball, jump rope, and all the games that are or were available on city streets. Biblical matriarchs are known for the sons they bear, and mothers in the Bronx were known only by the names of their children: "Butchie's mother, Sydelle's mother, Ruthie's mother" interrupting the sweet hours of play with calls from open windows advocating late-afternoon glasses of milk or admonitions to "come in before it rains."

"Why do they always wear housedresses and why are they so fat?" I once asked my mother.

"From having children," she tartly replied.

Married women, it turned out, had no time to primp and fuss, to wear high heels and flowered silk dresses and fragrances like "single" women—my Aunt Ida and a Cousin Naomi—did.

Small wonder I had confided to my grandfather at five that I did not plan to marry until forty so that I could travel first and see the world. The Bronx is its own educator.

And I was not alone. My best friend, Joyce, and I received inspiration from similar sources: the daring adventures of Wonder Woman, the nefarious pursuits of the Dragon Lady—the first to be emulated, the second, exposed and eradicated. Comic-strip figures whose prototypes go back through millennia.

After living in the Bronx for two years, I was sure we would be there forever; we had never before been in the same apartment for longer than a year. I was wrong. Not only were we going to change apartments, I learned at my favorite holiday of the year—the Passover seder—we were going to move out of New York—upstate to Albany. Or "Albania," as my mother initially introduced it to me, to avert the Evil Eye. And "Albania" was what I told my teachers at school, who politely wondered if I had not made some error.

So far as I was concerned, moving to Albany was the error. The first two years in that gloomy capital, I pretended that this was all a dream, and I would awake to find myself back in the

Bronx. When we returned for a visit, I was eleven, and went to find my old friends. Joyce had since moved, but others were still there. I had a strange accent they said, and did I want to go to the park to pick up boys? In Albany, the closest I had come to boys were chaperoned dances at the local "Y." Sure, I said, and eventually found myself uncomfortably circling Indian Lake deep in Crotona Park with a Yeshiva boy named Heschie, who threatened to pull down my bloomers. You Can't Go Home, et cetera.

Despite the distinctly European bearings of my family and those formative early years, by the time I was in my teens, I had totally embraced the American Dream and was dedicated to emulating the current plastic replica of the all-American girl —snub-nosed, shiny-haired, peppy, popular, and not too bright. My own nose did not happen to turn upward, though I diligently guided it in that direction before falling asleep each night. My tryouts for cheerleading proved more successful.

Outfitted in maroon and gray on crisp football afternoons, I enthusiastically cheered for Our Side—although I was nearly always myopically unsure of where it was.

In short, it was a kind of tangled adolescence, scarcely unusual for those of us who shared it in the fifties, in which scholarship for women was suddenly suspect—"boys didn't like smart girls" was the terrifying refrain that dictated our dumbness—although high academic standing (at least in my family) was taken for granted. My own temperament propelled me toward cheerleading and dance, theater and dating, sexual excitements and concomitant guilts.

While I dropped the cheerleading early in college, my involvement in acting and dance was more serious, and persisted when I moved to New York after college.

Those then were my early years in New York: occasional acting jobs (just barely enough to render me eligible for the unemployment line with my other colleagues), dance classes, acting workshops (of course, a method actress!), and low-rent apartments.

Somewhere along the way, I decided that I both needed and would profit from psychoanalysis, which quickly plummeted me into the necessity for entering a higher income bracket—even at one or two sessions a week. I could, after all, teach, the analyst pointed out (even painters need money for their materials), and that would provide me with a more regular salary than acting or the other odd jobs I picked up. I found every reason to say that I couldn't, but, in fact, finally did. The notion that I could both teach and look for work in the theater was illusion. After one semester in the nightmarish setting of a vocational high school to which I had been dispatched, I found myself retiring after school each day by crawling into bed and reading Henry James. Indeed, I think my survival at that point depended on alternating between the chaos of my daily life and the elegantly ordered world of Jamesian novels.

After a couple of years of this, I left for Europe with a friend and stayed as long as my money held out—painting, writing, and wandering about. On returning, of course I had to work again—at that dreadful high school that had driven me to James.

In November of that year, my mother called to tell me that Bubbe Jenny had died. I hadn't seen her in years—that tiny, frail woman whom I dimly remembered now in the balcony of the synagogue or sitting at the curtained window of her living room, *siddur* in her lap, reciting prayers, her lips moving with no sound for hours and hours at a time. I arrived at the funeral chapel, strained and out of breath—my teaching relief was late, subways never seemed to arrive, it was an uphill climb—and quickly sat down beside my family in their pew. The sight of that closed pine box struck me with an unexpected force. It looked so tiny, as though I could have picked it up in my arms and cradled it, and a memory of my grandmother erupted as though layers of time had been stripped away—neither the constrained image in the synagogue balcony nor the veiled figure at the window silently mouthing the words of the siddur, but my grandmother laughing, doubled over with laughter while the two of us played our language game, a language made up of sounds that we spoke to each in the kitchen of the Bronx, both of us laughing, doubled over with laughter. And now the sharp, harsh sting of tears.

The following year, a rabbi who never knew her delivered what he no doubt considered the appropriate oration at the ritual unveiling of her gravestone. It was awful. He extolled her for virtues she never possessed and he knew nothing of those she had. Platitudes about motherhood and pious references to those of us who stood about her grave that violated the truth of each life and annihilated hers. An inchoate rage welled up in me at this hideous display that could only find its outlet in tears. I cried and cried, and of course everyone found it appropriate—the grandchild mourning her grandmother. But I knew it as anger—at him, at her, at myself—all of us standing nodding at this travesty of an unveiling that proved the ultimate veiling.

An old Hebrew proverb observes that a grandfather teaches Talmud but one learns Torah from a grandmother. Torah, in this context, refers to the very heart or essence of belief; Talmud to its exegesis or elaboration.

When I signed the contract for this book more than five years ago, I hadn't expected it to take the length of time or the form that it has. I found myself increasingly impelled to trace the images of women further and further back in time, as if I were trying to strip away the veilings of inappropriate and damaging elaboration—dry convention, stereotype, false assumptions—to arrive at some sense of the essence of being, of what it means to be a woman. If there are some glimpses of that illumination, then perhaps that is the Torah I learned from my grandmother.

Introduction

At the beginning of the 1970s, America was ripe for the transformations suggested by the feminist movement. Traditional patterns of family and sexual behavior had broken down; a sex-based division of labor was incompatible with the economic and social realities of contemporary life. Comic-strip roles of man as breadwinner and woman as homemaker no longer made sense; women found them neither palatable nor appropriate. Lacerated by indictments of "momism" and the "castrating bitch" version of American women so popular in the fifties; by litanies of complaints from their husbands and lovers, fathers and sons; by admonitions masquerading as "insights" from psychoanalysts over the decades to "accept" their "femininity" with a corollary tendency to interpret all assertive acts as genital maladjustments—women began to question a role that had for centuries been defined by everyone but themselves, by priests and potentates who doled out prescriptions and proscriptions for the behavior of this alien majority in their midst. Those aliens turned at last to examine their own experience, giving credence to their own perceptions of self and world. In this climate of heightened awareness, women began to seriously challenge prevailing concepts of male and female, state and family, religious practice and institutional hierarchy.

As a writer, my involvement with "the movement" had been peripheral—partly the reason, perhaps, that in 1971 I was assigned to cover a speak-out on rape, having been credited with an objectivity enhanced by the absence of affiliation. Eager to avoid the stigma of parochialism, I lusted after the universal—what seemed to me, then, the more global event. Nor was I free from the contaminating vision of early suffragettes conveyed by fleeting references in high-school history books: dour portraits of tight-lipped spinsters and assorted freaks, ladies who, according to prevailing legends of the time, needed nothing more than a good——! Juxtaposed against the loose-lipped, bosomy, and infinitely more desirable heroines of Hollywood extravaganzas, poster art, and toothpaste ads, those grudging textbook portraits of Susan B. Anthony and Carrie Nation could scarcely fire the tumescent fantasies of adolescents in the fifties. Compared with the reigning billboard beauties of the period, the suffragettes—alas!—suffered very bad press.

Such then was my state of mind and arrested development when I arrived at the speak-out, held at a Manhattan church just two blocks west of Eighth Avenue's porno strip—a proliferation of shabby erotica promising such delights as "Pure Pleasure for Adults," "Sexual Freedom in Denmark," and "Rubber Anniversaries" (whatever *that* meant).

Whatever it meant, the women two blocks away weren't having any. Vulnerability, humiliation, fear, and anger were the feelings that prevailed as rape—metaphorical and real—was examined in detail.

My own ambivalence, uncomfortably embracing both skepticism and sympathy, shifted during the afternoon's testimony as a history of sexual antagonism emerged in my report:

> . . . In reviewing the afternoon's testimony, I attempted to trace sexual patterns—a kind of selective sexual history from the baboon to modern man.
>
> The strongest male baboon, I am told, banishes weaker males and takes all females for himself—establishing, perhaps, the prototype for viewing woman as the property of man. It remained for humans, however, to render that property an object of contempt. Rape is a human act, a crime of violence, expressing anger through the medium of sex. . . . Most sexual encounters fall short of rape, and many fall equally short of love, with women tending to idealize lovemaking and men to denigrate it. The Virgin, after all, was man's creation.
>
> And so the genesis for 1971's speak-out on rape unfolds, opening with Eve, that sorry rib, who took the rap for eating the apple and getting the family evicted from

Eden. After tainted Eve, tonsorial Delilah, and lewd Lilith, the world was ready for Christianity's clean slate, an immaculate conception placing Mother, the Eternal Virgin, at the top of the class and Magdalen, the Eternal Whore, at the bottom—with no one in between.

In this manner, the questionable proscriptions of an esoteric gang of Essenes riveted the archetypes of Virgin and Magdalen into woman's psyche and man's perception—a welding job that lasted for centuries, from the glittering age of chivalry, when knights rode out in shining armor, locking their ladies in drafty castles, through warmer seasons of burning witches, until Freud took the lid off the Victorian stew, pronouncing man and woman victims of the castration complex.

Men had It, and women (sore losers!) wanted It, so men had better watch out. At least, this was the inference drawn by the cult of Momists who emerged after World War II. Women had been drafted into the labor force during the war years, but when Johnny came marching home, he wanted Guinevere back in the kitchen, assuring her at the same time that she could never match the *real* women he had visited abroad—women who generously accepted their natural submissive roles (and who were invariably the struggling subjects of invaded nations).

As the Great Earth Mother evolved into the Big Ball Breaker, man continued to resent woman for withholding sexually, even though he had originally placed her in this bind. Momism burned itself out in the fifties, and Mom retaliated in the sixties. The burgeoning revolution in sexual mores pronounced virginity a disease, frigidity a crime, and orgasm a must. Books like *The Sexually Inadequate Female* appeared, exhorting women to fulfill their sexual *responsibilities*. The curious marriage between the Old Puritan and the New Libertine still managed to avoid vows of joy, ecstasy, or even friendly pleasure. . . .[1]

On and on I went, poking fun at the hallowed icons of established history, relishing my selective excursion into the past, little dreaming where it might lead.

The following year, America's first woman rabbi—Sally Preisand—was ordained at Hebrew Union College, a Reform rabbinical school in Cincinnati; and Sandy Eisenberg Sasso, a Reconstructionist rabbinical candidate from Philadelphia, addressed the American Jewish Committee's national meeting in New York.

"Judaism's predominantly male perspective must be balanced with a feminine counterpart," she urged her large audience. "To state that woman's status in Judaism is merely different but equal to man's simply ignores the facts."

Those facts succinctly followed:

- The exclusion of women from the *minyan* (quorum of ten males required for worship).
- The exclusion of women as witnesses in Jewish courts of law.
- Prohibitions against calling women to read the Torah.
- The refusal to consider the ordination of women as rabbis by Conservative and Orthodox schools.
- Laws of the *niddah* (emanating from ancient taboos) that require women to maintain significant distances from husband and temple during the seven days allotted for their menstrual flow and for seven days following it.
- Marriage ritual in which the groom repeats vows consecrating the bride unto himself while she remains silent.
- Procedures for divorce that remain the husband's prerogative and may never be initiated by wives.
- Life-cycle ceremonies in which a boy's birth is heralded with far greater celebration than a girl's.
- Daily prayer in which man thanks God for not having made him a woman.
- Traditional literature and creative arts that depict man in a variety of activities—singing, dancing, praying, studying Talmud—while woman eternally lights Sabbath candles or cradles a small child.

"I find myself very attracted to the ideas you express," a man in her audience responded to Sandy's recommendations for change, "but don't you think a tradition that has lasted for centuries might have some validity?"

A middle-aged woman leaped to answer him. "We've been smarting under those traditional patterns for years!" she exclaimed. "They no longer suit the lives we lead or want to lead." The words spilled out: "We're not telling you that we're *about* to turn over the apple cart; we want you to recognize that the apple cart *has been turned over!*"

A climate of change was clearly in the air. Unlike generations past, women today were literally descending from the balconies, some even ascending the pulpit, daring to enter male sanctuaries of religious scholarship and authority that had been closed to them for centuries. Surely, one must investigate.

I contacted Sandy Sasso, arranged for a magazine assignment on women in the rabbinate, and flew to Maine, where Sandy and her husband, Dennis, were working at a summer camp for children. We spent the week talking about Judaism's long and tortuous history, the conditions of life and belief in those civilizations from which it emerged, the voluminous body of traditional literature and law that had successfully sustained Judaic continuity through centuries of upheaval and dispersal. We also talked about Sandy's own transition—upon confrontation with those attitudes toward women that emerged during the detailed examination of Judaic law and civilization required by rabbinical study—from an initially compelling interest in Jewish mystical tradition to concern and dismay over woman's role in traditional Judaism.

How had that role evolved? Was woman's subordinate status in Judaism merely a reflection of conditions in surrounding civilizations? An accommodation to the mores and social patterns of Babylonia? Of Greece? Of Islamic Spain and medieval Europe? Or was it intrinsic to the very tenets of Judaism itself?

"Woe to the father whose children are female," mourned one talmudic sage. "A woman's wisdom lies only in her spindle," quipped another.

How deeply rooted was this unmistakable vein of misogyny?

How pervasive? What was its impact on those women who embraced Judaism and those who fled from it?

Given its strong patriarchal tradition and masculine bias, could Judaism *ever* genuinely endorse the aspirations for equality and desire for participation expressed by women today? What clues did the past hold for the future?

Such were the questions that emerged in July.

Late in August, I found myself ensconced in the Frederick Lewis Allen Room of the New York Public Library, immersed in the histories and legends of the Jews, conjecturing on Genesis (wasn't it Eve and Adam?), burrowing into a past I thought I had abandoned at my grandmother's grave, feeling as though I were treading on forbidden territory; all of it evoking some distant chord of memory, an eerie sense of having been here before, of having known all this somehow without ever being told; tales familiar not from my own childhood, to be sure, but from some far more distant past: vestigial memories plunging back through layers of time, moving from the limited, personal, idiosyncratic history of the self to the larger, infinitely more penetrating and powerful archetypes of the group.

Sources lie heaped on the desk before me: Torah and Talmud, Midrashic commentaries and Halachic decisions, esoteric mystical writings and abstruse philosophical ones, proliferations of legal codes and modern rabbinical responsa, sources that had, without my knowing it, shaped my life and thoughts, my view of self and world, of love and sex, of life and death—far more than I would have dreamed or might have wished.

Dark passages of cleft and womb. The magic and power of words. Ancient memories evoked. Revelations, like glowing amber crystals, retrieved from the shadows of a forgotten drawer.

Unveilings.

Glimpses and Revelations

> If a wife refuses to carry out such wifely duties as
> washing her husband's hands and feet, or serving
> him at table, she is to be chastised with rods.
>
> (Moses Maimonides)

A large volume, bound in gray and lettered in blood red: Maimonides' *Guide to the Perplexed*.[1]

I am perplexed.

The *Guide* falls open to Maimonides' discussion of form and matter—an elegant Aristotelian discourse, linking woman with turbid, transient matter while reserving loftier realms of the spirit for man. Calling on Solomon's analogy in *Proverbs,* matter is likened to a "married harlot":

> . . . for matter is in no way found without form and is consequently always like a married woman who is never separated from a man and is never free . . . she never ceases to seek for another man to substitute for her husband, and she deceives and draws him on in every way until he obtains from her what her husband used to obtain. This is the state of matter.

Since matter and form are inextricably joined in human life—the superior form incapable of existence divorced from base matter—man is urged to attain the eternal realm of spirit by overcoming the devious and compelling lusts of his earthbound flesh.

> . . . as it was necessary that man's very noble form
> . . . the image of God and His likeness, should be bound
> to earthy, turbid, and dark matter, which calls down upon
> man every imperfection and corruption; He granted it—I
> mean the human form—power, dominion, rule, and control
> over matter, in order that it subjugate it, quell its impulses,
> and bring it back to the best and most harmonious state
> that is possible.

That "most harmonious state," according to Maimonides, is one that shuns the sensuous and sensual, to which all men of superior sense and sensibility can testify. The others—ignorant multitudes who steep themselves in fleshly filth—"are separated from God by a veil." An anecdote serves to illustrate distinctions between these two classes of man.

Of the superior spirits: "This is like the case of a man with whom the ruler had become angry; he ordered him accordingly, with a view to humiliating him, to transport dung from one place to another. Such a man will endeavor with all his power to be hidden at the time . . . he will transport a small quantity to a nearby place, so that perhaps his hands or clothes will not be dirtied and no one else will see him. Free men would act in this manner."

Men of less fastidious inclination, however, are like the "slave" who "would rejoice in this and would not consider that he has been subjected to a great hardship. He would throw himself with his whole body into this dung and filth, soil his face and hands, and carry the dung in public, laughing the while and rejoicing and clapping his hands."

But what of man's relationship with woman on earth? What guides does Maimonides provide for human sexuality—that inevitable union of matter with matter by which man reproduces the undervalued substance for his overvalued form?

To speak of it as little as possible is Maimonides' advice, performing such acts only when absolutely "necessary" (to whom and for what is not quite clear), and in secret—emulating, no doubt, the fastidious manner of the unwilling dung carrier. Advocating an excess of moderation, Maimonides joins

Aristotle in abjuring any "cultivation of the sense of touch— that sense which is the greatest disgrace. . . ."

Throughout the *Guide,* woman is identified with transient, turbid matter, while man is urged to transcend the baser compost of his noble form. Woman, by implication and inference, is incapable of transcendence. Like Solomon's "married harlot," she remains glued to the gluttonies of the flesh. Man's matter, on the other hand, is evidently quite another matter.

Even the very language of Scripture reflects, for Maimonides, the mandatory veiling of one's privy parts.

"In this holy language," he observes, "no word at all has been laid down in order to designate either the male or female organ of copulation, nor are there words designating the act itself that brings about generation, the sperm, the urine, or the excrements . . . signified by terms used in figurative sense and by allusions . . . to indicate that the things ought not to be mentioned and consequently that no terms designating them should be coined."

How, then, is one to speak of country matters? Maimonides advocates use of the metaphor "when necessity impels mentioning them"; the veiled allusion, "just as the most diligent endeavor should be made to be hidden when necessity impels doing these things."

Biblical references to "these things" are cited by Maimonides with chapter and verse, to illustrate their appropriately modest derivation from less carnal terms. For the male organ, the Hebrew *gid* (sinew) and *shaphka* (instrument for pouring out); for the female, *qetaba* (her stomach) and *rehem*—"the term designating the part of the entrails in which the fetus is formed" —in referring to the vulva. A somewhat curious elision of anatomy!

Terms for excrement and urine follow; sperm is subsequently designated as *shikbath zera* (layer of seed). "The act of generation itself," Maimonides continues, "has no name at all, the following expressions signifying it: *yishkab* (he lies), *yib al* (he marries), *yiqah* (he takes), *yegalleh 'ervah* (he uncovers his nakedness), and no others." How curious that no terms are catalogued for woman's participation in the sexual act, although her "organs"—to be sure—are itemized and "covered." Despite the identification of woman with matter by Maimonides and her Scriptural association with temptations of the flesh in biblical imagery—Solomon's parade of married harlots and those Women of Virtue whom no man can find—the specifics of her participation in the human sexual drama apparently remain unmentioned, or unmentionable.

Some two hundred pages later in the *Guide,* the theme of abstinence reasserts itself in Maimonides' brief commentaries on biblical commandments.

Prohibitions against "illicit unions" are perceived as directed toward "making sexual intercourse rarer and to instilling disgust for it so that it should be sought only very seldom."

The reason for prohibitions against homosexuality and intercourse with animals, according to Maimonides, "is very clear. For if the thing that is natural should be abhorred except for necessity, all the more should deviations from the natural way and the quest for pleasure alone be eschewed."

Circumcision—apart from its covenantal significance—is viewed as "the wish to bring about a decrease in sexual intercourse and weakening of the organ in question" (such delicacy!) "so that this activity be diminished and the organ be in as quiet a state as possible. . . ."

Reasons for prohibitions against intercourse with menstruants and married women are brushed aside by the philosopher, who has so painstakingly sought and elaborated reasons for all else. "The reason . . . ," he simply states, "is too clear to be in need of search for a reason."

"Sexual intercourse," concludes Maimonides, "should neither be excessively indulged nor wholly abolished."

All joy is, somehow, drained.

The *Shulchan Aruch*[2] (the Set Table) or Code of Jewish Law is a four-volume handbook of detailed regulations for daily life and ritual observance—a product of the zest for elaboration and codification of Jewish law that flourished in the centuries following the master's death, inspired by his example. Compiled in 1565 by Joseph Karo, a Spanish refugee and mystic of the Sfad school, with glosses added by Joseph Isserlies in 1568 to incorporate Ashkenazic or European custom, the Code —in an unfortunately abridged form from which all minority and dissenting opinions have been excised—serves today as a guide for observant Jews throughout the world. Its most recent revisions are those of Rabbi Solomon Ganzfried of Hungary in 1870, contained in the abridged *Kitzur Shulchan Aruch.*[3]

While Maimonides' codifications and philosophical observations occupy revered shelves in the libraries of scholars, the *Shulchan Aruch* is available in every observant Jewish household, particularly since its fourth volume is almost entirely devoted to "Laws for Family Purity": regulations governing marriage, sexual intercourse, restrictions for the menstruant and ritual immersion, the birth and rearing of children, care during illness, rituals for death, interment, and mourning. Unencumbered by scholarly references or philosophical speculation, the volume serves as a veritable layette of prescriptions and proscriptions for the daily and nightly life of Orthodox Jewish women.

More than one hundred sexual proscriptions are contained in this slender volume, reflecting the ambivalence and temperamental variations of its contributing rabbis. While the Judaic ideal of sexual union, rather than celibacy, remains the norm, a proliferation of rules circumscribe the conditions under which that union is permissible. No fewer than thirty-eight are set down for the menstrual state alone.

> A woman from whose womb issued a drop of blood, be it ever so small, and whether or not it is her regular period of menstruation, and even if it is the result of an accident, is considered menstrually unclean until she counts seven days and takes the ritual bath of immersion. Both man and woman who have sexual intercourse after the menstrual flow has begun, incur the penalty of *Karet,* excision (being cut off from their people); and the temporal punishment for caressing one another is flagellation.

Clearly, woman is a dangerous creature; the menstruant, doubly so. Not only is sexual contact with her prohibited dur-

ing the seven days allotted her menstrual flow and for the seven
"clean" days that follow, in an elaboration of Levitical injunctions, but far more tangential association is forbidden as well:

"It is written (Lv. 18:19): 'And thou shalt not approach
unto a woman in her menstrual uncleanliness;' because it is
written 'Thou shalt not *approach*,' it is explained that any kind
of approach is forbidden; he should not play with her or indulge in foolery, or even speak words that may lead to
sin. . . ."

A pageant of avoidance follows: "The husband . . . should
not touch her even with his little finger. He is not allowed to
hand anything to her . . . nor to receive anything from
her. . . . He is not allowed to eat with her at the same table
. . . to drink what she left over in her cup . . . to eat of the
food she leaves over. They are not allowed to sleep in the same
bed . . . even if both have their clothes on and do not touch
one another. . . . If they lie on the ground, they may not sleep
facing one another, unless there is a big distance between
them. . . . They are not allowed to sit on the same swing
board, unless there is someone sitting between them. They
should not ride in the same wagon or take a voyage in the same
ship. . . . She is not permitted to pour a cup of wine for her
husband in his presence, nor to bring it and set it before him
upon the table, nor make his bed. . . ."

Orthodox Jewish men and women, of course, feel themselves
obligated to follow the letter of the law. Nonobservant ones
presumably do not. Decidedly more startling is the disturbing
awareness of the subtle but no less profound impact of such
codes and laws on the lives and attitudes of nonobservant
Jews, despite their ignorance or conscious rejection of them.

"If you don't find it aesthetically repugnant," responded a
secular Jewish gynecologist some years before when I—then un-
familiar with the Code—asked him, who shared my ignorance of
it, if it was "all right" to have sexual intercourse during menstruation. Ancient taboos and medieval prohibitions transposed
into a case for contemporary aesthetics. "Aesthetically repugnant"—what more?

The Code's laws of chastity require that "intercourse should be in the most possible modest manner. He underneath and she above him is considered an impudent act; both at the same level, a perverse act. . . ."

While it is incumbent upon men to gratify their wives, wives must clearly be recumbent for them to do so; the "missionary position" characteristic of patriarchal civilization, clearly spelled out in the Code of Jewish Law.

Like the biblical and rabbinic literature that preceded it, the Code recognizes woman's sexual needs and desires, urging their fulfillment, but only when expressed in an appropriately modest manner:

". . . when a man sees that his wife is coquetting and primping and trying to please him, he is bound to visit her. . . . However, if she demands it openly, she is a brazen woman . . . like a harlot, with whom he must not live together."

Don't call him; let him call you: An indirect appeal is the better part of discretion; a delicate balance between the fearful aspects of woman's desire and the recognition of her right to it. Those more frightening aspects emerge in the explicit regulations of a passage protectively peppered with Scriptural allusions:

"One is forbidden to look at the genital organ of his wife. Whoever looks at it is devoid of shame, and violates (Mi. 6:8): 'And walk humbly' (which also means 'in modesty'). For the one who is prudent is not apt to sin, as it is written (Ex. 20:17): 'And for the sake that His fear may be before you (and this means being bashful), so that you sin not.' Also, by this he stimulates lewd thoughts within himself. Certainly, one who kisses that place violates all this, and in addition he violates (Lv. 11:43): 'Ye shall not make yourselves detestable.'"

Clearly a volatile issue, emerging in a passage inundated with more biblical references than any that precede or follow it. Can the Old Testament really have concerned itself in such exquisite detail with sexual play and foreplay? Do observant Jews today refer to the Code at their bedside when more than the spirit moves them?

Meeting my mother on an excursion from the Allen Room, I

ask if she and my father observed these regulations in their own life.

"Your father," she giggles, "was more liberal."

While an aversion to sex characterized the medieval period, reaching a pinnacle in the writings of Maimonides and in the later abridged *Shulchan Aruch,* such views were ameliorated by the observations of Nachmanides and other rabbinical thinkers of the time who argued that "unorthodox conduct" was permissible. Saadia Gaon considered sexual intercourse the "greatest of all mundane goods."

Although one rabbi taught that children are born blind because the husband "gazes at that place," dumb because he "kisses that place," lame because he "inverts the table," a contrary ruling permits all of those variations (Neharim 20 a-b).

In his notes to the *Shulchan Aruch,* Rabbi Moses Isserles observes: "He can do as he wishes with his wife: He can have intercourse at any time he wishes; he can kiss any part of her body; and he can have intercourse both in the usual way and in an unusual way or on her limbs, provided that he does not spill his seed. Some are more lenient and rule that unnatural intercourse is permitted even if it involves a spilling of the seed, provided it is only done occasionally and he does not make a habit of it. Although all these are permitted, whoever sanctifies himself in that which is permitted to him is called holy."[4]

> Let the words of the Torah rather be destroyed by
> fire than imparted to a woman.
> > (Talmud: P. Sotah, 192)

Treading on ever more forbidden territory, I turn to older sources, which inform those medieval codes that penetrate contemporary life: images, legends, and life of the ancient Near East from which the Torah itself emerged; a voluminous body of exegetical literature that followed its dissemination and redaction, developing simultaneously in Palestine and Babylonia with the onset of Exile, the destruction of the Temple. Volumes of talmudic commentary on biblical text contain the precepts, opinions, and decisions that form the core of Judaism's Halacha or "way of life": principles for social, personal, and religious relationship and behavior. Earlier Midrashic forms merge with later Aggadic material—the why of Halacha: a proliferation of narrative and homily derived from Scriptural association that bears eloquent testimony to the rich and frequently misogynistic perception and imagination of the Rabbinic period (200 B.C.E.–500 C.E.).

"Whoever teaches a daughter Torah teaches her obscenity," warns Rabbi Eliezer ben Hyrcannus, recording his rancor in the Talmud.

Which, then, is obscene: Torah or daughter? Clearly, the austerity of your Palestinian school at the turn of the millennia informs the ambivalence of Jewish women today: those carefully preserved injunctions against unveiling sacred Torah to the lewd, unseeing eye of woman.

Have we no entrance to history, no voice in our own destiny, no observations that may be taken into account? Must we forever turn to view ourselves in the mirror of man's perception? Have we no souls and selves to speak of, no voices that may be heard? Is it truly better that the Torah be desecrated by fire than meet our eyes?

A softer voice speaks from the Talmud. "Woman," observes Judah haNasi in another age, "was endowed with more intelligence than man." Surely, a more benign view—yet clearly a minority opinion that has withstood the test of time less well in the perpetuation of official dogma. Inevitably it is the sourer view of woman that prevails in both Judaism and Christianity.

Indeed, all of Western history has been articulated by men; its forms and norms established and transmitted by them. Women appear only when they enter man's perception: as mothers, wives, and harlots. Those who object are not suffered kindly. More often than not, Scriptural allusion is introduced to sanctify malice and indifference.

Like Maimonides, opponents of the Equal Rights Amendment before New York State's Legislature in 1975 cited Solomon's definition of a "virtuous woman" to enthusiastic applause from those who supported their views. ". . . She looked well to the ways of her household." More, it would seem, is still unseemly even near the turn of the next millennia.

"When those who are opposed to all reforms can find no other argument," exclaimed Elizabeth Cady Stanton more than a century ago, "their last resort is the Bible. It has been interpreted to favor intemperance, slavery, capital punishment, and the subjection of women." Her own attempt at Scriptural exegesis, published in 1895 as *The Woman's Bible*,[5] was condemned by the reigning clergy as an unwholesome collusion with the devil.

Happily reissued by the Seattle Coalition Task Force on Women and Religion in 1974, Stanton's Bible—loosely termed "a woman's Talmud"—reveals her as a woman of keen intelligence and spirit, albeit wanting—as she was the first to admit—in biblical scholarship.

Yet those women who were recognized biblical scholars were excluded from participation in official revisions of Scripture, despite extensive criticism during the nineteenth century of the Authorized Version of the Bible published in 1611 and the public rankling of women over the Scriptural roles assigned them.

Among eighteen grievances in a Declaration of Sentiments presented at the first Woman's Rights Convention in 1848 were two that dealt specifically with woman's place in Church and Scripture:

"He (man) allows her in Church, as well as State, but a subordinate position, claiming Apostolic authority for her exclusion from the ministry, and with some exceptions, from any public participation in the Church. . . .

He has usurped the prerogative of Jehovah himself, claiming it as his right to assign her a sphere of action, when that belongs to her conscience and her God."[6]

Nonetheless, in 1870, when the Church of England appointed groups of scholars to prepare a revision of the Authorized Version—with similar groups formed in the United States—no woman was invited to participate, despite the eminence of female scholars like Julia Meade, who had made five translations of the Bible from Hebrew, Greek, and Latin, considered by some to be the most literal translations to date.

In her own commentary on Scripture published in 1895,

Stanton took immediate issue with the founding myth of Genesis: "Genesis Chapter I," she wrote on its frontispiece, "says Man and Woman were a simultaneous creation. Chapter II says woman was an afterthought. Which is true?"

"The work of women and the devil!" responded one clergyman.

"Let the words of the Torah rather be destroyed by fire . . ."

"Woe to the father whose children are female."
Woe, woe to the females who are children of such fathers!

Moving from sources, I turn to the Source.

How did it all begin?

2

Origins

"Mommy, where did I come from?" The child's question is echoed by the group in its persistent quest for origins: the source and meaning of life.

How did it all begin? The question is always and everywhere the same, reflecting that curious and pervasive human need to define itself, to comprehend its relationship to culture and cosmos; to wrest some meaning from what might otherwise seem—and, indeed, well may be—the ultimate absurdity of human existence: a pulsing pimple on the vast, indifferent face of time, afflicted with memory and desire, driven by the need to examine and justify itself; a palpitating bubble that seeks to learn what it can never hope to know, to discern what it can never hope to fully see, probing the darkness from which it emerged and to which it must return, consumed by its own nature, painfully aware of those very limitations it continues to defy: its own existence little more than an ephemeral moment in time, bound by birth and death—those constant and irrevocable parameters of physical life. Yet this curious creature persists in its futile and inevitable pursuit for coherence, for meaning, for dignity, and for purpose in the scheme of life.

Who am I? Where did I come from? What will become of me? The questions are universal and discrete, emerging from those unfailing constants of the human condition: birth and death. The answers are multitudinous and diverse, reflecting a variety of cultural norms and forms, rooted in variables of space and time, externals of climate and landscape, social structure and ideological bias; illuminating yet another dimension of human experience: man's inner life, the resolution of his deepest fears and needs. Question and answers together comprise humanity's most potent myths: civilization's formally stated assumption of common ancestry, a cohesive cultural force that endows human society with meaning, lending perspective to its past, defining the quality and purposefulness of its present, determining the direction of its future.

The creation myths of a civilization reveal its attitudes toward the men and women in it, their relationship to each other and to the world. Just as the child finds his place in the world by identifying his parents and determining the relationship between them, so does the group define itself in the elaboration of its myth of common origin.

Western civilization today finds its source in the Old Testament's version of creation, orally transmitted for centuries, before its recension and redaction as the opening chapters of Genesis, generating a proliferation of interpretive glosses and exegetical assumptions.

In Genesis I, Elohim, a God popularly and syntactically perceived as male—despite theological assertions of noncorporality—shapes the universe within the course of a week, separating heaven and earth, dry land and sea, eliciting form from the whirling flux of chaos. His light penetrates primeval darkness, establishing day and night. He sets the sun, moon, and stars in the sky; vegetation and animal life upon the earth. As the culminating event of such cosmic ingenuity, Elohim creates "ha-adam" (mankind) on the sixth day, in its suggestion of androgyny—"male and female created He them"—establishing their dominion over those creatures that preceded them. On the seventh day, Elohim rests, instituting sanctification of the Sabbath.

In Genesis II, drawn, as biblical scholars have pointed out, from another stream of ancient Near Eastern narrative, Adam (one half the original couple) arrives much earlier on the scene, is placed in a pretty garden and presented with creatures of land, sea, and air, whom he is privileged to name for all time. When he finds no suitable mate among them, Adam beseeches Lord Elohim, who responds to his request by fashioning a helpmeet from Adam's side in the most astonishing feat of antique surgery ever recorded:

"And the Lord God caused a deep sleep to fall upon the man . . . and He took one of his ribs, and closed up the place with flesh. . . . And the rib which the Lord God had taken from the man, made He a woman, and brought her unto the man."

Upon awakening, Adam is thus presented with the substance of his dream. Who could ask for more? Yet more there is! For just as he named those creatures that preceded her and failed to please him, so does Adam name this final creation:

"This shall be called woman, for from man was this taken."*

Indeed, such ultimate indignities served to define the status relationship between man and woman for generations to come. As traditionalists are quick to point out, it is woman's origin as rib that renders her subservient to man. Witness the commentary to Genesis included in the 1975 Soncino edition of the Pentateuch:

"We have here a wonderfully conceived allegory designed to set forth the moral and social relation of the sexes to each other, the dependence of woman upon man, her close relationship to him, and the foundation existing in nature for the attachment springing up between them. The woman is formed out of the man's side; hence it is the wife's natural duty to be at hand, ready at all times to be a "help" to her husband; it is the husband's natural duty ever to cherish and defend his wife, as part of his own self."[1]

Nature indeed! This curious reversal of *natural,* ordinary perception in which woman—not man—gives birth, is less a tribute to natural order than to the power of the myth that may obliterate and supersede it.

Despite her humble origins as rib and belated birth in Genesis II, *ishshah* quickly proceeds—via seduction by a walking snake in Genesis III—to lure Adam into tasting of the forbidden

* In Hebrew, *ishshah* (woman), an etymologically inept play on the Hebrew word *ish,* the generic term for man; the English is perhaps more to the point: wom(b)man—from the womb of man!

fruit, getting them both evicted from the pretty garden with its intimations of innocence and immortality.

When admonished by Lord God prior to eviction, Adam quickly pleads innocence. Untarnished by the chivalry of a later age, he immediately lays the onus on his wife: "The woman whom Thou gavest to be with me, she gave me of the tree, and I did eat."

Lord God, however, in his eternal and supernal wisdom, doesn't accept Adam's story and sends both of them out. At this point, Adam—arrogant to the end—renames his wife "Havvah" or Eve, "mother of all living." A midrashic gloss on the biblical text informs us that Adam subsequently revenges himself on the wife he had initially requested by refusing to sleep with her for generations to come.[2]

That such may often be the way of all marriage—made in heaven or not—is perhaps less to the point than the substance of the adumbrations that later fell upon these simple tales, a heavy weight of interpretive dogma linking them with notions of evil and Original Sin. Like their illustrious, lonely, and ambivalent forebear, Adam's descendants could never forgive Eve.

"From a woman did sin originate," observed the acerbic Jesus Ben Sirach in his Apocryphal wisdom and corruption of Pentateuchal text, "and because of her we must all die."[3]

"A Man has no need to cover his head," commented the Apostle Paul, advocating the veiling of women in the first of his letters to the Corinthians some two centuries after ben Sirach: "Man is the image of God and the mirror of His glory, whereas women reflects but the glory of man. For man did not originally spring from woman, but woman was made out of man; and man was not created for woman's sake, but woman for the sake of man. . . ."

In this manner and much to woman's dismay, myths of Creation and Fall have echoed down centuries, sanctifying male dominance and female subordination.

Generations of serial adumbrations heaped upon Genesis I, II, and III by prophets and priests, rabbis and Church Fathers, schools of biblical analysis and psychoanalysis—Jungians and Freudians, those shamans of the twentieth century who speak to and for our ailing souls—continue to perpetuate this sorry state of affairs, their interpretations more often serving to obscure, rather than reveal, the essence of the text.

From where and how, then, have these myths emerged? What inner fears and needs do they resolve? What counterparts have they in earlier Near Eastern narratives? And how have those elements—images, symbol, and ritual—borrowed from epics and pantheons of earlier civilizations been transformed by the monotheistic vision?—a transformation that, in turn, set the pattern for social and personal relationships in generations to come. For the myth itself often conceals more than it reveals, functioning in both normative and formative fashion by positing a common past, described in terms of those values the group deems important, which then serve as a prescription for patterns of social organization and relationship in the future.

It is difficult, indeed, to analyze the source and structure of a myth in which one is inevitably a participant—for myth, by its very nature, requires participation on a level of feeling that plunges far deeper than we would consciously care to admit and is far less accessible to the sunny light of reason than we choose to pretend. For the truth and potency of myth does not lie in its historicity—the narration of actual event—but rather in its evocation of the human spirit, its revelation of the interior life and imagination of man.

The impact of our mythic past upon the lives we live today may be more fully appreciated if we step outside our own Judaeo-Christian tradition, for the moment, to examine the legends and folklore of cultures presumably different from our own—those in which we are less blindly immersed—whose stories of origin are less tinged for us with notions of divine ordinance.

The Kikuyu people of central Kenya provide us with this opportunity to step outside ourselves. Their legends, recorded by Jomo Kenyatta,[4] who learned them from the elders of his tribe, vividly pinpoint certain universal themes, articulated with enviable simplicity, precision, and good humor.

Kikuyu tradition is still transmitted orally, as our own once was. "The spoken word," Kenyatta reports, "is handed down from generation to generation with great care, since it is the group's only record of their history and traditions before the white man came."

While small consolation to librarians and archivists, the oral tradition undoubtedly retains for its participants certain advantages that are lost in more codified and rigid written forms. Its greater intimacy and flexibility provides a sense of continuity and connection with the traditions of the group, while maintaining the capacity to subtly transform itself through the retellings of subsequent generations, to the immediacies and concerns of changing times. Indeed, rabbinic commentators of pre-Christian times indicated their awareness of such advantages during a period of prolonged debate over whether or not oral law should be committed to writing. In some cases, moreover—as will soon become clear—the oral tradition may well recall what the written has chosen to forget.

Nowhere is this more apparent than in the changing letters of Scripture to which we are heir. The findings of archaeologists and biblical scholars in recent years point to far greater divergence in the transmission of the written word than is comfortable for Fundamentalists, and those who advocate literal adherence to the Word. While revelation may have initially been divine, its transmission has proved all too erringly human.

Here then, the story of the Kikuyu—much as Jomo Kenyatta tells it—happily unburdened by assertions of divine authorship.

"Legends tell us that the Kikuyu have always lived in the same country. Long before the dawn of history, in the beginning of things, when the Lord of Nature separated land from water, forest from grassland, plain from hill, and mountain from desert, they came into being in tropical East Africa.

"According to the earliest legends, the tribe first established its homes around Kere-Nyaga, the mountain of mystery, now known as Mount Kenya, which was the abode of Mwene-Nyaga† the supernatural power. . . . On this mountain,

† Mwene-Nyaga ("possessor of brightness") is one form of Kikuyu address for Ngai, the Supreme Creator.

Mwene-Nyaga appeared to the man Kikuyu, founder of the tribe. He took Kikuyu to the top of the mountain, among the glittering snow-covered peaks . . . and showed him the beauty of the surrounding country."

Here the beauty of the landscape is poignantly evoked: "rivers sparkling in the sun, herds of antelope . . ." truly an Eden from which the tribe is not evicted. In thanking Mwene-Nyaga for the abundance of life he has bestowed upon him, Kikuyu vows to serve him, "to act in accordance with your will."

Mwene-Nyaga is moved by Kikuyu's words and promises him sons and daughters who "shall roam and multiply, enjoying at the same time the beauty of the country and the fruits thereof, always remembering that it is I who have bestowed them upon you." With the Great Elder's blessing, Kikuyu is told to build his homestead in a clearing surrounded by fig trees (Mekoyo). Soon after, he is given a wife named Moombi, "the creator" or "molder." Kikuyu and Moombi live happily together and have nine daughters but no sons.

Remembering Mwene-Nyaga's promise of generations to multiply and inherit the land, Kikuyu approaches him. Mwene-Nyaga bids him to leave the sacrifice of a lamb at a sacred grove, returning when his offering has burned. When Kikuyu returns to the site of the dying embers, he finds nine young men standing there, as bridegrooms for his daughters. Great rejoicing ensues; but before the marriages may take place, Kikuyu exacts the condition that all will live together in one village around his homestead and that the women must be heads of their households. In this way, the nine clans of the Kikuyu tribe were founded, taking their names from Kikuyu's nine daughters.

Kikuyu traditions speak of four time periods and at least two significant revolutions within the history of the group. Most important of these was the revolution in which the women, who had ruled the country for many generations after the death of Kikuyu, were deposed by the men. According to the victorious men who now tell the story, the women chose to ignore these responsibilities incumbent upon positions of power, retaining only the privileges of leadership. They grew more and more tyrannical, until the men could no longer stand it and determined to overthrow the women's rule.

Their methods for doing this were particularly ingenious, pertinent to our own further exploration of Genesis, articulating the eternal theme of sexual attraction and antagonism, expressed in other legends of women's rule.

Meeting secretly, the Kikuyu men agreed upon a suitable date for the initiation of their plan. On the appointed day, the men approached the women leaders with great enthusiasm, cajolery, and flattery, inducing them to have sexual intercourse. Unaware that this was but the initial step of a well-planned revolt—introduction to their own downfall—the women succumbed to the flattery, cheerfully participating in their own seduction.

Time and patience served the men well. After "six moons," they saw clearly that their plan would soon materialize. Groups were organized immediately, and the revolt was carried out; the women, very nearly paralyzed by their last stages of pregnancy, could scarcely resist.

Several changes were introduced once the men took over government. Instituting the system of chieftainship, they appointed as their first, a man who took the name Kikuyu after the founder of the tribe. By way of further punishing the women, Chief Kikuyu abolished polyandry—customary under the old order—and introduced polygamy.

"Under the old custom," Kenyatta explains, "the women could have as many husbands as they liked, and were especially partial to young ones; the old men were overlooked, or were made to do all kinds of menial work, while the women had leisure to amuse themselves in the company of the younger men."

With the introduction of polygamy, the chief and elderly men —once despised—became all-powerful, taking as many wives as their wealth would allow.

Other changes centered on renaming the tribe, as well as an attempt to change the names of the clans that had arisen under the earlier matriarchate. The tribal name was successfully changed from "the children of Moombi" to "the children of Kikuyu"; but when it came to renaming clans, the women balked. They informed the men frankly that if they dared change those names that stood as a recognition that women were the original founders of the clan system, they would simply refuse to bear any more children. As an opening gambit, they offered to kill all male children born from the initial act of the revolt.

Fearing the women's wrath, the men avoided conflict by agreeing to retain the original clan names—vestiges of matrilineal origins in a society that was to become almost totally patriarchal.

Indeed, in time, the chieftainship proved oppressive not only to the women but also to the men, especially those young men who had been the women's favorites during the age of polyandry. These young men were now placed under severe discipline and assigned the most arduous military duties. New laws forbade them to marry before they reached the age of twenty-five or more. So much they could endure; but as time went on, their ambitious sovereign demanded more and more service from his young warriors, enforcing continuous duty upon them in military camps that took them completely away from their homes and the cultivation of their lands. Their inability to participate in the cultivation of crops for food so sorely needed by all incensed other villagers, who supported the young warriors in their subsequent revolt against Chief Kikuyu.

With Chief Kikuyu deposed, the village elders and young warriors met together and drew up a plan for better government: one in which all those who reached maturity would take part. The age of maturity was determined by the initiatory ceremony of circumcision, performed on boys between the ages of fifteen and eighteen, on girls between the ages of ten and twelve. Itkiwa, the "dissolving" or "relinquishing" ceremonial, was instituted as a ritual form within which the elder generation could relinquish office to the following one.

So the legends of the Kikuyu unfold, emphasizing those processes crucial to the transformation of their society, as well as the individuals within it. Those events that mark the evolution of Kikuyu society from matriarchate to patriarchate, from monarchy to democracy are paralleled in the dynamics by which each of us moves from birth to adulthood: the overthrow of women's rule (separation from the mother), followed by the rebellion of the sons against the father in which they succeed or replace him.

The theme of women's rule—while absent, expurgated, or obscured in biblical text—is one that occurs in various forms among many groups in diverse parts of the world. Invariably, the legend tells of a time more primitive than the present, when women ruled or were sole possessors of magic art.

For example, among the Ona Indians, a hunting tribe of Tierra del Fuego, the idea is fundamental to the story of origin of the lodge or *Hain* of the men's secret society.[5]

In primeval times, according to the legend, witchcraft was known only to the women of Ona-land, who kept their own secret society, which no man dared approach. Girls, as they neared womanhood, were instructed in magic arts, learning to bring sickness and even death to all those who displeased them.

The men lived in abject fear and subjugation, their simple bows and arrows inadequate weapons against the potency of female witchcraft. The tyranny of the women escalated—as it did in the legends of the Kikuyu—until the men could no longer bear it, and it occurred to them that a dead witch might well be less dangerous than a live one, whereupon they conspired to kill off all women old enough to practice witchcraft. A great massacre ensued, from which none escaped alive.

Since even young girls just beginning their studies in magic were killed with the rest, the men now found themselves without wives and with a long waiting period before their youngest girl children—the only ones spared—would grow into women. Meanwhile, the great question arose: How could men keep the upper hand now that they had won it? There was always the danger that once the girl-children reached maturity, they would band together once more and regain their former ascendancy. To forestall all this and keep the women in their place, the men inaugurated a secret society of their own, banishing forever the women's lodge in which such heinous plots had been hatched against them. Women were forbidden from approaching the *Hain* under penalty of death.

A new branch of Ona demonology was invented by the men: a rich pantheon of demons—some of them female—whose common bond was their hatred of women and their concomitant benevolence toward men. These demons could be readily invoked by the uncanny sounds and cries that issued periodically from the secret recesses of the *Hain;* indeed, their more tangible forms were occasionally reported to be seen roaming the land. A frequent participant in Hain activities was the monster Short, a lichen-colored figure (gray down from young birds supplied the coloring), reputed to be extremely dangerous to women and inclined to kill them. When Short was reported in the neighborhood, women would hasten home from their firewood or berry gathering in the forests, bolt their doors, and lie face downward with their children on the ground, covering their heads with any garments they could lay their hands upon.

Only one creature of the *Hain*—the very young and small Kterrnen, son of Short—was reputed to have any kindly inclinations toward women, who were even allowed to look up when he passed. His appearances, however, were infrequent.

Reflected in the legends of Kikuyu and Ona, as well as in our own myth of Genesis, is the eternal enigma of male and female: their coupling and separateness, their sexual differentiation and relationship to each other and to the social order of the group. Status is invariably introduced once differentiation is perceived, appreciated, or demanded. Distinctions between sexual roles tend to elicit value judgments, culminating in the struggle for supremacy of one over the other. The cliché dictum of "separate but equal" simply cannot apply to the position of men and women in a society that depends upon their coupling for its own continuity, yet insists upon their separation in public life, allocating administrative powers to one sex rather than the other.

Legends of man's rebellion against woman's rule illustrate a process by which sexual definitions culminate in hierarchical distinctions. Whether the overthrow of "woman's rule" is perceived as actual historical event (an earlier matriarchy superseded by patriarchal order) or as a metaphor for the sequence of inner dynamics by which the child frees himself from dependence on the once all-powerful mother, the struggle for ascendancy of male over female remains abundantly clear. The intensity and pervasiveness of the struggle suggest an overwhelming early fear of woman—a perception of her as alien and threatening, possessed of special powers or "magic" directly linked with her sexuality—awesome capacities that must be subdued.

Our own myth of Genesis simply begins where the legends leave off. Eve is a postrevolutionary figure; she emerges only after the battle has been won, all power drained from her by virtue of her status as rib—man's model for woman in a patriarchal age that has successfully suppressed all memory, fear, or possibility of another order and time. Vestiges of matrilineal origins—so vividly expressed by the Kikuyu in their conflict over the renaming of tribe and clans—are summarily and symbolically erased from our own history when God bestows the power of naming on Adam, setting the precedent for viewing the world through man's eyes—the dominant male perspective buttressed by pseudohistorical reiterations of endless genealogies in subsequent chapters of Genesis, claiming descent from those unknown fathers created by the ineffable and unknowable Father of all.

The dubious gains of such ill-won contests must be guarded at all costs against all possibilities of reversal. The Ona males and other primitive warrior groups consolidated their victory against the women of the tribe through the institution of secret initiation into the *Hain* or men's lodge from which all women were excluded. Judaism and Christianity similarly exclude women from the higher echelons of religious authority, the zealously guarded canons of church and synagogue, the all-male sanctuaries of talmudic study and commentary.

"Let the words of the Torah rather be destroyed by fire than imparted to a woman," exclaimed Rabbi Eleazar with appropriate scholarly fervor. So too are the bull roarers and secret incantations of the *Hain* taboo to women of the tribe. In Judaism today, the atavistic dread of women that inspires such fervent insistence upon her exclusion is cleverly coupled with the political manipulation of legalistic rationales that presumably prohibit her inclusion. But it is fear—not Torah—that remains the source for the antagonism and intensity of contemporary reactions against woman's appearance in pulpit, quorum, or Torah reading articulated by those who claim Orthodox adherence to the law, as well as those more discreetly concerned with "conserving" traditions of the past. Such righteous orthodoxies and conservatisms should be seen for what they are: the displacement of revelation by cult fetish and magic. For knowledge of the Torah—in this context—like the bull roarer and secret incantations of the *Hain,* is rendered the cult object of man's domain: his magic, his sexual prerogative, his potency.

Judaism, like so many other systems of custom and belief, adheres to a distinction between the sexes, a separation of their roles in areas far removed from their genital origin: the initial coherence of procreation and the sexual act. Why such insistence on distinctions between male and female beyond their obvious genital difference?

Despite the havoc it wreaks, the drive for sexual distinctiveness persists, recurring in all myths of origin, in all legends of the group, in all cultural solutions to the basic ambiguities inherent in sexual definition. Distinctions between appropriate behavior for male and female vary from culture to culture; yet the insistence on preserving such distinctions is as very nearly universal as it is arbitrary. Among the Dogon of West Africa,[6] for example, weaving was given by the gods to man; our own tradition—emanating in part from ancient Greek myths in which the weaving Fates, those dark female forces who preceded Olympian Zeus, spin out human destiny—proclaims weaving "woman's work." Work, feelings, thoughts, attitudes, and expression—all are endowed with masculine or feminine attributes, as though some compelling need insisted on the enforcement of distinction for its own sake, some primeval terror of the merging of male and female in one body, a consuming fear of return to a fluid and androgynous source.

Such a source is vividly suggested by the Dogon, who believe that each individual is born both male and female, physically manifested in the male's foreskin—the female component of his genital organization—and the female's clitoris, the male aspect of her sexuality. At puberty, according to the Dogon, each sex must divest itself of its bisexual component through rituals of circumcision and excision in which male and female—potentially bisexual—are thrust into the single-sex role demanded of each.

Dogon myths of creation echo the theme of original androgyny or bisexuality, as well as an aversion to it. At an early stage of creation the god Amma flung clay into space forming the earth, perceived as feminine, its sexual organ an anthill, its clitoris a termite hill. Lonely and desiring intercourse, Amma approached the earth, incurring a first breach in the order of the universe.

At his approach, the termite hill rose up, barring passage and displaying its masculinity; intercourse could not take place. But Amma, all-powerful, cut down the termite hill and copulated with the excised earth, from which defective union was born—in place of the intended twins—the solitary jackal. Further intercourse with his earth wife (the excision of the offending termite hill having removed the cause of the initial disorder) produced the twin spirits or Nummo, ancestors and guardians of mankind.

The solitary jackal, meanwhile, sought out his mother earth for intercourse. She resisted the incestuous act by burying herself in her own womb; disguised as an ant, she burrowed into the anthill. But the jackal persisted, and the earth eventually had to admit defeat, prefiguring for the Dogon "the even-handed struggles between men and women, which, however, always end in the victory of the male."

Menstrual blood flowed from the incestuous act; Amma rejected his original spouse and decided to create living beings directly. Modeling a womb in damp clay, he placed it on the earth; in the same way, he modeled a male organ.

At this point, the Nummo pair appeared on the scene and foresaw that the original rule of twin births was bound to disappear and that errors might occur comparable to that of the jackal whose solitary state led him to seek out his own mother.

The spirits then drew two outlines on the ground, one on top of the other, one male and the other female. Man stretched himself out on these two shadows of himself, taking both of them for his own. Woman did the same. Thus it came about that each human being from the first was endowed with two souls of different sex.

Since human life was incapable of supporting dual being, each person would have to merge himself in the sex for which he appeared best suited. The Nummo accordingly circumcised the man, removing from him the femaleness of his prepuce. The man then had intercourse with the woman, who later bore the ancestors of the Dogon people. In the moment of birth the pain of parturition was concentrated in the woman's clitoris, which was excised by an invisible hand.

Stripped of local particulars, conjectures on the nature and origin of human life elicit the inevitable sequence of birth, sexuality, and death—the passage for all life everywhere. Mysteries of birth and death are attended by anxiety, focused in the taboos and restrictions imposed on sexuality, the nexus where birth and death meet. For it is out of that curious conundrum of male and female—their coupling and separateness, their similarity and distinctiveness—that the group achieves its less than satisfactory measure of continuity. All myths of origin, all systems of belief, all attempts to endow human life with meaning and significance reveal the quintessential paradox of existence: man's lust for immortality in the face of temporality; the confinement of the eternally androgynous and ambivalent soul in a physical, temporal, and sexually distinct body. This very paradox generates a profound fear of woman, a perception of her as dangerous and alien; her sexuality is indisputably linked with life and, by implication, death. All birth issues from her, suggesting the awesome capacity to give life. All life—human, animal, and vegetable—in time dies, withers, and seres; woman, thus perceived as giving life, is endowed, by association, with the power to take it, to bring death. At its source then, the age-old lyrical pageant of "boy meets girl" carries awesome undertones of life and death.

"Mommy, where did I come from?" The child invariably asks the question of his mother, the source of his own life, as well as those brothers and sisters who issue from her womb. The father remains a remote figure, born of woman as the child is, yet not clearly implicated in the process of birth. Maternity is a matter of direct observation; paternity, one of inference. A certain measure of sophistication is required to appreciate Daddy's more subtle contribution to the blessed event. For the child as for the primitive, life initially issues from the loins of the mother—surely a mysterious and terrifying event—unmuted by the antisepsis and curtained delivery rooms of modern hospitals. What venerable powers is woman thus endowed with through her capacity to give birth, to bleed periodically—unlike man—without dying; to hold, by implication, awesome power over both life and death. What else, but such power, is the "women's magic" of which the Ona speak? What else but overwhelming fear of so primal a power would generate such intense and wide-ranging efforts to subdue it?

The written history of man is, in part, a testament to those efforts. Yet so emphatic a vision—so deeply rooted a perception of female power over life and death—is not easily erased, despite subsequent attempts to transform the terror of woman into a more manageable contempt. Such early fears are reflected in the taboos surrounding woman's sexuality; they live on in the legends of women's rule, in the construction of elaborate cosmogonies transferring the powers of generation to male gods or ancestors: the Australian Karora giving birth to mankind from his navel and armpits; the Heliopolitan Atum—the Memphite Ptah—spitting out the gods after swallowing his own semen; the Canaanite Humarbi similarly initiating the species through the act of masturbation; the Greek Zeus giving birth to Athena from his head, Dionysius from his thigh; Eve born of Adam via Elohim in the Old Testament's version of Genesis—a rib myth of origin that at once robs woman of divinity and power, justifying her subordination for generations to come; a brilliant resolution of man's perpetual dilemma.

Perplexing rib! Despite centuries of earnest exegesis by theologians and scholars, pop singers and psychoanalysts, its source remained buried with the forgotten civilization of Sumer, some forty feet deep beneath the arid, windswept flatlands of southern Mesopotamia—lost to memory for more than two thousand years. Less than a century ago, excavations in southern Iraq began to unearth the ancient cities of Ur and Nippur, Lagash and Erech; tens of thousands of clay tablets inscribed with Sumerian cuneiform were pieced together; the script was deciphered less than fifty years ago.

Sumerologist Samuel Noah Kramer—first to decipher Sumerican cuneiform—suggests a startling solution to the puzzle of Eve's biblical derivation from the rib.[7] In Sumerian script, Dr. Kramer points out, the words for "life" and "rib" are both represented by the symbol "TI." NIN.TI may thus be read either "Lady of Life" or "Lady of the Rib," effecting a play on words that cannot be duplicated with the Hebrew *tzela* for rib and *hayyah* (or eve) for life.

In the Sumerian Paradise Myth of Enki and Ninhursag,[8] the mother goddess Ninhursag agrees to cure her ailing spouse, Enki, by placing him in her vulva and giving birth to a series of gods and goddesses—eight in all—to cure each of his ailing parts. NIN.TI is the seventh of these, produced by Ninhursag when Enki complains of his aching rib.

"My rib hurts me!" he cries.

"Ninti I have caused to be born for thee," she responds. Ninhursag subsequently assigns cosmic roles to her offspring; Ninti, in this version, is designated "Queen of the months." (In other Sumerian tales, Ninti simply refers to a goddess of life.)

Confronted with the Sumerian original, suggests historian of religions Theodore H. Gaster, the biblical scribe may well have confused the sign TI for "rib," thus producing the curious mélange of *tzela* and *hayyah* in Genesis II.

". . . NIN.TI—that is, 'Lady of TI,'" comments Dr. Gaster, "could be interpreted either as 'Lady of Life' or as 'Lady of the Rib.' The former interpretation . . . led to the designation of the first woman as *Eve,* for this represents the Hebrew *Hawwah,* which is connected with the word *hay,* 'living.' Eve, as the Scriptural writer says explicitly (3:20), received her name because she was 'the mother of all living.' The latter interpretation, on the other hand, led to the tale that she had been formed from the rib of the first man."[9]

Alas for Eve, poor dislocated rib!—tribute to the failing eyesight and faltering philology of an early scribe, reinforced by an unmistakable current of misogyny that runs through millennia. For the revelations of twentieth-century archaeology still fail to touch the hearts and minds of those who hold woman's origin as rib so dear.

Yet the sequence of Genesis itself, in which male and female are first created simultaneously, followed by a Paradise myth in which death states its presence in human life (no sooner is Eve born of Adam's side, in a reversal of natural order, than she introduces him to his own mortality)—a sequence so puzzling to scholars and theologians for two millennia—reveals, on its deepest levels, despite the denial implicit in its reversal, that earlier, primal vision of woman as source of life and death.

3

Eve

From a woman did sin originate and because of her
we must all die.   (Sirach: *Apocrypha*)

Her grave is open. . . . (Arab expression referring to the state of the mother's womb
during the forty-day period following
childbirth when she is taboo).[1]

And God created man in his image. . . .
Male and female created He them.   (Gn. I:27)

Then God Yahweh cast a deep sleep upon the man
and . . . took one of his ribs. . . .
                                        (Gn. II:21–22)

Enter Eve.

A vast literature elaborates on the sequence of creation, the
reasons for Eve's origin as rib and its significance in determining
the character and inferiority of woman, thereby justifying and
sanctifying her subordination.

According to one speculation on Eve's belated arrival, God
originally foresaw that Adam would eventually complain about
his mate; she was, therefore, not given him until he asked for
her. Other Midrashic sources emphasize God's compassion for
Adam's loneliness: "The Divine resolution to bestow a companion on Adam met the wishes of man, who had been overcome by a feeling of isolation when the animals came to him in
pairs to be named."

Some suggest that Adam became conscious of sexual instinct only when he saw Eve before him. A distinctly less high-minded gloss maintains that Eve was only given Adam when his copulation with the animals proved unrewarding:

". . . God had set Adam to name every beast, bird, and other living thing. When they passed before him in pairs, male and female, Adam—being already like a twenty-year-old man—felt jealous of their loves, and though he tried coupling with each female in turn, found no satisfaction in the act. He therefore cried: 'Every creature but I has a proper mate!' and prayed God would remedy this injustice."

That God's remedy failed to please Adam's descendants is made abundantly clear in subsequent speculations on why the rib was chosen to ameliorate Adam's loneliness.

"When God was on the point of making Eve, He said: 'I will not make her from the head of man, lest she carry her head high in arrogant pride; not from the eye, lest she be wanton-eyed; not from the ear, lest she be an eavesdropper; not from the neck, lest she be insolent; not from the mouth, lest she be a tattler; not from the heart, lest she be inclined to envy; not from the hand, lest she be a meddler; not from the foot, lest she be a gadabout; but from a chaste portion of the body, urging to every limb and organ as He formed it: 'Be chaste! Be chaste!' "

Yet even God's will apparently proved no match for woman's. Despite such painstaking precautions, her intransigence—according to the commentator—persisted in the behavior of all her descendants, those mothers and daughters of the Old Testament we have been taught to revere.

"Woman has all the faults God tried to obviate," despairs the sage. "The daughters of Zion were haughty and walked with stretched forth necks and wanton eyes; Sarah was an eavesdropper in her own tent when the angel spoke with Abraham" (ah, that laugh! Sarah's eternal laugh—that she *dared* listen when they spoke of her!); "Miriam, a talebearer accusing Moses; Rachel, envious of her sister, Leah; Eve put out her hand to take the forbidden fruit; and Dinah was a gadabout."[2]

Such summary treatment of our biblical foremothers—those

chosen few who pass briefly through the Old Testament—requires a word in their defense. On what are the exegete's indictments based?

Dinah, Leah's daughter, is introduced solely for purposes of endorsing endogamy in Genesis 34:1–31; her "rape" is incidental to the violence that meets the idea of intermarriage. On her way to visit women friends in the countryside, Dinah is seduced by the uncircumcised Shechem, son of a Hivite prince ("he took her, he lay with her, he humbled her"), who falls in love with Dinah ("he spoke tenderly to her") and seeks her hand in marriage. When Shechem's father approaches Dinah's father, Jacob, to negotiate bride price and marriage, Dinah's two brothers, Simeon and Levi, insist that all male members of Shechem's tribe undergo circumcision—a condition to which they foolhardily agree, providing the duplicitous brothers with an opportunity for mayhem. Just two days after the circumcisions, Simeon and Levi take full advantage of their neighbors' weakened condition to remove Dinah from Shechem's house, slaughtering all the males of the tribe, including their future brother-in-law, after which they plunder the city and carry off its women—all in the name of avenging a sister's "dishonor"!

Dinah, meanwhile, is consulted not at all—neither about her honor, her marriage, her brothers' plans, nor the bleak future that awaits her. Jacob, to give him his due, is angered by his sons' violence—not, to be sure, for Dinah's sake but because they have given him a bad name; he curses them on his deathbed. But not a word for Dinah. Once the men play out their drama, she simply disappears from biblical text, reappearing for only a moment centuries later to be labeled a "gadabout" in rabbinic indictment of *her* behavior!

That aversion to exogamy for which Dinah's brothers slaughtered her newly circumcised intended is the very subject of Miriam's "talebearing." In Numbers 12:1–16, Miriam and Aaron make some derogatory remarks about their brother Moses' marriage to a Cushite woman ("They blamed him for his Cushite wife") and question his pre-eminence in conversations with the Lord ("Has He not spoken with us as well?"). For this breach of filial devotion, Miriam is stricken with leprosy. Aaron asks Moses to intercede for her with God: "Let her not be like something stillborn, whose flesh is half eaten away. . . ." Moses pleads with God to heal his sister; God agrees to limit her affliction and concomitant isolation to seven days (curiously, the Levitical time period mandated for seclusion of the menstruant). Later glosses on the text attempt to justify the unequal punishment accorded Miriam and Aaron for their joint indiscretion. Miriam, the rationale suggests, suffered greater punishment because she spoke *first;* the High Priest Aaron merely followed her example. Hence he suffered a leprosy of shorter duration—just five minutes!—too short a time, really, for anyone, including the biblical narrator, to take notice. So much for "talebearing."

The rivalry between Rachel and Leah centers on their relationship with Jacob: two wives competing for the love of a single husband by the serial bearing of children—a function of polygamous, patriarchal life. While themes of sibling rivalry recur in biblical texts[3] among brothers as well as sisters, brothers usually vie for status within the larger social order: the shepherd vs. the agriculturalist in the Cain/Abel story; the younger vs. the elder, countering traditions of primogeniture, in the Jacob/Esau tale. Rivalry between women, on the other hand, invariably centers on their capacity to bear children, a circumstance clearly mandated by patriarchal narrative and cultural milieu.

Returning to Eve, the *midrashim* proliferate, attributing psychological and social differences between the sexes to their myth of origin: man's as earth and woman's as bone. One view holds that the physical formation of woman is far more complicated than that of man because of her childbearing capacities; similarly, her intelligence matures more quickly.[4] A far less sanguine comparison is presented in the form of a hypothetical dialogue:

"Rabbi Joshua was asked: 'Why does a man come forth at birth with his face downward, while a woman comes forth with her face turned upward?' 'The man,' he replied, 'looks toward the place of his creation (the earth), while the woman looks upward toward the place of her creation (the rib).'

" 'Why must a woman use perfume,' continues the straight man, 'while a man does not need it?' 'Dust of the ground remains the same no matter how long it is kept,' suggests the rabbi, 'while flesh putrefies without salting.' "

We similarly learn that "the voice of women is shrill, not so the voice of men; when soft foods are cooked, no sound is heard; but put a bone in a pot, and at once it crackles. A man is more easily placated than a woman because a few drops of water suffice to soften a clod of earth, while a bone stays hard after days of soaking."

Differences between the sexes in dress, social forms, sexual dynamics, and moral obligations similarly derive from their reputed origins: " 'Why does the man make demands upon the woman, while the woman does not make demands upon the man?' 'The man . . . seeks what he has lost (his rib), but the lost article does not seek him.' 'Why does a man deposit sperm within a woman while a woman does not deposit sperm within a man?' 'This is like a man who has an article in his hand and seeks a trustworthy person with whom he may deposit it.' Woman covers her hair in token of Eve's having brought sin into the world; she tries to hide her shame. Women precede men in funeral cortege because it was woman who brought death into the world. The precept of menstruation was given her because she shed the blood of Adam. Those religious commands addressed to women alone are connected with the history of Eve. Adam was the heave-offering of the world, and Eve defiled it. As expiation, all women are commanded to separate a heave offering from the dough.* And because woman extinguished the light of man's soul, she is bidden to kindle the Sabbath light."

Here woman is clearly linked with death; her very creation, a reminder of man's loss; her presence, the source of his distress; her sexuality, punishment for that unspeakable First Crime. While the concept of Original Sin is a Christian rather than a Judaic precept—developed far more fully in later Christian theology—the seeds for its genesis may be readily discerned in

---

* Kneading of the challah for the Sabbath.

certain strains of earlier Apocryphal and rabbinic writings such as this.

Despite her humble origins as rib—a myth unparalleled in ancient Near Eastern or Mediterranean cosmogonies[5]—woman is rendered responsible for man's mortality, a paradoxically ambivalent interpretation that evokes the earlier, primal archetype of a terrible and powerful mother goddess who reigns over life and death. In this context, an early fear of woman merges with a political exploitation of biblical text to justify her subordination—a process that is explicitly articulated in the preceding *midrash,* as well as those that follow, mandating woman's very real "expiation" for an imagined crime.

Man's insatiable lust for immortality continues to override all the profound considerations and refinements of his theology, the evolution and sophistication of his philosophy. The one thing he cannot bear to face is his own end. In his denial of death, his futile and poignant clinging to a paradisiac vision of eternal life, he continues to render the rib—that woman, Eve!—culpable for the dissolution of his dream.

The twentieth-century translators and editors of this excerpt from the early Midrash Rabbah attempt to mitigate its misogyny with a meandering footnote that succeeds only in further "damning with faint praise."

After pointing out somewhat gratuitously that Judaism's attitude toward women is revealed in the replies attributed to Rabbi Joshua, the editors proceed to hoist themselves by their own petard—or rather, one that the rabbi may have slyly prepared centuries ago.

"Woman in accordance with Scripture," comment the editors, "is charged with having brought death into the world through her disobedience, yet her punishment is not to be accursed, but . . ." the talmudic but!—"hers is the privilege to emphasize the inviolate character of woman" (surely not in Rabbi Joshua's view), "to sanctify the bread one eats and spread the cheer of the Sabbath as symbolized by light." Some privilege.

Whether so bumbling and ill conceived a rationale for so virulent an etiology of these few forms of worship permitted woman—the lighting of Sabbath candles—can bolster the spirits of those women who remain faithful to Judaic precepts is more than dubious. More often than not, the pious mother of the family who welcomes each Sabbath by lighting candles and blessing them each Friday evening is blissfully unaware of Rabbi Joshua's dissertation on the reasons for her sacred task; such learned inquiries remain the province of male domains of scholarship and spiritual authority from which she is—by virtue of her "inviolate" sex—excluded.

Other speculations on Genesis question Eve's originality. Attempts to reconcile the disparities[6] between Genesis I and Genesis II produce the suggestion that the first being was an androgyne—male and female, created back to back. When God observed that among other things, this curious position rendered speech and locomotion difficult, he split the androgyne in half. Such, perhaps, is the source of a much later—and far more romantic—speculation that views male and female as two halves of an original soul, each seeking the other to regain the wholeness and integrity of its original unity.

Yet another "first Eve"—predecessor to the lady so fond of serving fruit—is posited, by some, created for Adam before his deep sleep.

"God created a wife for Adam before Eve, but he would not have her because she had been made in his presence. God let him watch while He built up a woman's anatomy: using bones, tissues, muscles, and glandular secretions, then covering the whole with skin and adding tufts of hair in places."[7]

Adam's response?

"Better death than that green slobber!" exclaimed the Bride of Frankenstein, hair electrically awry, when she viewed her groom in Edward Fields' version of the same.[8] So too, did Adam speak on viewing the first Eve.

"The sight caused Adam such disgust that even when this woman, the First Eve, stood there in her full beauty, he felt an invincible repugnance. God knew He had failed once more and took the First Eve away." Where she went, nobody knows. . . .

An even more demeaning gloss suggests that God created Eve not from Adam's rib, but from his tail, ending in a sting that

had once been part of his body. God cut this off, and the stump
—now a useless coccyx—is still carried by Adam's descendants.

The sting, if not the tail, persists in further elaborations on
woman's creation. When Adam woke from his deep sleep, according to one variation, he saw Eve before him in all her
beauty and grace and exclaimed, "This is she who caused my
heart to throb many a night!" Yet despite his initial infatuation,
he immediately discerned woman's true nature. She would, he
knew, seek to carry her point with man either by pleading and
tears or by flattery and caresses. "This," he thus pronounced,
"is my never-silent bell!"[9]

Indeed, perhaps the final word on the sequence of creation
and its significance is provided by a twentieth-century biblical
scholar who is both an Orthodox Jew and a woman. If man's
creation after the animals suggests his superiority and lordship
over those creatures that preceded him, observes Nechama Liebowitz with wry good humor, then surely woman—God's ultimate creation—was meant to become the lord of man![10]

Yet the mystery of the first persists—predecessors and descendants of the ancient NIN.TI, so recently recovered from
Sumerian script, so erringly joined by the biblical scribe to
man's rib. Even the early *midrashim,* as well as later medieval
legends—untouched by the archaeological revelations of recent
years, the recovery of a written literature that moves back the
dates of recorded time by more than a millennium—questioned
the originality of the rib.

If not Eve, who then?

4

The Demon Lilith

In the midst of the huluppu tree, the vampire Lilith
built her house. . . . Gilgamesh . . . slew the snake
. . . at the base of the tree . . . and Lilith tore down
her house in the middle of the tree and fled to her
desolate haunts.

> (*Gilgamesh and the Huluppu Tree*,
> Sumer c. 2500 B.C.)

God then formed Lilith, the first woman, just as He
had formed Adam, except that he used filth and sediment instead of pure dust. . . . Adam and Lilith
never found peace together. . . .

> (*Alphabet of Ben Sira*, A.D. 10th Cen.)

Some claim Lilith for Adam's wife—a woman who preceded
Eve and was created from the same earth as he. Expurgated
from biblical texts,* Lilith emerges in folklore as Adam's first
wife who fled the Garden when he insisted she lie beneath him.

"Why should I lie beneath you," she sensibly remarked,
"when God created us out of the same clay?"

Adam tried to force her, and Lilith recoiled, enraged. Uttering God's ineffable name, she rose into the air, leaving her
earthbound spouse far behind. Opting for independence over
subservience, she fled to the Red Sea, where she coupled co-

---

* Save for the fleeting reference in Is. 34:14: ". . . the ruins of Edom
will be haunted by demons; the night hag [Lilith] will make her home
there . . ."

piously with all manner of demons, producing—legend has it—
more than a thousand demon children a day.

Adam bewailed her loss and cried out to God. Ever sensitive
to man's despair, God immediately dispatched the angels
Sanvi, Sansanvi, and Semangelef to secure Lilith's return. The
angels found her in the midst of the sea, riding the crests of its
emerald-green waves.

"Return to Adam at once," they commanded, "or we will
drown you!"

Lilith laughed. "How can I return to Adam," she teased,
"and live like an honest wife after my stay by the Red Sea?"

"It will be death to refuse!" they thundered. An empty
enough threat, as Lilith clearly perceived, knowing full well
that both her life and flight from Adam preceded the Fall.

"How can I die?" she blithely replied, "when God has ordered me to take charge of all newborn children: boys up to
the eighth day of life—their day of circumcision; girls up to the
twentieth day."

Unwilling to admit defeat, the angels negotiated a compro-
mise. Eager to be rid of them, Lilith agreed to leave newborn
children unharmed when an amulet with the names and images
of Sanvi, Sansanvi, and Semangelef was displayed above the
newborn child. Yet Jewish folklore could scarcely allow Lilith's
intransigence to continue unchecked. Accordingly, God punished her by making one hundred of her demon children die
daily; when the magic amulet prevented her from destroying a
human infant, she was reputed to spitefully turn against her
own.

Yet Lilith's power, while transmuted to the netherworld of
shades and demons, remained unsuppressed. Seductress and
strangleress, she visited men in their sleep, initiating nocturnal
emissions from which she bore countless demon children. She
coupled once more with Adam, after his separation from Eve,
giving birth to all the plagues that would beset mankind.
Women in labor trembled at the thought of her; she was known
to invade the souls of newborn children, drawing them to the
demon world over which she reigned. Charms and amulets,
magic circles and incantations were employed against her.

She lives under various names everywhere—Circe, Strega, Lamashtu, Obizuth, Langsuyar, Bruxa. Her forms are multiple: glittering and wild-haired, winged and birdlike, dark-haired and golden, boldly naked and terrifying, seductively sheathed in shimmering velvet. Her career is the most fantastic and long-lived of all. Some say she ruled as Queen in Zemargad, and again in Sheba; others name her the demon who destroyed Job's sons. The Kabbalists linked her with Sammael, Prince of Darkness, and again with God—after the Shekinah, his first consort, joined the exiled nation of Israel when the Temple fell. She was challenged by Elijah and by Solomon—to no avail. She outlived them all, free from the curse of death that overtook Adam, since she had fled from him long before the Fall.

Nineteenth-century poets, playwrights, and novelists sought her as their muse. Some twentieth-century women have found in her the source and springboard for their own vitality, retrieving Lilith from millennia of darkness, to restore her in a world of light.

For Lilith's origins far precede her entry into Adam's life; she is older than biblical time. The earliest notes we have of her biography date back to the third millennium B.C.E. The name of a demon, similar to Lilith, can be found in the Sumerian King list (c. 2400 B.C.E.), recording the father of the hero Gilgamesh as a Lillu demon. The Lillu was one of four demons belonging to a vampire or incubi-succubae class. The other three were Lilitu (Lilith), a she demon; Ardat Lili (or Lilith's handmaid), who visited men by night and bore them ghostly children; and Irdu Lili, probably a male counterpart who would visit women and beget children by them. Originally these were storm or wind demons, derived from the Sumerian *lil* (wind). Eventually, a mistaken etymology linked Lilith with the Semitic *layil* (night), and she was rendered a night demon.

Babylonian references to Lilith dub her "the beautiful maiden"; yet she was also believed to have been a harlot and vampire who, once she chose a lover, would never let him go, without ever giving him real satisfaction. According to some versions, she was unable to bear children and had no milk in her breasts. (Consistency is never the hobgoblin of mythology).

Lilith's abode in the desert—referred to by the prophet Isaiah —finds its source in the story *Gilgamesh and the Huluppu† Tree* from the Sumerian *Gilgamesh Epic,* dating from about 2000 B.C.E.

Once upon a time—the story begins—a huluppu tree, planted on the banks of the Euphrates and nurtured by its waters, was uprooted by the south wind and carried away on the waters of the Euphrates. The goddess Inanna, strolling nearby, saw it, picked it up in her hands, and carried it to her city of Erech, where she planted it in her garden. She tended it carefully, planning, when the tree had grown large, to use its wood for a throne and couch for herself.

Years passed. The tree matured and grew tall, but its trunk stood bare with neither branch nor leaf. For at its base, "the snake who knows no charm" had built its nest; in its crown, the fierce Imdugud bird had placed its young; and in its middle, the vampire Lilith had built her house.

Inanna turned to her brother, Utu, for help when her sacred tree was invaded by the snake, the fierce bird, and the vicious Lilith. As dawn broke and the sun god Utu came forth, Inanna tearfully told him all that had befallen her tree. But Utu would do nothing to help her.

She then appealed to Gilgamesh, who determined to stand by her. Donning his armor and taking up his ax, Gilgamesh approached the tree and slew the snake at its base. Seeing this, the Imdugud bird fled with its young to the distant mountains, and Lilith tore down her house in the middle of the tree and fled to her desolate haunts.

Gilgamesh and the men of Erech who had accompanied him then cut down the tree and gave it to Inanna for her throne and couch. The story goes on at some length, but Lilith—having fled to the desert, where Isaiah marks her presence centuries later— no longer appears in it.

A Sumerian terra-cotta relief, identified as Lilith and roughly contemporary with the Gilgamesh story, reveals her as a slender, shapely nude with wings and clawed feet. She stands erect

† Probably a willow.

on two lions who face in opposite directions, flanked by two large owls, suggesting her nocturnal aspect. She wears a horned, Hathor-like headdress and holds a ring and rod in her raised hands.

As early as the eighth century B.C.E., the seductive aspect of Lilith became fused with what had originally been the quite distinct demonic figure of the child-stealing witch, known to Mesopotamians as Lamashtu. A small amuletic plaque, dating from the period and found in Arslan Tash, portrays the beldam in two aspects: as a vixen swallowing a tiny human figure and as a winged monster. Designed to protect expectant mothers from Lilith's assaults, the small limestone plaque is pierced at the top for suspension and inscribed with the following incantation:

> O Flying One, thou Goddess
> ‒‒‒ ‒‒‒
>
> O strangleress of lambs
> the house I enter,
> enter not,
> and the court I tread
> tread not, for there hath been
> made with us a bond
> everlasting! . . .
>
> . . . .
> By the bond of heaven and earth,
> (for)ever be (exorcised), by the bond of Ba'al
> . . . .
> O thou that fliest into darkened chamber(s)
> pass over, right now, right now, O Lili(t)!
> Kidnaper, crusher of bones, begone!
> . . . May her (wom)b be opened
> and may she give birth!
> St! Zt! (when) the sun rises,
> travail and give birth![1]

The child-devouring aspect of Lilith has worldwide analogues. The Hittites called her "Wesuriyanza" (strangleress). Among the Semites of Mesopotamia she was portrayed as a hideous hybrid monster with lion's head, ass's teeth, and bird's claws, holding a snake in either hand and suckling a dog and a pig at her breasts. On Akkadian cylinder seals, she is imaged as a demon with bird's feet, holding a crouching man in her talons and another in each hand.

The ancient Greeks knew her under several names and several guises. In classical Greece, Ovid identifies the child-stealing demon with the night owl: "Greedy birds there are . . . that fly by night and seek out babes when their nurses are absent. These they carry away, and mar their bodies with their talons. The bowels of sucking bairns they are said to rip out with their beaks, and they have their throats full glutted with the blood they drink. . . ."

In a Hellenistic work, at least five of the host of demons who parade before King Solomon may be readily identified with Lilith. *The Testament of Solomon* is a Greek work of the early Christian era based on Judaeo-Hellenistic magical beliefs and practices with Persian, Arabic, and Egyptian influences. King Solomon is engaged in building the Temple as the Testament opens. The vampire spirit, Ornias, descends upon his servant; and Solomon prays for help. The archangel Michael brings him a ring that endows its possessor with power over all demons. Solomon subsequently summons the demons before him, one by one, and tests them, asking their name, their province, and the name of their antagonistic or frustrating angel. Solomon thus gains ascendancy over the demons and enlists them in the building of his Temple. Ironically, he succeeds in vanquishing the demon world, only to fall prey to the "spell" of an ordinary woman.

Ornias is the first to appear, a male demon, containing three forms, one of which is the Lilith aspect: "Whenever men come to be enamored of women, I metamorphose into a comely female; and I take hold of the men in their sleep, and play with them."

Onoskelis appears next—a shapely, fair-skinned woman. Like the seductive, wind-spirit Lilith, Onoskelis' dwelling place constantly shifts. "At one time," she informs Solomon, "I strangle men with a noose; at another, I creep up from the nature to the arms. My most frequent dwelling places are the precipices, caves, and ravines. Often I consort with men in the semblance of a woman. . . ."

The child-strangling aspect of Lilith is embodied in the demon Obizuth, a Medusa-like figure with no limbs, a "bright and greeny glance," and wildly disheveled hair. Mocking Solomon, she eventually describes herself: "I am called among men Obizuth. By night I sleep not, but go my rounds over all the world, and visit women in childbirth. Divining the hour, I take my stand; if I am lucky, I strangle the child. If not, I move on to another place; for I cannot for a single night retire unsuccessful. I am a fierce spirit of myriad names and many shapes. . . . Though thou hast sealed me round with the ring of God, thou hast done nothing. I am not standing before thee, and thou wilt not be able to command me. For I have no work other than the destruction of children, and the making their ears to be deaf, and the working of evil to their eyes, and the binding of their mouths with a bond, and the ruin of their minds, and paining of their bodies."

Only the name of her frustrating angel, Raphael, written on a woman in childbirth, can prevent Obizuth from entering her womb. (The name of Ba'al is similarly exhorted to banish Lilith in the Canaanite amulet dating from the eighth century B.C.E.; the angels Sanvi, Sansanvi, and Semangelef—as well as the prophet Elijah—are called upon to diminish Lilith's hold in medieval amulets and incantations.)

Yet another major female demon appears before Solomon to prophesy his doom. The three-headed, many-armed Enepsigos predicts the destruction of the Temple (a *fait accompli* at the writing of the piece) and the breaking of the jars in which he has shut up the evil spirits, disseminating them throughout the world for centuries to come, until the Messianic Age—predicated, here, upon the Virgin Birth.

The Queen of Sheba‡ also appears, classified here as a demon or "witch." After trying Solomon with her riddles, she is

‡ The Queen of Sheba is linked with Lilith in numerous sources, originating in the *Targum to Job* 1:15. The implication, clearly, is that a clever and powerful woman simply cannot be a human one.

so dazzled by his wit and strength that she generously contributes to the Temple.

Solomon, alas, outwits all the demons only to meet his nemesis in a young Shunammite woman, the Jezebel—if not the Lilith —of his day. He falls "violently in love" with the Shunammite and asks to have her join his contingent of wives; but the priests of her tribe refuse unless he is prepared to make sacrifices to their gods. Desperately clinging to his faith, Solomon refuses; the priests insist, craftily enlisting the Shunammite in their cause.

"When I answered that I would on no account worship strange gods, they told the maiden not to sleep with me until I complied. . . . Crafty Eros brought and laid by her for me five grasshoppers, saying: 'Take these grasshoppers, and crush them together in the name of the god Moloch; then I will sleep with you.'"

Thus, alas, stirrings of the flesh—or ego—brought Solomon to defeat. Once he had crushed the grasshoppers before the altars of the foreign gods, his strength and powers departed, and the maiden had her way with him. "The spirit of God departed from me, and I became weak as well as foolish in my words. And after that I was obliged by her to build a temple of idols to Baal and to Rapha and to Moloch. . . . My spirit was darkened, and I became the sport of idols and demons."

While the author (or authors) of this unusual, amusing, and highly syncretistic document does not identify the female demons with the human maiden, the modern reader can easily discern—even in the Shunammite—the same old story once more recast: the seductive siren leading man to his doom. Lilith alive in the land.

Even the relatively austere Talmud takes notice of her presence, referring to her as "long-haired" and "winged." In the tractate Shabat (151 b), Rabbi Hannina warns men against her incursions: ". . . whoever sleeps in a house alone is seized by Lilith." Among the ten curses bestowed upon Eve as a result of the Fall, one gloss (PR.100b) observes, "She grows long hair like Lilith, sits when making water like a beast, and serves as a bolster to her husband."

Despite the resemblance between postexilic Eve and Lilith glancingly noted in the preceding gloss, folklore of the talmudic period clearly—and curiously—renders Lilith the enemy of women as well as of men. For women, she presumably poses the greatest danger during the periods of their sexual cycle: before defloration, during menstruation, pregnancy, and childbirth —periods in which a woman's sense of her own sexuality is invariably heightened, marking her distinctly different from man— an alien and frightening being, whose sexual life and expression he cannot emulate. The capacity to give birth, of course, is the most dramatic of these differences. Significantly, it is in the hour of childbirth that mother and newborn infant were considered most vulnerable and in need of protection from Lilith.

Dozens of bowls, inscribed with magic incantations against Lilith, dating from C.E. 600 (just a century after the completion of the Babylonian Talmud) and excavated at Nippur—where a large Jewish colony flourished—testify to the hold Lilith had on the popular imagination of the time. A rough drawing sketched on one of these bowls shows Lilith naked, with long, loose hair, pointed breasts, no wings, strongly marked genitals, and chained ankles. The female Liliths were reputed to couple with men by night, and the male Lilis with women, generating demonic offspring. Once these spirits succeeded in attaching themselves to a human, they acquired rights of cohabitation, and had to be exorcised by a letter of divorce. Such bills of divorce are inscribed on many of the bowls with accompanying exhortations. In one of these, Lilith and her companions are banished from the house "in the name of Yahweh" and tendered a formal divorce:

". . . A divorce writ has come for you from across the sea. . . . Hear it and depart from the house and dwelling of . . . You shall not again appear to them, either in a dream by night or slumber by day. . . . Your divorce and writ and letter of separation . . . sent through holy angels . . . the Hosts of fire in the spheres . . . the Beasts worshiping in the fire of his throne and in the water. . . . Amen, Amen, Selah, Halleluyah!"

In another bowl, both male and female demons are given

their *get* (letter of divorce) to rid the house and its inhabitants of them: "This is the *get* for a demon and spirits and Satan . . . and Lilith in order to banish them. . . . I adjure you . . . whether you are male or female, I adjure you. . . . Just as the demons write letters of divorce and give them to their wives and again do not return to them, so take your letter of divorce, accept your stipulated share (*ketubba*), and go and leave and depart from the house. . . . Amen, Amen, Amen, Selah."

A medieval story, preserved in Hebrew and Arabic versions, tells of a youth, Dihon ben Shalmon, who marries the daughter of Ashmodai (king of the demons), then gives her a bill of divorce, whereupon she kills him with a kiss.

From early post-talmudic times, these succubae were reputed to be extraordinarily jealous of their bedpartners' human mates, to hate those children born of ordinary human wedlock, to attack them, plague them, suck their blood, and strangle them. Lilith was also rendered responsible for miscarriages, barrenness, and any complications occurring during pregnancy or childbirth.

Lilith's fame spread from Babylonia eastward into Persia. Among Babylonian Jews under Persian rule, she was designated mother of Ahriman, chief of all devils, and king of evil, darkness, and death. Persian magic bowls were used against her in much the same manner as those from Nippur. She is addressed and banished on one with the following inscription: "The evil Lilith, who causes the hearts of men to go astray and appears in the dream of the night and the vision of the day, who burns and casts down with nightmare, attacks and kills children, boys, and girls—she is conquered and sealed away from the house and from the threshold. . . . Vanquished are the black arts and mighty spells, vanquished the bewitching women. . . . Vanquished and trampled down are the bewitching women, vanquished on earth and vanquished in heaven. Vanquished are their constellations and stars. Bound are the works of their hands. Amen, Amen, Selah."

Yet another Persian bowl provides an even more powerful incantation to render Lilith harmless. After the usual adjurations to cease haunting the home of a particular Persian citizen, she is immobilized in the following prose: "Bound is the be-witching Lilith with a peg of iron in her nose; bound is the be-witching Lilith with pinchers of iron in her mouth; bound is the bewitching Lilith . . . with a chain of iron on her neck; bound is the bewitching Lilith with fetters of iron on her hands; bound is the bewitching Lilith with socks of stone on her feet. . . ."

In the Middle Ages, fear of Lilith spread throughout Europe in both the Christian and Jewish worlds. Men held her respon-sible for their nocturnal emissions; women, for their failures in childbirth. A demonic projection of man's fears and woman's ambivalence, she embodied for both a morbid dread of their own unbridled passions and sexuality. More often represented as a scraggly-haired crone than as a seductive sylph or the winged goddesslike figure of Sumerian times, her reign over realms of darkness and death remained undisputed. Charms and amulets, magic incantations and rituals were widely used to keep her at bay. A proliferation of texts elaborated on her ori-gins and influence.

The *Alphabet of Ben Sira,* a Jewish work of the tenth cen-tury, recounts the story of Lilith as Adam's first wife, their sub-sequent dispute, her flight, her interlude at the Red Sea and confrontation with the three angels who exact her promise that she will leave mothers and newborn infants unharmed upon sight and sound of their three names. While based on earlier material[2] that designates Lilith as the "first Eve," created at the same time as man, the *Alphabet* endows that earlier story of or-igin with a further misogynistic embellishment: "God then formed Lilith, the first woman, just as He had formed Adam, except that he used filth and sediment instead of pure dust. . . ."

The concept of woman created independently of man proved far too subversive a view to survive for long in the patriarchal ethos of the times. Lilith's bid for equality in refusing to submit to Adam's will and her subsequent decision to leave him were consequently interpreted as contrary to the will of God. After leaving Adam, Lilith could only become—in this context—a pro-miscuous, insatiable female spirit forever seeking attachments to men. A further wedge was driven between the spirit of Lilith and the aspirations of ordinary women by insisting on Lilith's hatred and antagonism to human women. Her insatiable and wanton need for men clearly ran counter to the pallid affections of Eve's docile daughters, whose required submissiveness was presumably mandated by Divine will, just as Lilith's intransigence was censored and punished by it. Even Lilith's propensity for snatching children was attributed to her enduring jealousy of Eve—an eternal, vengeful mourning at being replaced by another woman!

The figure of Lilith is further amplified in the Zohar, the major text of Kabbalism, an elite and esoteric mystical movement that began to emerge in the twelfth century. Here Lilith's descent is traced in an intricate cosmogony, one version of which presents her as Sammael's (Satan's) other half, wrought from the stern and punitive aspect of God—one of His ten mystical attributes (Sephirot) whose lowest manifestation has affinity with the realm of evil, referred to as "the dregs of the wine":

". . . out of the dregs of the wine there emerged an intertwined shoot which comprises both male and female. They are red like the rose, and they spread out into several sides and paths. The male is called Samael, and his female (Lilith) is always contained in him. Just as in the side of Holiness, so in the Other (Evil) Side as well, male and female are contained in one another. The female of Samael is called Serpent, Woman of Harlotry, End of All Flesh, End of Days."

The coupling of Lilith and Samael in the netherworld thus echoed the mating of Adam and Eve in the human sphere, as well as the link between God and the Shekinah—his feminine aspect—in the celestial realm. Such a construct served as foundation for Lilith's subsequent ascendance to the throne of God, a theme introduced in the Zohar and developed in later Kabbalistic works. This high point in Lilith's career (and low point in God's) presumably occurred upon the destruction of the Temple in Jerusalem, when God lost the Matronit [his coruler in the celestial sphere, roughly comparable to the Shekinah] and attached himself to the Other Place . . . the "slave woman," Lilith.

A slightly different view of Lilith's rise and fall holds that God's degradation came about through the evil of men, which had precipitated the destruction of the Temple and the exile of the nation of Israel. The Shekinah—that pure and divine female essence or aspect of the Godhead—was then compelled to leave God's side to join the exiled nation on earth, providing the ambitious Lilith with an opportunity to move up in Her place.

Yet another Zoharic reference identifies the earthbound Shekinah with the demon herself: "When Israel was exiled, the Shekinah, too, went into exile, and this is the nakedness of the Shekinah. And this nakedness is Lilith, the mother of a mixed multitude."

Kabbalistic development of Lilith's impact on human life reflects the belief that all behavior is prey to both good and evil forces. The sexual act itself may either evoke the divine and sacred or the base and demonic, depending upon the circumstances surrounding it and the impulse that elicits it. On the one hand, union between man and woman within marriage is considered a holy act—a kind of meditation in which the nation of Israel, represented by the Shekinah, reunites with God.

"Wasting of the seed," on the other hand, either through masturbation or coitus interruptus (decried even in biblical times), is viewed as a destructive act, through which not the holy, but the "other side"—Lilith and her retinue—gains ascendance. An extreme cult of "purity" furthered the notion that not only improper acts, but also the mere flickering of lascivious desire would prompt her presence. Elaborate rites were prescribed to assure her exclusion.

"In the hour when the husband enters into union with his wife," the Zohar advises, "he should turn his mind to the holiness of his Lord and say:

> Veiled in velvet—are you here?
> Loosened, loosened (be your spell)!
> Go not in and go not out!
> Let there be none of you and nothing of your part!
> Turn back, turn back, the ocean rages,
> Its waves are calling you,

But I cleave to the holy part,
I am wrapped in the sanctity of the King.[3]

"Then, for a time, he should wrap his head and his wife's head in cloths, and afterward sprinkle his bed with fresh water."

Indeed, Lilith's seductive and destructive aspects are vividly enumerated in yet another passage, which describes her transformation once men succumb to her:

"She adorns herself with many ornaments like a despicable harlot, and takes up her position at the crossroads to seduce the sons of man. When a fool approaches her, she grabs him, kisses him, and pours him wine. . . . As soon as he drinks it, he goes astray after her. When she sees that he has strayed from the path of truth, she divests herself of all ornaments . . . her hair is long and red like the rose, her cheeks are white and red, from her ears hang six ornaments, Egyptian chords and all the ornaments of the Land of the East hang from her nape. Her mouth is set like a narrow door comely in its decor, her tongue is sharp like a sword, her words are smooth like oil, her lips are red like a rose and sweetened by all the sweetness of the world. She is dressed in scarlet, and adorned with forty ornaments less one. Yon fool goes astray after her and drinks from the cup of wine and commits with her fornications and strays after her. What does she thereupon do? She leaves him asleep on the couch, flies up to heaven, denounces him, takes her leave, and descends. That fool awakens and deems he can make sport with her as before, but she removes her ornaments and turns into a menacing figure. She stands before him clothed in flaming fire, inspiring terror . . . making body and soul tremble . . . in her hand a drawn sword dripping bitter drops. And she kills that fool and casts him into Gehenna."

This burning image of Lilith inflamed not only the minds of the mystical elite in medieval times, but also seared the popular imagination as well, eliciting a proliferation of folk rituals to diminish her hold.

The observation of *Wachnacht*[4] (Watchnight)—in which vigil was maintained over mother and child to guard against the invasion of Lilith from the moment of birth until conclusion of the circumcision ceremony—is mentioned by Jewish writers as early as the twelfth century, although its origins are not specifically Jewish. Relatives and friends would gather in the home on the eve of circumcision to study Torah all night, to read the Psalms, and to recite the "Shema Yisrael. . . ."

Some other prophylactic measures during the Middle Ages included the placing of Torah scroll and phylacteries on the mother's bed or at the door of her room, the lighting of candles on her behalf, and the closing of all windows at night (a practice maintained to this day by some Jews in the Caucasus and Morocco). Amulets inscribed with conjurations against Lilith and her retinue were suspended on the walls of the room. During the last days before delivery, the mother would keep a knife with her when alone, reflecting the superstition that demons—born in the Stone Age—were repelled by iron, the later metal. According to some reports, the metal key to the synagogue was placed in the mother's hand during labor; when no synagogue key was available in isolated homes and villages, a church key was occasionally substituted.

Often, a magic circle was drawn around the lying-in bed and an inscription (reading "Sanvi, Sansanvi, Semangelef, Adam, and Eve, barring Lilith") was chalked upon the walls or door. Medieval amulets and inscriptions generally followed the same formula as the much older Canaanite incantation, as well as those found on sixth-century bowls in Persia and Nippur, reflecting folk belief and magical practice that has spanned the centuries. Demons, according to this belief, may be exorcised or rendered powerless upon confrontation with their own image (usually bound or manacled), the recital—in the case of Lilith—of her various names and aliases, or the names of her antagonists (the three angels, Elijah, Adam, and Eve).

Yet another ceremony, with interesting parallels to the exorcism of Lilith during the Wachnacht, despite its derivation from Teutonic mythology, gained wide popularity among Jews in medieval Germany. The practice of the Hollekreisch marked the secular naming of children, in which the child's secular name* was shouted out to ward off the demon Holle. Guests specially invited for the occasion lift the baby into the air three times, shouting the child's name in unison each of the times. A typical formula, used well into the seventeenth century, begins: "Hollekreisch! What shall this child's name be?" followed by calling out the name. Another variation: "Holle! Holle! This child's name shall be . . ."

And who was the fearful lady Holle? Among the ancient Teutons, Holle, Holda, or Hulda was represented as an ugly crone with long, matted hair and protruding teeth. She was accordingly held responsible for entangling hair at night. By medieval times, she had developed into the demon who gobbles children. Indeed, the parallels between the Oriental Lilith and the Teutonic Hulda are stunning. Both are demons of the night, distinguished by their long hair; both have an insatiable appetite for newborn human children; both make their attack before the child is named.

Jewish folklore of the time welcomed Holle-Hulda with open arms, transforming her in the process from a child-snatching crone to a corrupted Venus of sorts, goddess and patroness of lovers. Lilith did not fare so well.

Yet for Jews, Lilith remained the more enduring figure; Holle-Hulda was merely a passing secular name. Born in ancient Sumer, Lilith traveled far and wide; her presence was simultaneously remarked in Europe, North Africa, and the Middle East. An eighteenth-century Persian amulet portrays a rather pot-bellied Lilith with arms outstretched and appropriately shackled. Across her body, Hebrew letters once more "protect this newborn child from all harm." The names of Adam and Eve, together with the matriarchs and patriarchs, appear on either side of her. She is further restrained, above and below, by the initial letters from passages in Numbers and Psalms.

* Hebrew names are customarily given male children on the day of circumcision; female children, on the first Sabbath after birth. Since the earliest days of the Diaspora, however, Jews have also borne names from the nomenclature of the countries in which they live—their *secular* names, as distinct from the Hebrew or classical name.

Even Solomon's early dominance over the demons (attested to in his third-century "Testament") has been evoked in Middle Eastern Jewish exorcisms of Lilith as recently as the early twentieth century. Those vulnerable to her designs are advised to "Draw a Seal of King Solomon . . . who adjured Lilith that when she would see his seal she and her cohorts would flee. . . . And if it be placed on a house, she would not enter it, neither she nor any one of her band. If it be engraved upon pure silver, it is even better. And this is its shape:"

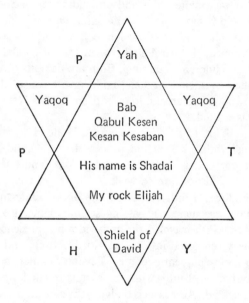

(From Raphael Ohana, *Mar'eh HaYeladim*, as reproduced in Raphael Patai's *The Hebrew Goddess*)

Lilith, nonetheless, managed to survive both spells and seals. She moved into the nineteenth century to become the muse of poets, playwrights, and novelists. The British Congregationalist minister George MacDonald became enamored of her. At twenty-six, he left the ministry to devote his life to writing and became a celebrated and popular author of the time. In his adult fantasy novel *Lilith,* published in 1858, the hero is drawn toward a rediscovery of reality through a series of dreamlike episodes that brings him closer to the enigmatic and often terrifying female figure.

His contemporary, poet-painter Dante Gabriel Rossetti, was equally taken with Lilith's fatal charm. He recasts the story of Creation and Fall in the long ballad *Eden Bower,* in which Lilith, Adam's first wife, is set in opposition to Eve:

> Lilith stood on the skirts of Eden;
> (And O the bower and the hour!)
> She was the first that thence was driven;
> With her was hell and with Eve was heaven.

For Rossetti—as for so many others—despite the moral driven, Lilith's hell emerges as far more vivid and engaging than the purity of Eve's heaven. The two are again coupled in matching sonnets, "Soul's Beauty" (Sonnet LXXVII), featuring Eve; and "Body's Beauty" (Sonnet LXXVIII), also titled "Lilith: For a Picture."

> Of Adam's first wife, Lilith, it is told
> (The witch he loved before the gift of Eve.)
> That, ere the snake's, her sweet tongue could deceive,
> And her enchanted hair was the first gold.
> And still she sits, young while the earth is old,
> And, subtly of herself contemplative,
> Draws men to watch the bright web she can weave,
> Till heart and body and life are in its hold.
>
> The rose and poppy are her flowers; for where
> Is he not found, O Lilith, whom shed scent
> And soft-shed kisses and soft sleep shall snare?
> Lo! as that youth's eyes burned at nine, so went
> Thy spell through him, and left his straight neck bent
> And round his heart one strangling golden hair.

Such wistful nostalgia for the fatal snares of love continued to stir the hearts and minds of vulnerable adolescents nearly a century later. It was Rossetti, incidentally, who introduced Lil-

ith to contemporary American historian James Flexner in the
years of his youth. ("Lilith was my first girlfriend.")

In eastern Europe, Lilith retained her hold on the folk imagination—delaying men on their way home for the Sabbath, in-
vading the sleep of husband and wife. The simplest *stetl* Jew
lived in a world rich with demonic possibilities. Such numinous
perceptions of life on earth linked with the life hereafter and
fraught with temptations from the "other side" found their way
into the brilliantly conceived Yiddish stories of Isaac Leib
Peretz in the nineteenth century and those of Isaac Bashevis
Singer in the twentieth.

In France, the aristocratic recluse Remy de Gourmont re-
created the Genesis myths in *Lilith,* a dramatic dialogue, first
published in 1892. An interest in occultism and illuminism—
typical of the period—found rich source material in Apocryphal, talmudic, and Kabbalistic writing. The resurgence of these
sources in new French translations combined with Gourmont's
own inflamed fantasy to produce a work that is, at the same
time, both an awkward and a compelling blend of eroticism,
mysticism, and misogyny. After fashioning the perfect Adam
with loving care and tenderness, for example, a rather bumbling
God turns to the creation of Lilith. In his enthusiasm for building up her breasts and hips, adding layer after layer of clay,
God runs short of clay before completing Lilith's head. Impatiently, He grabs a chunk out of her belly, leaving "a great cav-
ity," but endowing her with a head of sorts. "Give me a man!"
are the first words out of newborn Lilith's mouth, as she un-
dulates before God, "fondling her full breasts." Unwilling to
burden perfect Adam with lascivious Lilith, God bestows her
on Satan. Adam, meanwhile, is puzzled by the one organ of his
body that seems to serve no function. To provide it with purpose, God hastily fashions Eve from Adam's displaced rib—a
vapid, childish creature who, nonetheless, manages to precipi-
tate his downfall—aided by Satan and Lilith, who then couple
with the human pair.

A gentler and more wistful note is introduced in Anatole
France's short story "The Daughter of Lilith," part of his col-
lection *Balthazar,* first published in 1889. As the story opens,

M. Ary, a troubled young man, visits his old priest and philosophy teacher who has been immersed in the study of arcane matters for the preparation of a book on which he awaits his *monseigneur*'s blessing. The younger man's troubles gradually unfold. He had been happily engaged to a young woman whom he loved when Paul, a friend from student days, returned to Europe from a diplomatic mission in the East with a new companion—the beautiful and enigmatic "Leila." Leila exerts a strange and compelling attraction for the young Ary; he falls madly in love with her, forgetting all else—his work, his friendship with Paul, his betrothal. At the height of his abandonment to this consuming new passion, Leila abruptly vanishes, leaving behind only a sealed message, which Ary has not yet opened. The old priest recognizes, in the young man's confessional, the person of Lilith's daughter. The book on which he awaits ecclesiastic approval, it turns out, is an exegesis of the Genesis story, based on the incorporation of Lilith as Adam's first wife. As the story closes, the *monseigneur* rejects the old priest's book, and Ary opens Leila's note to read:

"The Prayer of Leila, Daughter of Lilith. My God, promise me death, so that I may taste of life. My God, give me remorse, so that I may at last find happiness. My God, make me the equal of Eve's daughters."

Yet Leila's words are those of Anatole France. Despite a presence that has endured for millennia and an antagonism that spans centuries, we have heard neither from the daughters of Lilith nor from the daughters of Eve. We do not know how women perceived these two mythologems, set in opposition to each other, as models for their own behavior.

What assured Lilith's powerful hold on man's imagination? How did so malevolent a spirit endure so long—long after belief in other demons had faded? Merely one among many spirits in the ancient world where such belief was literal and where all the forces of nature were endowed with human attributes, Lilith moved from a minor role four thousand years ago in Sumer —a passing wind-spirit who briefly invaded the goddess Inanna's garden before being banished to the desert—to the status of a major demon, linked with birth, sexuality, and death, in the feverish constructs of early Christian and medieval times. Even in the nineteenth century, when belief in the animism of nature had long since vanished, fear of Lilith and fascination with her fatal charm continued to prevail. The more men decried her, the more they sought her out—this seductress who lured them to their doom, this harridan who threatened the lives of their wives and children. Until recent years, we learned all we knew of Lilith through the words of men, intrigued, beguiled, repelled, and fascinated by her. Why was this demon more tenacious than all others? What is the secret of Lilith's hold on the minds of men?

The unveiling of such mysteries now rests in the hands of women. For the first time in more than four thousand years, the daughters of Eve and Lilith have begun to speak for themselves. And in their words, the lie is given to those images of Eve and Lilith that have haunted men and plagued women for centuries. Prompted by a new sense of self-assurance, illuminated by feminist insight, women in the twentieth century have turned to re-examine the cultural origins of their oppression—the myths and images that kept them in their place. Man's curious vision of woman as angel/demon, saint/sinner, virgin/whore, Eve and Lilith breaks down under the impact of such scrutiny—dissolves and scatters, ephemeral as the wind out of which Lilith was born.

In the struggle to find their own voices, in the re-creation of their own origins, women have succeeded in transforming those very myths that sanctioned their subordination. For Jewish feminists, particularly—and for the first time in recorded history—the figure of Lilith serves as a springboard to the rediscovery of themselves.

The Coming of Lilith, written by Jewish feminist theology[5] lecturer Judith Plaskow in 1973, reunites Lilith with Eve in the Garden, symbolically restoring to woman the power and spirit denied in her rib myth of origin.

Some years ago, a Moroccan woman gave an amulet inscribed with the image of Lilith to a friend of mine, Lilly Rivlin, to guard against barrenness. For the Moroccan woman, Lilith had ironically become a symbol of fertility.

Both the link between her own name and that of the ancient demoness, as well as her identification with the struggle of contemporary women to emerge from the confinement of those "names" bestowed upon them by men in generations past, moved Lilly Rivlin to explore the impact of the Lilith figure on the lives of women and their responses to it. In an article published by *Ms.* magazine in 1973, she analyzes the political use of the Lilith myth to suppress women and the essential inadequacy of both Lilith and Eve as models for woman's experience.

Other women, as well, have turned to the legend of Lilith as a source for their own re-creation. In the past few years alone, essays, poems, short stories, parables, and theater pieces about Lilith, written by women, have proliferated. The publication of *Lilith,* a national quarterly magazine, dedicated to the pursuit of feminist ideals in Jewish life, was launched by a Jewish feminist collective in New York in June of 1976.

The Bat Kol† Players, a traveling feminist theater group led by rabbinical candidate Lynn Gottlieb, has introduced a treatment of Lilith into their repertoire. Written by Ms. Gottlieb, the Lilith piece is the most radical departure, thus far, from traditional concepts of male and female elements in myths of creation:

In the beginning God created the earth and the sky and the sea
And God reached into the waters
Formed a womb in her hands
And placed it in the heavens
Then with her own life breath
God filled the womb with the spirit of Lilith
First woman.

Lilith gives birth to herself, bursting through the watery womb of God, to be embraced by the sky: "Lilith embraced all of life/Her wings of fire not knowing where sky began and her own self ended." Lilith thinks she has found another like her-

† *Bat kol:* literally, "daughter of the voice"; used as a figure of speech, since biblical times, to mean "the gift of prophecy."

self when she sees her own reflection on the waters, but when she speaks to it, the image does not answer, and Lilith experiences her first loneliness. God then creates a companion for her:

> And God said: It is not good for woman to be alone
> I will make her a companion
> As Lilith is sky
> So man shall be earth.

The first woman and the first man meet; she perceives a difference between them, while he—frightened by her fiery wings—falls to the earth, whereupon she names him "Adam, child of Adama."‡ She tells him they are meant to be mates, but Adam is still frightened, and

> Lilith
> Needing her companion
> Removed her wings of fire
> Hurled them to the heavens
> Where they became the sun.

Once they begin to know each other, Lilith assumes that Adam will no longer fear her, and she calls to the sun to return her wings of fire. But Adam, still "afraid of woman's fire" and angry that he has shown this fear, forces Lilith to the ground. Thus the first rape, in which man uses his greater physical strength to crush the spirit of the first woman, produces the version of creation with which we are familiar:

> Deep inside her own darkness
> Under the fear of man
> Lilith forgot her sky birth
> And awoke without memories
> Eve
> Second woman.

Although it draws strongly from Judaic sources—using both Midrashic form and content in the elaboration of the biblical

---

‡ *Adama,* Hebrew for earth, is always in the feminine gender.

myth of origin for man and woman, Bat Kol's *Lilith* succeeds in transforming creation itself, as well as those meanings traditionally drawn from it. God weeps at the transformation of the relationship between man and woman, at woman's subjugation. Death is introduced to provide the passing of generations, so that a future man and woman may retrieve the potential for equality initially intended in their creation.

When Eve eats of the Tree of Knowledge, faint memories stir of her earlier self. But Adam sees only death and insists they leave. God sends two swords of fire to the Garden to remind them of the past. But Adam, once more, is frightened of the fire and flees, taking Eve with him:

> And Eve left the garden wtih her master
> Mourning a self not quite remembered.

The theater piece concludes with both a claim and a plea for woman's recovery of the fullness of her spirit, symbolized by Lilith's wings of fire:

> Lilith
> We are your children
> We are the changing generations
> Help us recover our wings of fire
> So we can come together
> Woman and man
> As intended at Creation.

5

The Suppressed Goddess

Do you not see what is going on in the cities of
Judah and in the streets of Jerusalem? Children are
gathering wood, fathers lighting fires, women kneading dough to make crescent cakes in honour of the
queen of heaven. . . .   (Jr. 7:17–18)

. . . there I saw women sitting and wailing for Tammuz. . . .   (Ezk. 8:14–15)

Everything in the sphere of this first attachment to
the mother seemed to me so difficult to grasp . . . so
gray with age and shadowy . . . as if it had succumbed to an especially inexorable repression. . . .
            (Sigmund Freud, *On Female Sexuality*)

Shards of goddesses buried deep under the earth: stout Paleolithic Venuses more than twenty thousand years old, tinged
with red ocher, surrogate for blood, female genitalia inscribed
on sacred caves—uterine forms of worshiping places that precede the soaring towers and ziggurats of prebiblical times;
queens buried in splendor in Anatolia and Ur, in Thebes and
Upper Egypt—images retrieved from the womb of the earth:
mute, enduring testimony to female power and mystery, descending back through layers of time, long before the advent of
recorded history.

The suppression of powerful female deities, mandated by
monotheism's vision of a single, syntactically male god, continued throughout the biblical period, even into the days of the

Israelite monarchy, when women of the Old Testament were offering crescent cakes to the Queen of Heaven—the Sumerian Inanna, the Babylonian Ishtar, the Canaanite Asherah. They continued to weep for Tammuz, the young fertility god retrieved from the underworld and restored to life by the older goddess Ishtar. Weaving tapestries for Asherah in the temples of Yahweh, they incurred the wrath of Israel's prophets—these Old Testament women erecting pillars to Asherah on sacred temple grounds, paying homage to the Queen of Heaven, goddess of the sea and sacred groves.

That inexorably repressed "first attachment to the mother"— to which Freud alludes in another context—emerges from the shadows of abrogated memory, as archaeological revelations of the twentieth century render the distant past far more accessible than ever before. Buried civilizations, lost from memory for thousands of years, have been unearthed within the past two centuries.

"More has been dug up in the last hundred years," comments biblical scholar Theodore Gaster, "than in the past two thousand!" Yet archaeologists estimate that less than 1 per cent of extant materials have thus far been unearthed, deciphered, and translated. Meanwhile, refinements of dating and decipherment continue to revolutionize biblical scholarship, as well as our knowledge of human history, unveiling the richness and significance of the past in ways undreamed of less than a century ago. The analysis of artifacts and skeletal remains plunges back dates for the inception of human life on earth by hundreds of millennia; the discovery and decipherment of vast libraries of cuneiform tablets reveal the literary texts and legal codes of those ancient Near Eastern civilizations from which the biblical ethos emerged, both illuminating the Old Testament and antedating it by more than two thousand years.

Despite such truly remarkable advances in scholarship within the past few decades, the image and role of woman throughout the ages remains relatively unexplored. My own purpose in undertaking the journey back through time is to examine the sources of those myths and attitudes that have defined women in various civilizations, unveiling the abundance of that past from which the present is derived.

Moving back through the aeons, a series of images unfolds, suggesting a pattern in which an early primal vision of woman as source of life and death—of birth and regeneration—gives way to the gradual ascendance of the male (reflected in imagery of mother and son or goddess with young god), followed by the subordination of female power, manifest in prebiblical texts when an older goddess is overthrown by a young hero or god, culminating with the ultimate suppression of female force in the sweeping vision of monotheism that informs the Old Testament and biblical period—the source of Western civilization as we know it today. Closer examination of this pattern of evolution and transformation offers considerable insight into those very human conflicts and passions—projected onto the images of deities and heroes—that continue to pervade contemporary life and threaten to contaminate the future.

Among the first images created by humankind are the Stone Age Venuses, striking Paleolithic figures of the female in bas-relief and plastic forms. Well over twenty thousand years old, these prehistoric idols appear across a wide area, extending from western Asia across the Russian steppes and valley of the Don into Europe, the Mediterranean, and Asia Minor—with a preponderance occurring on those eastern sites from which the goddess cults emerged thousands of years later.

Two major types prevail among these archaic images. The first, typified by the Aurignacian Venus of Willendorf, is squat and corpulent, with pendulous breasts, broad hips, rotund buttocks, and protruding abdomen, suggesting pregnancy. The second, far more stylized in execution—like the elegant Magdalenian ivory Venus from Lespugne—is slender and elongated, with willowy waist and neck, buttressed by broad hips and thighs. Traces of red ocher, which can still be detected in the porous limestone from which many of these figures are formed, indicate the use of red pigment as a life-giving agent and surrogate for blood, both in Paleolithic and later rituals, linking the idols with human and animal birth and generation, as well as with fertility and fecundity of the earth.

Suggestions have been made that prehistoric food-gathering groups venerated the fecundity represented by the corpulent female idol, while hunting groups elevated the importance of the chase, depicted in the caves of Altameira, typical of the Magdalenian era in southern Spain. Yet the cave itself, observes Rachel Levy, is uterine in form—precursor for the labyrinth of later mythologies—the journey to the shrine at its inmost point, symbolic of generation and rebirth by passage through the female.

Plastic figures of the female, however, are invariably found outside of caves. While no written texts accompany their appearance, these numinous figures—many of them no more than fifteen inches high, sculpted in sandstone and limestone, in bone and ivory—speak to us today from shrines and worshiping places of the past of an archaic awe and wonder at the prodigious capacities of the female form and spirit.

From Neolithic times onward, phallic emblems become increasingly prominent. Nonetheless, four times as many female figurines appear on Neolithic sites as do male ones, and the female principle—eventually personified as a mother goddess—continues to assume a leading role, particularly in western Asia, as well as in Crete and the Aegean, where the young male god remained subservient to the older goddess until well into the Iron Age.

In eastern Europe, figures dating from about 7000 B.C.E. take on a highly stylized form, triangular or fiddle-shaped with striations that emphasize a strongly marked navel. Similar forms occur some two thousand years later in the Chalcolithic mound of Tel Archipayah, near the ancient city of Nineveh.

A breakthrough to 6000 B.C.E. was made in Asia Minor when excavations at Catal Huyuk (Anatolia) unearthed the earliest pottery images of the goddess linked with pigs, dogs, cattle, and wheat. Among figures found at Huyuk are those of a mother and child, twelve inches high; the ceramic image of a female—presumably a goddess—giving birth; and a sculpted piece in greenish stone of two goddesses, back to back, with a male child between them. The continuous association of the goddess with vegetation, as well as animal and human life, persists from prehistoric times into early written history.

In Mesopotamia (roughly identical with modern Iraq), excavations at the Chalcolithic mound of Arpachiyah (the beginnings of which go back to before 4000 B.C.E.) have retrieved an abundance of figures concentrated about the tholoi or ancient shrines. Almost all the human figurines are plastic representations of nude, painted females, with head barely indicated, but with exaggerated portrayal of breasts, abdomen, buttocks, and vulvar region—reminiscent of earlier Aurignacian images. Most are in squatting position, indicating approaching delivery. Some occur in the stylized, striated, fiddle-shaped forms that appeared earlier in eastern Europe. A large number of animal figures represent cattle, sheep, pigs, and the dove—closely associated with the goddess in later Near Eastern texts and art. Figures dating from about 3200 B.C.E., unearthed at Erech and at Ur (that ancient site in southern Mesopotamia from which the biblical patriarchs subsequently departed) include slender female nudes with well-modeled bodies, feet together, with an incision marking the pubes and division between the legs, and hands at waist or hips, some holding a child to the breasts. Yet another striking group of clay images incorporates the slender, well-modeled female body with a grotesque, elongated head and reptilian features.

Long before their appearance in the eastern Mediterranean, images of the goddess associated with the double ax and dove, the bull's head and the serpent, were in common use in northern Iraq, dating from about the fifth millennium B.C.E. Later Babylonian images (c. 2500 B.C.E.) portray the goddess standing on a lion; an abundance of Syro-Hittite cylinder seals (c. 2000 B.C.E.) depict her standing on a bull. Both American Semitics scholar William Foxwell Albright and British Orientalist Edwin Oliver James suggest that the unmistakable affinities of these figures with the archaic Stone Age images provide a significant link between the Paleolithic cultus and its later Chalcolithic and Bronze Age manifestations in Anatolia, Crete, and the ancient Near East.

In Egypt, Hathor—frequently referred to as "the cow goddess"—is depicted either as a female with horned headdress or as a giant cow. Egyptian art and theology portray the sky as female—personified in the goddess Nut—who bears the male earth-god Geb and is, in turn, impregnated by him each night as the sun sets, the following day's rising sun described as the calf born of her each morning. The very ancient goddess Neith from the western delta, eventually identified with Hathor and Isis, is also described as "the great cow that gave birth to Re"— the later sun god. Originally, however, she seems to have been a personification of the primeval watery depths from which all creation emerged—much like the Sumerian Nammu and later Babylonian Tiammat, vestiges of which appear in the biblical story of Creation as the watery chaos (*tehom*) from which the Old Testament God fashioned Creation. Like Nut, Neith possessed the power to conceive and give birth to the new sun god daily. Initially, however, she appears to have been eternal and self-produced, personifying from very early times a sense of the female principle as self-sustaining and all-pervasive.

The well-known image of the goddess Isis, seated with the young god Horus on her lap, was eventually transformed into the throne—lap of the goddess—from which ancient Egyptian monarchs ruled.

By contrast, Memphite theology ascribes creation to the male god Ptah, who brought forth all things virtually *ex nihilo*—like the Old Testament God—through thought and word. A more graphic version of the Ptah myth portrays him as creating the gods by masturbating and swallowing his own semen. So, too, the Hittite Kumarbi—suggesting a kind of "womb envy," resolved with the usurpation of female power and the assumption of maternal procreation by male gods. Similar themes occur later in Greek mythology, when the archaic earth-mother Gaia is replaced by the monarchic Zeus, leader of the Pantheon, who literally gives birth to Athena from his head and Dionysius from his thigh or side, much as the biblical Adam conceives Eve in Genesis II.

The extensive interchange among nations of the ancient Near East through trade, political alliances, and military occupations is amply documented. Literary texts and plastic imagery reveal a concomitant exchange of ideas and theological concepts.

Among more than three hundred female figurines unearthed in Palestine—dating from the third through the first millennium B.C.E. (including the period of Israelite settlement)—a large number resemble Mesopotamian, Syrian, and Egyptian images from both earlier and later periods. The Qadesh type found in Palestine exhibits a variety of features: figures with arms extended to the side or holding stalks of grain, as well as nude females standing on lions. Several wear the Hathor headdress. Another series presents the female in maternal aspect, either pregnant, giving birth, and holding or suckling a child. A group of pillar figurines portrays the female with hands on breasts or encircled by a serpent—motifs that recur in Minoan and Mycenean Crete. Some few archaic figures with pierced ears and arms supporting breasts are succeeded by a proliferation of more delicately modeled types that found their way into Palestine from Mesopotamia around 2000 B.C.E., where they persisted as a motif for the mass production of figurines for more than six hundred years. In both Mesopotamia and Palestine, the form eventually degenerated into the "Venus *pudique*" type, with one hand over the breast and the other coyly covering the genitals—providing visual correlation for the debasement of the goddess in later literary texts.

The transformation of that early primal female image—reigning over life and death—to subordinate status in the pantheons of the ancient Near East, toppled by an ascendant male god or epic hero—may be traced through literary documents, beginning with the ancient civilization of Sumer.

The excavations at Nippur and Lagash, at Erech and Ur, together with the recent decipherment of cuneiform texts, reveal the existence of a remarkable people—the ancient Sumerians, non-Semitic in origin—whose legal codes and literary works, theological concepts and rituals, writing, and mathematical systems—served as the prototypes for those Semitic civilizations that succeeded them.

Sumer, the land that came to be known in classical times as Babylonia, consists of the lower half of Mesopotamia, roughly identical with modern Iraq, from north of Baghdad to the Persian Gulf—an area approximately ten thousand square miles, slightly larger than the state of Massachusetts. Hot and arid, wind-swept and barren, the land would seem empty of promise, except for the extraordinary creativity of the Sumerians, who occupied it from about 4000–2000 B.C.E., channeling the rich silt-laden waters of the Tigris and Euphrates to irrigate the barren inland soil, baking river clay and mud with plaited dried marsh reeds for huts, inventing brick molds for shaping and building, devising the potter's wheel, wagon wheel, the plow, sailboat, arch, vault, and dome, casting in copper and bronze, riveting, brazing, and soldering, sculpting in stone, working with engraving and inlay, and ultimately originating the system of writing on clay that was borrowed and used throughout the ancient Near East for some two thousand years. It is those very clay documents, inscribed in cuneiform script, from which Babylonian, biblical, and modern counterparts can today be derived.

The Sumerian myth of origins—most significant in any given culture—describes the goddess Nammu, written with the ideogram for the sea, as "the mother who gave birth to heaven and earth." This concept, later adapted in Babylonian cosmogonies, views heaven and earth as the products of primeval waters. Other sources refer to Nammu as "the mother, the ancestress who gave birth to all the gods." Within this framework, a heaven and earth (Anki) were originally united. An (heaven) was male, and Ki (earth), female. They were separated by their offspring, the air god Enlil, who carried off his mother, Ki, while An carried off heaven, thereby setting the stage for the organization of the universe, the creation of man, and the establishment of civilization.

A large pantheon eventually supervised, operated, and directed the universe, functioning as an assembly with a King at its head. The seven gods "who decree the fates," together with fifty deities known as the "great gods," constituted the Pantheon's most important groups. Those accorded highest status were the creative gods in control of heaven, earth, sea, and air.

Mankind emerged as something of an afterthought, created

primarily to serve the gods. One story has it that the hungry gods, grumbling about how difficult it was to procure their own bread, complain to Enki, god of water and wisdom. But Enki, fast asleep in the Abzu, his watery dwelling place, fails to hear them. Thereupon his mother Nammu, the primeval sea, brings "the tears of the gods" before Enki, advising him to give some thought toward fashioning servants, capable of reproducing themselves, for the divine family.

Following his mother's advice, Enki leads forth "the host of good and princely fashioners" and asks Nammu to bind upon the creature she conceived "the image of the gods." Sumerian man is thus created in similar image as biblical man, although, of course, the relation of human to divine is markedly different. Among other things, the polytheistic gods are far more capricious, conveying a sense of the arbitrariness of those natural forces they personify.

The female divinity in the Sumerian version of man's creation, however, plays a far more important role than in later Babylonian myths, or in the Old Testament story in which she is virtually erased. In the following excerpt from the Sumerian tale of creation Enki speaks to his mother, Nammu:

Mix the heart of the clay that is over the abyss,
The good and princely fashioners will thicken the clay,
You, do you bring the limbs into existence;
Ninmah [an earth-mother goddess] will work above you,
The goddesses [of birth] . . . will stand by you at your fashioning;
O my mother, decree its [the newborn's] fate,
Ninmah will bind upon it the mold of the gods,
it is man. . . .

Nammu, the original creatrix, recedes once the universe is set in motion and mankind is created to serve the gods. The air god Enlil eventually replaces his father An (heaven) as head of the pantheon. Enlil and the mother goddess Ninhursag usually head lists of the gods; they hold seats of honor at divine meetings and banquets; together with the water god Enki, they often serve as a group, performing significant acts.

The Paradise story of Enki and Ninhursag provides striking parallels and contrasts with the biblical story of creation and expulsion from Eden. In the Sumerian paradise, eight plants are made to sprout by the mother goddess Ninhursag, through an intricate process involving three generations of goddesses, born of Ninhursag and inseminated by Enki. Most significant is the ease with which Ninhursag gives birth—"one day being her one month/ two days being her two months," etc.—compared with the curse placed upon Eve for her disobedience in Eden: "I will increase your labor and your groaning, and in labor you shall bear children." (Gn. 3:16)

Like the biblical Elohim, Ninhursag warns Enki not to eat of the plants. But Enki, wanting to "know their heart," disobeys her and proceeds to taste each of the plants in turn. Angered at his disobedience, Ninhursag curses him with death and disappears.

Enki pines away, growing weaker each day. A fox comes to his rescue, negotiating with the air god Enlil for a reward, if he should be able to return Ninhursag to the assembly of the gods. The fox succeeds in securing Ninhursag's return, just as Enki is at the brink of death. Ninhursag seats him in (or by) her vulva and asks what hurts. For each of Enki's eight ailing parts, she gives birth to a healing god or goddess, thereby restoring him to life.

> Ninhursag seated Enki in her vulva. . . .
> "My brother, what hurts thee?"
> "My rib hurts me."
> "Ninti* have I caused to be born for thee. . . ."

Ninhursag subsequently assigns cosmic roles to her offspring (Ninti, as queen of the months; Abu, king of the plants, etc.). Vegetation and life are thus restored, both to Enki and the earth.

Clearly, the female remains pre-eminent in the Sumerian story; a further reversal occurs in the biblical account, where it is the woman Eve, rather than the male, who is tempted to taste

* See p. 27 for the probable erroneous derivation of woman as rib.

of the forbidden tree. The Sumerian paradise is inhabited only
by the gods; disobedience incurs the threat of death, but ultimately results in restoration to eternal life. In the biblical counterpart, paradise is created for the first humans; disobedience
results in expulsion from Eden and the loss of eternal life—essentially an etiological explanation for human suffering and
death, poignantly at odds with man's unattainable vision of immortality.

While the procreative powers of the female, retained in Sumerian myths about Nammu and Ninhursag, provide a literary
link between the archaic Stone Age goddesses and later Babylonian and biblical narratives, it is through the adventures of
the remarkable goddess Inanna—patroness of the arts of civilization and tutelary deity of Erech—that the female potential
reaches its greatest magnitude and fullest expression.

Three tales are central to an appreciation of Inanna's mul-
tifaceted powers as reigning deity and to the hymns of praise
heaped upon her by the Sumerian people. The first is the story
of the transfer of the arts of civilization from Eridu to Erech;
the second, the poems and rituals associated with the Sacred
Marriage; and the third, the tale of Inanna's descent to the
netherworld.

According to the first tale, the goddess was eager to increase
the welfare and prosperity of her city and to establish it as the
center of Sumerian civilization, Inanna—daughter of the moon
god Sin and the goddess Ningal—sets out to obtain the *mes,*
principles by which the universe is governed, from the water
god Enki, who holds them in the Abzu of Eridu, the watery
abyss where he lives. The ambitious Inanna realizes that if she
can obtain the valuable *mes* and bring them to Erech, its glory
and her own will be unsurpassed.

As her boat approaches the Abzu of Eridu, Enki—taken with
Inanna's charm—sends his messenger Isimud to greet and wel-
come her. A lavish banquet is prepared, at which Enki proceeds to get increasingly drunk. At the height of besotted con-
geniality, he magnanimously proffers the *mes* to Inanna:

> By the name of power, by the name of my power,
> To holy Inanna . . . I shall present the divine decrees.

He thereupon presents, several at a time, the more than one hundred divine decrees that guide the universe. Delighted, Inanna accepts the gifts with dispatch, loads them on her "boat of heaven," and embarks for Erech.

Once the flush of the banquet has worn off, Enki notices the missing *mes* and regrets his earlier magnanimity. Determined at all costs to retrieve the *mes,* he dispatches Isimud together with a group of sea monsters, instructing them to seize Inanna's boat at the first of seven stopping stations between Eridu and Erech.

Following orders, Isimud overtakes Inanna's boat and informs her that Enki has changed his mind. While she is free to go on to Erech, the boat with its cargo must be returned to Eridu.

Inanna furiously berates Enki for breaking his word, and turns to her messenger Ninshubur for help. Ninshubur succeeds in rescuing the boat from Isimud and the sea monsters, allowing Inanna to continue her journey. But Enki persists, dispatching Isimud and the monsters again and again to seize the boat. Each time, Ninshubur successfully rescues his mistress, until the boat and its valuable cargo arrive safely at Erech, where Inanna carefully unloads the precious *mes,* one by one—amid great jubilation and feasting among the city's delighted inhabitants, happily celebrating the pre-eminence that is now assured their city and its patroness, Inanna.

While the story of the *mes* clearly asserts Inanna's ambition, cleverness, and power, the lush and explicit sexual imagery of the songs associated with the Sacred Marriage renders her a revered and unparalleled goddess of love and fecundity. Going back to before 3000 B.C.E. and annually celebrated throughout the ancient Near East for two thousand years, the Sacred Marriage is predicated on Inanna's choice of a mate. Both the shepherd and the farmer vie for her hand, each offering the bounty of his domain. Inanna chooses the shepherd, Dumuzi, bestowing upon him "godship of the land." Bathed and dressed in her special "garments of power," she has Dumuzi brought before her. His presence fills her with such desire that she composes a paean to her vulva on the spot, comparing it to a horn, "the

boat of heaven," the new crescent moon, fallow land, a high
field and a hillock, concluding:

> As for me, my vulva,
> For me the piled-high hillock,
> Me—the maid, who will plow it for me?
> My vulva, the water ground—for me,
> Me, the Queen, who will station the ox there?

Dumuzi cheerfully accommodates:

> Oh Lordly Lady, the King will plow it for you,
> Dumuzi, the King, will plow it for you.

Inanna happily accepts:

> Plow my vulva, man of my heart!

After bathing her holy lap, they cohabit, and vegetation
flourishes about them:

> At the King's lap stood the rising cedar,
> Plants rose high by his side,
> Grains rose high by his side,
> . . . gardens flourished luxuriantly by his side. . . .

Each year, the King—standing in for Dumuzi—similarly
"married" a representative of the goddess Inanna, to assure his
people bountiful crops and prosperity. Festivities began with
the King's journey to the temple of the goddess, culminating in
his copulation with a priestess of Inanna—symbolically assuring
the flourishing of vegetation for the following year—and concluded with lavish feasts and banquets at the King's palace on
New Year's Day.

More than a dozen Sumerian Sacred Marriage Songs have
now been translated, providing significant parallels with the
biblical Song of Songs and its cuneiform prototype. Generations
of embarrassed rabbis, as well as Church Fathers, confronted
with the tender and voluptuous sexual imagery of the biblical
book—by then canonized and ascribed to King Solomon—painstakingly sought new interpretations. The rabbis settled for allegory, determining that the sensual lyrics of Song of Songs sym-

bolized the relationship between God and the people of Israel. Subsequent biblical scholars pooh-poohed such allegorical allusions, asserting that the biblical lyrics were exactly what they appeared: a story of sexual desire and fulfillment. More recently, scholars—among them Sumerologist Samuel Noah Kramer—suggest that both assumptions—the allegorical and the simple love story of a shepherd for his maiden—fall somewhat wide of the mark; that, in fact, the biblical lyrics are rooted in the ancient rites of the Sacred Marriage. Given the greater abundance of joyous Sumerian Sacred Songs now available, most of them translated by Kramer himself, parallels between the Sumerian poetry and the Hebrew Song of Songs may now be drawn with far greater accuracy and sophistication, a project on which scholars are now embarked and that Kramer discusses in some detail in his text *The Sacred Marriage Rite* (Bloomington, Ind.: University Press, 1969).

Most significant and intriguing for women today is the story of Inanna's descent to the netherworld—virtually the only prototype for woman's passage through life, in which the central female figure, rather than the traditional epic hero undertakes a difficult journey from which she emerges victorious.

Abandoning her various temples in the land of Sumer "where the sun rises," Inanna determines to plumb the darkest heart of the netherworld, ruled by Ereshkigal†, the Sumerian goddess of death. Protectively garbed and jeweled, Inanna collects the appropriate divine laws (*mes*) and prepares for her descent to that land from which none have ever returned, instructing her messenger Ninshubur to set up a lament for her if she is not back within three days.

On approaching the lapis-lazuli palace of the netherworld, Inanna demands entrance. When the gatekeeper asks why she has come, the "pure" Inanna dissembles, pretending an interest in witnessing the funeral rites for Ereshkigal's husband. While Inanna waits, the gatekeeper consults with Ereshkigal, who in-

† Ereshkigal is originally described as a sky goddess brought to the netherworld (possibly by the monster Kur). Enki sets out to retrieve her but fails, and she reigns thereafter as Queen of the Netherworld.

structs him to bring Inanna through each of seven gates leading
to the heart of the netherworld.

At each gate, Inanna is required to relinquish an article of
jewelry or clothing—until, upon passage through the seventh
gate, she finds herself in naked confrontation with Ereshkigal:

The pure Ereshkigal seated herself upon her throne,
The Anunnaki, the seven judges, pronounced judgment
    before her,
They fastened [their] eyes upon her [Inanna], the eyes
    of death,
At their word, the word that tortures the spirit . . .
The sick woman was turned into a corpse,
The corpse was hung from a stake.

When Inanna fails to return within three days, Ninshubur,
following her instructions, laments before the assembly of the
gods, tearing at eyes, mouth, and clothes—beseeching each god
in turn. Neither Enlil nor Nanna will stand by her; none can return from the netherworld, Nanna informs Ninshubur, such is
the unbroken law. What makes his daughter, the goddess Inanna, presume to be the exception?

The water god Enki, however, who "knows the heart of all
things," comes to her rescue. Fashioning the kurgarru and the
kalaturru, two sexless creatures whom he gives the "food of
life" and the "water of life," Enki instructs them to refuse all
offers of food or drink from the underworld, but to ask rather
for the corpse of Inanna, upon whom they are to sprinkle the
gifts with which they have been entrusted.

Enki's creations gain entrance to the netherworld and access
to the lifeless form of Inanna.

Sixty times the food of life, sixty times the water of life,
    they sprinkled upon it,
Inanna arose. . . .

The Anunnaki flee, and Inanna ascends from the netherworld, preceded by the dead whom she has literally raised. Accompanied by the shades and demons of Ereshkigal's domain,
Inanna proceeds through the land of the living. First to meet

her is the faithful messenger Ninshubur, dressed in sackcloth, who prostrates himself before her. The demons are eager to carry him off, but Inanna restrains them, praising his devotion to her. In similar fashion, Inanna moves from city to city, followed by her grizzly entourage. Each monarch, in turn, prostrates himself before the goddess; and Inanna prevents the demons from carrying him off.

Only in Kullab, a district of Erech where Inanna's spouse, Dumuzi, rules as shepherd-King, is there celebration and rejoicing. Rather than bewailing the loss of his wife, Dumuzi has "put on a noble robe" and "sat high on a throne." Enraged at his arrogance, Inanna looks down upon him with "the eye of death" and turns him over to the demons, eager to carry him off to the netherworld.

Weeping, Dumuzi appeals in turn to his sister Geshtinanna, divine poetess, singer, and interpreter of dreams, and to Inanna's brother Utu, the sun god. Both Geshtinanna and Utu attempt to save Dumuzi through a series of ruses, all to no avail. The demons pursue him relentlessly, routing him from each hiding place. Penetrating each of his various guises, they stone him, torture him, and ultimately carry him down to the netherworld, where the once-powerful Dumuzi serves as substitute for his once-adoring wife, the goddess Inanna.

Once Dumuzi is gone, Inanna laments his death and tenderly recalls her love for him. When his sister Geshtinanna offers to take Dumuzi's place in the Land of No Return, Inanna decides Solomon-like that Dumuzi will remain in the netherworld for half the year, and his sister for the other half.

From Mesopotamia, the theme of the dead Dumuzi and his resurrection (repeated with some modifications in the later Akkadian story of Ishtar's descent to the underworld to save the dying Tammuz) spread to Palestine, where the women of Jerusalem—much to the dismay of Israel's prophets—annually mourned the death of Tammuz at one of the gates to the Temple in Jerusalem (Ez. 8:14). To this day, there is a month called Tammuz in the Jewish calendar; its seventeenth day is a day of fasting and lament that may originally go back to the mourning for Dumuzi, although later tradition attributes it to the destruction of the Temple at Jerusalem.

While Akkadian mythology (emanating from the Assyrian conquest of Sumer, c. 2100 B.C.E. and the subsequent Babylonian Empire) derives largely from Sumerian prototypes, those new elements that are introduced reveal an increasing distrust, as well as disgust with the goddess (manifest in Gilgamesh's diatribe against Ishtar), and a gradual diminishment of her power, most vividly pronounced in the *Enuma Elish,* the Babylonian myth of creation recited annually at the New Year, in which the hero-god Marduk slays the primeval sea-mother Tiammat and re-creates the world from her carcass.

The serial adventures of Gilgamesh, popular throughout the ancient Near East for thousands of years, is perhaps the oldest model for the heroic epic. Son of a mortal father and a divine mother, Gilgamesh rules the ancient city of Gish with an iron hand. When its citizens beseech the goddess for relief, she creates the hairy Enkiddu, who lives in the fields, in harmony with the wild beasts. To tame his ostensible rival, Gilgamesh dispatches a town harlot to the fountain where animals water in the evening. The mortal woman seduces the immortal Enkiddu, and they make love for seven days and seven nights. Poor Enkiddu! His former friends, the wild beasts, will now have nothing to do with him; moreover, his congress with mortal woman‡ has robbed Enkiddu of that eternal life conveyed by his divine birth—a matter of considerable consequence later in the epic.

The "harlot-lass" convinces Enkiddu to return to town with her to meet the folk. On New Year's Day, following the ceremony of the Sacred Marriage, Enkiddu challenges Gilgamesh to a wrestling match. Neither wins; and the two become fast friends, embarking on a series of adventures together, only to be interrupted by the goddess Ishtar. So taken is Ishtar with the

‡ The ancients believed that contact between the sexes conveyed the quality of one to the other, a notion reflected in the ban on sexual relations among warrior Arabs, as well as other groups who abstain from sexual contact on the eve of battle, fearing they will contract the "weakness" of those women with whom they have lain.

beauty of Gilgamesh that she offers him all the wealth of her realm if only he will lie with her.

Gilgamesh gallantly responds by telling off the goddess in no uncertain terms. He berates her promiscuity, blames her for the death of Tammuz, and castigates her for inconstancy, comparing her to "a brazier that goes out in the cold, a palace that crushes the valiant, pitch that soils its bearer," and "a shoe that pinches the foot." He then runs down a list of all those lovers whom Ishtar has presumably destroyed, culminating with his own revulsion at her invitation to "taste" such "stench and foulness."

Enraged, Ishtar ascends to heaven, where she convinces her father, Anu, to unleash the Bull of Heaven to smite Gilgamesh and avenge her honor.

Gilgamesh and Enkiddu, however, succeed in slaying the bull. Furious, Ishtar springs upon the ramparts of the city, cursing them: "Woe unto Gilgamesh because he insulted me by slaying the Bull of Heaven!"

Insult is heaped upon insult when Enkiddu tears loose the right thigh of the bull and throws it in Ishtar's face. The goddess calls forth her hierodules to mourn the death of the Bull of Heaven, while Gilgamesh gets his gang together—craftsmen, armorers, and artisans—to admire his handiwork in slaying the bull.

The gods, nonetheless, are angry and ordain Enkiddu's death.

In a magnificent passage, Enkiddu's life passes before him, and he regrets that earlier intercourse with mortal woman that has rendered him vulnerable to death. Gilgamesh is so shaken by Enkiddu's death that he sets out in quest of eternal life. After a series of adventures, including a flood that he manages to survive, Gilgamesh secures a plant that promises immortality. While crossing the waters with the herb, a sea serpent takes the plant from Gilgamesh and eats it—the reason why the serpent is immortal* and man is not.

Ambivalence toward the female is far more pronounced in the Babylonian epic than in its Sumerian prototype. Gilgamesh

* The ancient belief in the immortality of the serpent is derived from its ability to shed its skin.

and Enkiddu are unquestionably happier when unencumbered by women, mortal or divine. When the Sumerian Gilgamesh encounters Inanna, his relationship with the goddess is cordial but not conjugal. In the story of the huluppu tree† for example, he rids Inanna's garden of the serpent and the Lilith demon by hewing down the tree they have seized and making a throne for the goddess. In the Sumerian quest for immortality, Gilgamesh settles for fame—a realistic resolution, compatible with the high status of the goddess. Significantly, the Sumerian Sacred Marriage ceremony is consummated when the King visits the priestess in Inanna's temple; in later Babylonian Sacred Marriage rites, it is the priestess who is taken to the palace of the King.

The shift in attitude toward the procreative gifts and powers of the female is even more marked when we compare a creation story of the First Babylonian Dynasty (c. 2057–1758 B.C.E.) with the *Enuma Elish* (c. 1000 B.C.E.). In the earlier fragment (part of which was used as the introduction to an incantation to facilitate childbirth), the goddess Mami (or Ninhursag) is credited with the creation of mankind:

> Thou art the mother-womb,
> The creatress of mankind. . . .

In the later *Enuma Elish* composed to provide cosmological reasons for the advancement of the new god Marduk from chief deity of Babylon to head of the pantheon, and recited annually at the New Year, the hero-god Marduk slays the primeval sea-mother Tiammat (analogous to the Sumerian Nammu) and re-creates the world from her carcass.

Marduk first speaks of Tiammat's enmity to his grandfather Anshar:

> My father, Tiamat, our bearer, hates us.
> She has formed an army and is raging furiously.
> All the gods have gone over to her;
> Even those whom ye have created march at her side.
> . . . .
> They rage and plot, not resting day or night. . . .[1]

† See p. 41.

Marduk then proceeds to describe the gruesome monsters and demons that have been unleashed, "sharp of tooth," their bodies filled "with poison instead of blood." He alleviates the older god's ensuing gloom by assuring him that he—Marduk— will vanquish Tiammat:

> What man is it who has brought battle against thee?
> Ti'amat, who is a woman, is coming against thee with arms!
> . . . rejoice and be glad;
> Soon thou shalt trample upon the [neck] of Ti'amat!

With the aid of Anshar, Marduk prepares to do battle with Tiammat:

Ti'amat and Marduk, the wisest of the gods, took their stands
    opposite each other,
They pressed on to the battle, they approached in combat.
The lord spread out his net and enmeshed her,
The evil wind, following after, he let loose in her face.
When Ti'amat opened her mouth to devour him,
He drove in the evil wind, so that she could not close her lips.
As the raging winds filled her belly,
Her belly was distended, and she opened wide her mouth.
He shot off an arrow, it tore her belly,
It cut through her inward parts, it pierced [her] heart.
When he had subdued her, he destroyed her life;
He cast down her carcass [and] stood upon it.

. . . .

The lord trod upon the legs of Ti'amat,
And with his unsparing club he split [her] skull.
He cut open the arteries of her blood. . . .

The older gods, rejoicing at Marduk's victory over Tiammat, heap gifts and praise upon Marduk. Marduk, meanwhile, pauses to consider "how he might divide the colossus [and] create wondrous things. . . ."

> He split her open like a mussel into two parts;
> Half of her he set in place and formed the sky. . . .

After setting up the sky like a giant canopy in which he places its luminaries—sun, moon, and stars—Marduk fashions the earth from Tiammat's other half, dividing it into waters and dry lands. Having taken the Tablet of Destinies from Tiammat's favored son, the giant Kingu, Marduk brings him bound before the assembly of the gods, who cut open his arteries and fashion mankind from the titan's blood.

The *Enuma Elish* concludes with Marduk's ascendance as head of the pantheon, to whom all other gods and man pay homage:

When the great gods had assembled,
They extolled the destiny of Marduk, they bowed down.
. . . .
When they had granted him the exercise of kingship of
    the gods,
When they had given him dominion over the gods of
    heaven and underworld,
Anshar pronounced supreme his name . . . [saying]:
"Let us do obeisance at the mention of his name,
To his utterance let the gods give heed,
Let his command be supreme above and below!"[2]

Yet another Akkadian myth, concerned directly with sovereignty[3] of the netherworld, tells how the god Nergal, originally a sky god, became King of Hades, whereas until then the goddess Ereshkigal had reigned supreme. The story begins with an invitation from the gods for Ereshkigal to send an emissary to a forthcoming heavenly banquet. Ereshkigal accepts, dispatching Namtar, who arrives in heaven and is welcomed by all the gods, except for Nergal, who remains seated when all the others rise to greet Namtar. To avenge such insult, Ereshkigal demands that Nergal be extradited to the netherworld. The gods, however, agree to protect him with special instructions for his behavior, buttressed by the companionship of fourteen demons to stand guard at the gates of the netherworld. On first approaching Ereshkigal,[4] Nergal bows down before her and ends up in bed with her, where they make love for seven days and seven nights. She mourns his departure:

Tears were running down her cheeks.
"O Erra‡ my voluptuous mate,
I was not sated with his charms [and] he has left me. . . ."

Upon his return, Nergal grabs Ereshkigal by the hair and drags her from the throne, ready to do away with her. She pleads with him to save her, and Nergal agrees to become Lord of the Netherworld, with Ereshkigal as his Queen. They kiss and make up, again embarking on seven days and seven nights of love.

This, then, was the ethos from which the seminomadic ancestors of the ancient Hebrews emerged, moving along well-traveled caravan routes from Ur at the mouth of the Persian Gulf, northwest through Babylon to Haran, where the biblical Terah, father of Abraham, lived (c. 2000 B.C.E.); moving again from Haran southwest along inland or coastal routes on the Mediterranean through territory roughly identical with the modern nation of Syria, into Egypt, and ultimately across the Sinai to settle in Canaan (c. 1250 B.C.E.), where the ancient nation of Israel was founded.

Within the past fifty years, discovery of materials in Ugaritic script—closely akin to ancient Hebrew and dating from about 1450 B.C.E.—has further illuminated biblical writing and reference, more fully defining the clash between the monotheistic vision of the ancient Hebrews and the polytheistic beliefs of the Canaanites with whom they came into contact. Canaanite imagery and poetic forms infuse early biblical writing; Old Testament injunctions against worship of Baal and Asherah refer to Canaanite deities.

Headed by El[5] and his consort Asherah, the Canaanite pantheon divided the world among three major gods, each of whom claimed he possessed the earth. Yam (god of seas and rivers), as the eldest, first assumed sovereignty, asking excessive tribute, including the jewels and ornaments of the goddesses. When the goddess Astarte walked naked before Yam in an attempt to seduce him, and Yam—like Gilgamesh—refused, Baal (god of heavens and rain) fought Yam, presuma-

‡ Another name, or term of endearment for Nergal.

bly to avenge Astarte's honor, and wrested sovereignty from him.

The next sequence of events concerns the rivalry between Baal and Mot, god of the underworld, death, and dry places. Narrated in a series of poems usually referred to as the Baal-Anath cycle, Baal's victory over Mot—aided by his sister, the goddess Anath—is particularly rich in imagery suggesting the opposition of life to death and fertility to barrenness. Most striking is the figure of Anath—at once the most savage and warlike of ancient goddesses,* while maintaining gifts for rendering the earth fertile. Both aspects of Anath's character are revealed in the following sanguinary passage, narrating her response to the invasion of her quarters by a pro-Mot faction:

> But Anath gives battle
>   mightily she cuts in pieces the sons of the two cities,
> She smites the people of the Seashore,
>   she exterminates the men of the Sunrise.
> Beneath her are heads like balls,
>   over her are palms of hands like locusts,
>   like grasshoppers without number the hands. . . .
>
> . . . .
>
> (She smites exceedingly, and says:)
>
> Anath hews in pieces and rejoices,
>   her liver extends with laughter,
>   her heart is filled with joy,
> for in Anath's hand is success,
>   for she plunges her knees in the blood of swift ones,
>   her thighs in the gore of fast ones.
> She battles in the house until she is sated,
>   she hews in pieces between tables. . . .

(Once victory is won, Anath assumes her virginal/maternal aspect:)

* Cyrus Gordon (*Loves and Wars of Baal and Anat*) suggests that Anath's ferocity is more closely akin to that of the brutal Egyptian goddess Sekhmet, who "went berserk and would have exterminated the human race had she not been stopped . . ." than to any images from Mesopotamian sources.

The blood of fast ones is wiped away from the house,
    oil of peace is poured out in the rooms.
The Virgin Anath washes her hands,
    the Mother of Nations, her fingers . . .

Again, in a subsequent segment, Anath is visited by the gods. Fearing bad news, she begins to recount her sanguinary victories:

Behold, I smote El's Beloved Sea [Yam]
    I destroyed the Great Rivers of El,
I muzzled Tannin [the Sea Dragon] . . .
    I smote the Crooked Serpent,
    the monster of seven heads,
I smote the Beloved of the "might" of the netherworld,
    I cut off El's calf . . .
I smote the godly bitch, Fire,
    I destroyed El's daughter, Flame,
I fought and took possession of the gold. . . .

Aware of the extremities within Anath's nature, the gods reassure her that Baal wants to make peace, to which she readily responds:

I shall withdraw war from the earth,
    I shall set upon the land love,
I shall pour forth peace in the midst of the earth,
    I shall increase love in the midst of the fields.

Nor does Anath fear her father, the great god El. When Baal tells Anath that he wants a palace built for him, she agrees to help him by securing support from El. If El should refuse, Anath threatens:

I shall trample him down like a lamb to the ground,
    I shall bring down his hoary head with blood to the grave,
    the gray hair of his old age with his gore.
Thus shall a house be given to Baal like the gods',
    a court like Asherah's children's.

True to her word, the goddess Anath ascends to heaven to confront her father, El:

> She broke in and entered the domain,
>   the bases of the pavilions quake.
> Bull El, her father, lifted up his voice,
>   and hid himself in seven chambers,
>   inside eight enclosures.

From his hiding place, El warns that he shall withhold the sun from the heavens out of love for the vanquished Mot, rather than provide a palace for Mot's rival. Anath coolly lets El know what she has in mind for him should the great god persist in his refusal to give Baal the palace:

> Thou has wept, O god, at thy calamity,
>   rejoice not when I attack,
>
> . . . .
>
> I shall seize thy curls with my right hand,
>   thy locks with the great power of my hand,
>   I shall pluck out the hair of thy pate.
> I shall bring down thy hoary head with blood to the grave,
>   the gray hair of thine old age with thy gore.

Still in hiding, El acquiesces:

> I know thee, my daughter, that thou art invincible
>   that it is impossible to withstand the goddesses.
> What is thy request, O Virgin Anath?

Here twentieth-century translator and biblical scholar Umberto Cassuto suggests that El yields to his daughter's wishes because he recognizes that her strength and courage "are irresistible, just as in general, the gods are unable to stand against the goddesses."

Yet the biblical Yahweh did, indeed, stand against the goddesses with considerable success. Monotheism's victory was not easily gained, however, and reversals to polytheism persisted for centuries. Elijah's contest with the 450 priests of Baal and the 400 priestesses of Asherah during Ahab's reign in the Northern Kingdom of Israel calls for a miracle from Yahweh to convince the populace that they must turn away from the Canaanite deities. To ensure their good faith and in retribution for the earlier slaying of Yahwistic prophets by Ahab's queen, Jezebel, the 450 prophets of Baal are summarily slaughtered. Even so, Baalism continued to flourish. Not until the ninth century did the Yahwistic movement clearly gain the upper hand. Devotion to Asherah lasted even longer, well into the last days of the monarchy (c. 600 B.C.E.), when Jeremiah noted with dismay "children gathering wood, fathers lighting fires, women kneading dough to make crescent cakes in honor of the Queen of Heaven. . . ."

What is the powerful appeal of the goddess, and what loss did her suppression incur? Castigated by Jeremiah for their continued recognition of Asherah even after the exile, the people declared that they would continue to burn incense to the goddess and pour drink offerings to her as their Kings and princes had done always, for then there was food in abundance and the people were well and knew no evil.

Subsumed by the austere monotheistic vision, the human need for female eminence continued to erupt throughout the ages, manifesting itself in mystical constructs of a heavenly family and in the emergence of the Shekinah, identified with the nation of Israel, in conjugal relationship with its god.

For women today, the multidimensional aspects of the goddess are particularly compelling contrasted against the fragmented images of sanguine Eve and malevolent Lilith. A figure like Inanna, embracing a far wider range of possible behaviors and passions, clearly provides a more comprehensive archetype for female experience than those constricted images foisted on women in recent centuries. The current resurgence of interest in the goddess does not suggest a polytheistic revival, but rather a deep yearning to retrieve a lost sense of self, to emerge from the confinement of inadequate models.

The Hebrew Bible, observes Rabbi Everett Gendler, came on the scene at a period in history when the struggle for masculine dominance had reached its peak, justifying the shift to the new dominant masculine order. The popular attribution of male character to the biblical god—despite theological assertions of noncorporality—is further reinforced by the gender-laden syntax of Hebrew in which all pronouns, verbs, and adjectives describing the deity are grammatically masculine.

What, then, of woman in the Bible?

6

Woman in the Bible

In the Bible as in soap opera, woman's concerns center almost exclusively on childbearing and on her relationships with men. Viewed from a predominantly male perspective, biblical women appear only when they enter man's perception—as mothers, wives, or harlots. They are literally not born, nor do they experience that passage from birth through childhood to maturity essential for an appreciation of the fullness of female experience. Like Sleeping Beauty awakened by the prince's kiss, biblical woman springs to life the moment man sees her; all other moments and levels of her experience remain shrouded in mystery. That the birth and childhood of daughters go unrecorded proves no small obstacle to Jewish and Christian women today who turn to biblical sources to define their origins and their place in the history of the group.

Such errors of omission have been further compounded throughout the ages by the impact of a monotheistic vision and its covenantal arrangements in which a syntactically male God binds Jewish men to Him through the rites of circumcision, leaving helpmates to stumble on alone. The biblical Yahweh, however, signifies His covenant with Abraham* *and* Sarah by changing both their names: Abram to Abraham and Sarai to Sarah. Of utmost significance during biblical times, the process of naming retreated from view in later exegetical works, submerged by a proliferation of interpretations placing man at stage center while woman perpetually waited in the wings.

* Even in this context, Yahweh's discourse with Abraham is far more extensive, appearing in dreams, visions, etc.

In social and economic spheres, woman's legal status reflects the patriarchal norms of surrounding civilizations. Biblical woman does not own property; she is dependent on father, husband, or sons (in the case of a widow) for economic sustenance; her vows—a matter of considerable consequence in biblical times—may be annulled by father or husband; she cannot initiate divorce, while her husband (the Hebrew word is *baal* [master]) may separate from her at will, simply by uttering a declaration that severs their relationship.

Yet the Old Testament itself—unlike literature that preceded it—is not primarily a narrative about the nature of man nor the acts of a god or gods. It is essentially the story of the relationship between a people—the nation of Israel—and its God—a god who transcends nature and acts through historical event to forge the destiny of His people. The concept of moral causality —absent from prebiblical narrative—permeates the Old Testament and subsequent Judaic thought. To put it simply: When the people act in harmony with their god, life goes well for them; when they turn away from their god—usually by worshiping foreign divinities or idols—a series of disasters befalls them. Historically, the disasters frequently take the form of military defeats; mythically, they occur in the flood that only Noah and his family survive; and to some extent, in the expulsion from Eden as a result of the first couple's disobedience in tasting the forbidden tree.

In this context, the string of barren women—among them Sarah, Rachel, and Hannah—who proceed through the Old Testament further reinforce the concept of a transcendent deity, a god outside of nature, running counter to prevailing polytheistic personifications of natural forces. For Canaanite and Babylonian women, fertility rested in the powers of the goddess, represented in a proliferation of plaques and amulets unearthed in the area. Biblical thought transferred such powers to Yahweh or Elohim, who renders the barren women of the Old Testament fertile (Sarah, even in her ninetieth year!), endowing them with those sons who perpetuate patriarchal history.

Yet despite the clearly patriarchal ethos that pervades the Old Testament and the masculine bias of its narrative, closer examination of those women who appear in the Bible reveals a far greater latitude and diversity of experience than might be expected.

DEBORAH, JAEL, MIRIAM, AND HULDA

The oldest fragments of biblical text include references to the refrain sung by Miriam, leading the women after crossing the sea:

> Sing to the Lord, for he has risen up in triumph;
> the horse and his rider he has hurled into the sea.[1]

and Deborah's exultant song of victory over the armies of Sisera:

> Champions there were none,
> none left in Israel,
> until I, Deborah, arose,
> arose, a mother in Israel. . . .[2]

The images of these extraordinary women run counter to those conventional assumptions about women derived from the myth of Genesis, the stories of the matriarchs, the later Book of Wisdom, and apocryphal, pseudepigraphal, and rabbinic literature. All, save Jael, are endowed with gifts of prophecy that transcend sex or gender. Deborah, moreover, presides as judge of Israel for a period of forty years.

The position of judgeship, like the gift of prophecy, was presumably divinely ordained: "The Lord set judges over them, who rescued them. . . ." (Jg. 2:16). The period of the judges followed Joshua's conquests in Canaan and preceded the monarchy. Settlement in Canaan evidently brought with it a resurgence of Baal and Asherah worship, biblically interpreted as cause for subsequent defeats. The judges, in this context, acted to reunite the people of Israel with their god. When the judge died, however, the people, more often than not, resumed idolatrous practices. Just such a time preceded Deborah's emergence as judge of Israel, during a period of severe oppression under Sisera, commander of Canaanite forces.

It was Deborah's custom to dispense justice while seated beneath a palm tree in the hill country of Ephraim. Moved by the suffering of her people, Deborah sends for Barak the tribal leader and advises him to bring together a group of ten thousand to confront Sisera's army, promising him that the Canaanite forces shall be delivered into his hands. Barak refuses to proceed unless Deborah is willing to accompany him. She agrees, acting as commander-in-chief in planning the strategy that succeeds in routing Sisera's army: ". . . the whole army was put to the sword and perished."[3]

Sisera, meanwhile, has fled by foot to the tent of Jael, wife of the Kenite Heber. Jael greets him hospitably enough, offers him milk, and agrees to stand guard at the tent door while Sisera sleeps. Once Sisera is asleep, the hardy Jael proceeds to split his skull open with a tent peg—fulfilling Deborah's prophecy at the outset that Sisera would "fall into the hands of a woman."[4]

When Barak approaches, Jael goes out to meet him, displaying the slain Sisera—finale for the Israelite victory over Canaanite forces.

That very same day, Deborah and Barak sing Deborah's Song—one of the oldest passages in the Bible—celebrating their triumph. The song recounts the heroic deeds of the Israelite army, led by Deborah, and further commemorates Jael's handiwork in a sequence reminiscent of Anath's gory victories:

> Blest above women be Jael,
> the wife of Heber the Kenite;
> blest above all women in the tents.
> He asked for water; she gave him milk,
> she offered him curds in a bowl fit for a chieftain.
> She stretched out her hand for the tent peg,
> her right hand to hammer the weary.
> With the hammer she struck Sisera, she crushed his head;
> she struck and his brains ebbed out.
> At her feet he sank down, he fell, he lay;
> at her feet he sank down and fell.
> Where he sank down, there he fell, done to death.

A poignant passage follows, portraying Sisera's mother peering through the lattices of her window, wondering why her son is so late in returning. The "wisest of her princesses" answers her, "Yes, she found her own answer." That answer is contained in the elaboration of a vision of Sisera gathering women and booty "to grace the victor's neck." The vision is dramatically counterpointed with the concluding peroration:

> So perish all thine enemies, O Lord;
> but let all those who love thee be like the sun rising in
>   strength.

The thirty-one verses of Deborah's Song culminate with the pronouncement that peace prevailed in the land for forty years afterward.

What is particularly significant in the biblical stories of Deborah and Jael—as well as in references to the prophetic gifts of Miriam and Hulda—is that the extradomestic dimension of their lives is not treated as unusual. (In 2 K. 22:14–20, Judah's reigning monarch dispatches a retinue, including his high priest, adjutant general, and personal attendant, to seek advice from the prophetess Hulda at her home in Jerusalem.) While the women, to be sure, are extraordinary enough, it is the quality of their leadership that renders them so—*not* their departure from the harem. Enormous power is concentrated in both the imagery and poetic rhythm—more resonant in the Hebrew repetition than in English translation—of Deborah's Song.

Such power and unquestioned prominence evidently proved problematic for later commentators who suggest, in conformity with that modesty that they advocated for women, that Deborah dispensed judgment in the open air because "it was not becoming that men should visit a woman in her house."[5] While granting Deborah her gifts of prophecy, commentaries introduce and elaborate on "the frailties of her sex," among them that "inordinate self-consciousness" that prompted Deborah to send for Barak, rather than going to him; and to "speak more of herself" in the song than was "seemly." Midrashic retribution for such unseemly behavior is posited in the assumption "that the prophetical spirit departed from her for a time while she was composing her song."

Midrashic literature is curiously more comfortable with elaborating on Jael's bloody act, embellishing it with a seductiveness that is totally absent from biblical text: "She was unusually beautiful, and her voice was the most seductive ever a woman possessed." This biblical "woman of the tents" is portrayed in midrash as adorned "in rich garments and jewels" on meeting Sisera in flight, having first prepared for him a bed "strewn with roses." So taken is Sisera with this desert beauty that he determines to take her home to mother as his wife. Alas, poor Sisera! Continually calling to God to strengthen her maiden hand, his intended drives a stake through the general's head. He-man to the end, Sisera utters his dying cry: "O that I should lose my life by the hand of a woman!"

THE FALL

The Fall was originally neither Fall nor breeding ground for the concept known as Original Sin until more than a thousand years *after* the redaction of Genesis and earlier segments of the Old Testament. Stripped of exegesis, the biblical story emerges as a simple etiological tale positing origins for the struggle and suffering implicit in the human condition.

In Genesis II, Yahweh makes trees spring from the ground in Adam's Eden, setting the tree of life and the tree of the knowledge of good and evil at the garden's center. Adam is placed in the garden with instructions that he may eat any tree save one— the tree of knowledge: ". . . for on the day that you eat from it, you will certainly die."[6] Eve is then created from Adam's rib to serve as his companion. Man and woman live together naked with no feelings of shame.

In Genesis III, the serpent appears in conversation with Eve.† "Is it true," teases the serpent, "that God has forbidden you to eat from any tree?" Eve replies that they may, indeed, eat the fruit of any tree, except for the one in the middle of the garden: "God has forbidden us either to eat or to touch[7] the fruit of that; if we do, we shall die."

Not so, maintains the serpent. Eating of the tree will confer upon woman that knowledge reserved for a god or gods. After meditating on the serpent's advice, as well as on the tree itself,

† Strictly speaking, biblical text does not refer to the woman as Eve until Adam calls her Eve, following their expulsion from Eden.

Eve tries the fruit and offers it to Adam: "When the woman saw that the fruit of the tree was good to eat, and that it was pleasing to the eye and tempting to contemplate, she took some and ate it. She also gave her husband some and he ate it. Then the eyes of both of them were opened. . . ." With the concomitant loss of innocence, man and woman become conscious of their nakedness and hasten to stitch some fig leaves together for covering their privy parts.

Yahweh meanwhile, strolling in the garden, calls to the couple who are hiding from Him. When Adam explains that he is hiding out of shame for his nakedness, Yahweh correctly surmises that the couple have tasted of the forbidden tree. Adam excuses his intransigence by placing the onus on his wife: "The woman you gave me for a companion, she gave me fruit from the tree. . . ." The woman, in turn, responds: "The serpent tricked me, and I ate."

The initial relationship between serpent and woman, together with the serpent's subsequent downfall, is particularly striking when viewed against the recurrent motif in polytheistic imagery linking the serpent with the goddess. Even in biblical text, the serpent is first referred to as the "craftiest" or "subtlest" of God's creatures, and it is the serpent—not man or woman—who is directly cursed by Yahweh:

> Because you have done this you are accursed
> more than all cattle and all wild creatures.
> On your belly you shall crawl, and dust you shall eat
> all the days of your life.
> *I will put enmity between you and the woman,*
> *between your brood and hers.*
> *They shall strike at your head,*
> *and you shall strike at their heel.* [emphasis mine][8]

Yahweh's subsequent statements are particularly significant in the light of later exegesis, which renders woman culpable for man's mortality. "The man has become like one of us, knowing good and evil; what if he now reaches out his hand and takes fruit from the tree of life also, eats it, and lives forever?" To preclude such a possibility, Yahweh expels the couple from Eden and places cherubim with flashing swords to guard the tree of life.

Clearly immortality was never meant to be man's destiny. Eating the fruit of the tree of knowledge, rather, rendered man conscious of his nakedness, his vulnerability, and his eventual death. Despite such immutable facts of human life and death, man perpetually tries to circumvent his mortality in subsequent exegetical interpretations.

Several periods are particularly significant in molding later exegetical thought. The Persian era (586–331 B.C.E.) introduced the concept of dualism with the polarization of good and evil, forever fighting each other on earth. Satan first appears during this period, together with a hierarchy of angels and demons. The messianic idea is predicated on the Persian notion of cyclic time in which the present tumult precedes a new world order. The Hellenistic period (331 B.C.E.–second century C.E.) introduced the discipline of philosophy, elevating the importance of mind and intellect.[9] For Semitic and Near Eastern peoples, emotion had been most important; the heart is the seat of perception and knowledge in the Old Testament; the Hebrew verb "to know" (*yodea*) means "to experience." In the Christian era, the messianic idea was realized by certain groups, and a curious aversion to sexuality was introduced and elaborated. This aversion permeated rabbinic as well as Christian writing, which viewed woman as temptress. While rabbis never celebrated celibacy, modesty—if not chastity—was advocated for women with an intensity that is totally absent in the Pentateuch.

Increasing concern with a sense of sin informed apocryphal and pseudepigraphal texts that attempted to grapple with the phenomenon of evil. Nonetheless, man's fall from an (imagined) state of grace was not initially attributed to the Eden story, but rather to the sixth chapter of Genesis, in which the sons of God (B'nai Elohim) have intercourse with mortal women, begetting the Nephilim, a race of giants. Later commentaries claim that the sons of God—referred to as "angels" by this time—were seduced by the women,‡ but the ele-

‡ I Enoch, in which the angels descend from heaven out of lust for the beautiful women of earth, thereby "defiling" themselves and produc-

ment of seduction does not appear in the biblical story. In the context of the Old Testament, the B'nai Elohim story emerges as an otiose survival of polytheistic beliefs. The tale is followed by God's sorry perception of man's evil acts and His determination to "wipe them off the face of the earth," giving rise to the flood that Noah—the only righteous man around—survives.

The notion of woman as source of sex and sin received added impetus in the *Testaments of the Twelve Patriarchs,* in which women were rendered culpable for the fall of the sons of God and the ensuing spread of corruption and evil:

> For evil are women . . . since they have no power or strength over man, they use wiles by outward attractions, that they may draw him to themselves . . . concerning them, the angel of the Lord . . . taught me, that women are overcome by the spirit of fornication more than men, and in their heart they plot against men; and by means of their adornment they deceive first their minds, and by the glance of the eye instill the poison, and then through the accomplished act they take them captive . . . thus they allured the Watchers who were before the flood. . . .[10]

Eventually the B'nai Elohim story as explanation for the origins of evil fell into disfavor and new models were sought, retaining the elements of female seductiveness. The seeds for Original Sin were sown early in the Christian era (between 40 and 300 C.E.), although it remained for the later Augustine to bring them to full flower. Eve's account of the fall in the *Apocalypse of Moses* (early Christian era) introduces an implicit sexual relationship between the first woman and the serpent.

---

ing the Nephilim—eventually identified with demons—who corrupt mankind.

The Book of Jubilees, with the modification that the angels were originally sent down to teach men righteousness. Only later do they choose mortal wives who bear the giants. Nonetheless, corruption and lawlessness increase; the angels are bound to remedy the situation; the giants slay each other; the flood sweeps the earth clean. The problem of the recurrence of evil in subsequent generations is resolved by an embellishment that maintains that 10 per cent of the giants were allowed to roam the earth.

The serpent is now either the embodiment or an envoy of Satan, using Eve to get back at Adam, whom he envies. The serpent "poured upon the fruit the poison of his wickedness, which is lust, the root and beginning of every sin. . . ." Both the *Apocalypse of Moses* and the related Latin *Life of Adam and Eve* tend to idealize Adam, rendering Eve culpable for all misfortunes that have befallen mankind.

While such themes inform one strand of Apocalyptic and Christian writing, other rabbinic and Apocryphal literature of the period does not at all depend upon the Eden story for an explanation of the origins of evil.* Christian Scripture, however, was substantially influenced by such motifs—undoubtedly an attractive means for transforming an early fear of woman into contempt, thereby justifying cultural norms of male dominance and female subordination. The later Church Fathers frequently blend the Watcher myth with the Eden story to further underline woman's transgression—now linked with lust—and her role in bringing death to the world.[11] Both Origen and Tertullian, intertwining the Watcher motif and its demonology with the Fall of Adam and Eve, lay the groundwork for Original Sin by insisting that Satan's poison has infected all posterity (the children of Eve), introducing the ritual of baptism by way of antidote. It remains, of course, for Augustine to ultimately reject the Watcher myth, replacing it with his theory—predicated on the Eden story—that Original Sin is transmitted from parent to child through that lust that is a result of the first sin and invariably accompanies the act of generation.

Apologists for woman's status in Judaism are quick to point out that the doctrine of Original Sin has no analog in Judaic belief, further maintaining—on precious little evidence—that Judaism has always revered its women to a far greater extent than those civilizations with which it came in contact. Yet that unmistakable streak of misogyny that gave birth to Original Sin continues to persist in Jewish writing—*sans* the doctrine—from the fall of the Temple to the present.

In recent years, however, increasing numbers of women have entered areas of biblical scholarship and theological specula-

* See the following chapter for discussion of the Talmudic Yetzer ha'ra.

tion. In a substantive challenge to prevailing dogma on the story of the Fall,[12] theologian Phyllis Trible points out that the biblical narrative does not sustain that judgment of woman's moral weakness and sexual vulnerability that was later foisted upon it. Eve's decision to taste the fruit of knowledge is an independent act. She neither consults her husband nor asks his permission. In subsequent dialog with Yahweh, she recognizes her transgression, as well as her deception by the serpent. Her response throughout is conscious and active. Adam, by contrast, emerges as a passive recipient; his response, one of quiescence rather than initiative. While the woman engages in theological speculation with the serpent and ultimately recognizes the deception when confronted by Yahweh, the man merely repeats that he followed his wife's suggestion. Both man and woman, however, are clearly judged equal in the responsibility for their transgression by the biblical Yahweh, who decrees their ensuing destinies. The etiological substance of the decree is descriptive, *not prescriptive,* reflecting the prevailing conditions of life for men and women of the time. While it clearly describes the human condition, it does not provide a mandate for future oppression. Such oppression, several scholars suggest, is implicit in the corruption of the Fall, in contrast to the inherent equality between the sexes at Creation.

Professor of Theology Phyllis Bird further emphasizes the theme[13] of alienation implicit in the Fall. Their transgression in Eden alienates both man and woman from their Creator. For man, the ground, source of his food and work, becomes his antagonist; for woman, man—initially her companion—now "rules over her."

"Israel's best statements about woman," observes Dr. Bird, "recognize her as an equal with man, and with him jointly responsible to God and to cohumanity. That Israel rarely lived up to this vision is all too apparent, but the vision should not be denied."

THE MATRIARCHS

Although the matriarchs—Sarah, Rebeccah, Leah, and Rachel—are celebrated primarily for the sons they bear, setting the scene for the emerging nation of Israel, a summary and comparison of their lives reveal an increasingly active role in determining the destiny of their sons, as well as a certain progression —within patriarchal context—of their own spiritual development.

Beauty and barrenness mark Sarah, wife of Abraham, whom we encounter in midlife. With the first matriarch, the theme of barrenness is introduced, together with the rivalry of women over the bearing of sons. When Sarai cannot conceive, she urges Abram to sleep with her Egyptian maidservant, Hagar, so that a family may be founded by the couple with the servant acting as intermediary (a recurrent practice in biblical narrative). Once Hagar conceives, she holds the barren Sarai in contempt; Sarai retaliates by mistreating Hagar, who runs away.

Having fled her mistress's harshness, Hagar pauses by a spring in the wilderness when an angel of God appears to her, telling her to return, even to endure Sarai's ill treatment, comforted by the prediction that she will bear a son called Ishmael, who will found a great nation. Hagar returns and gives birth to Ishmael when Abram is eighty-six.

When Abram is ninety-nine, Yahweh appears to him, introducing the ritual of circumcision to signify the covenant between them. Abram and his son Ishmael, who is now thirteen, are circumcised on the same day, together with all male members of the household. As part of the covenant, Yahweh changes Abram's name to Abraham, advising him: "As for Sarai your wife; you shall call her not Sarai [mockery] but Sarah [princess]; I will bless her and give you a son by her . . . she shall be the mother of nations. . . ."[14]

On hearing the news of this gerontologic birth, Abraham falls on his face, laughing. "Can a son be born to a man who is a hundred years old? Can Sarah bear a son when she is ninety?"

Three emissaries from Yahweh subsequently appear before Abraham's tent. With appropriate desert hospitality, Abraham welcomes them, urging Sarah to quickly prepare some cakes. The visitors predict that the following year at this time, Sarah will have borne Abraham a son.

Listening at the door of the tent, Sarah laughs to herself: "I am past bearing children now that I am out of my time, and my husband is old." When confronted about her laughter, Sarah denies it. But Yahweh insists that He has heard her, admonishing her with a question to serve as reminder: "Is anything impossible for the Lord?"

Evidently not, for the following year Sarah gives birth to a son named Isaac. Both the birth and her son's name† renew the source of laughter, but it is exceedingly unclear whether Sarah laughs from joy or fear that others will deride her. Indeed, when Ishmael makes sport of his baby brother, Sarah orders Ishmael and Hagar banished. Abraham reluctantly agrees after assurances from Yahweh that Ishmael, too, will be cared for.

Having run out of water, Hagar finds herself weeping once more in the wilderness of Beersheba, with Ishmael crying beside her. Again, the angel of God appears, encouraging Hagar to overcome her fears, reminding her that a great nation will be born of her son. A well of water springs up before her, saving both Hagar and Ishmael from that death she feared was imminent.

Sarah disappears from Old Testament text during the sequence in which Yahweh tests Abraham's faith by demanding the sacrifice of Isaac. She reappears with her death (in Gn. 23) at the biblical age of 127. Abraham mourns her and weeps for her, burying her in a plot of land he has purchased from the Hittites for 400 shekels, at Machapelah to the east of Hebron.

Isaac, meanwhile, has grown and is ready for marriage. To avert the possibility of marriage with a Canaanite woman, Abraham dispatches a messenger to his own country to find a wife for his son.

The story of Rebeccah presents several new elements: preference for patrilocal over matrilocal residence, consultation with Rebeccah during the courtship, the advent and quality of her pregnancy, and her dominant role in determining the destiny of her sons.

Shall Isaac take up residence among Rebeccah's people or will she come to live with him? Abraham insists upon the latter, absolving his servant of the oath to find a wife for Isaac, should the woman prove unwilling to return with him.

† The Hebrew *yitzchak* (he laughed).

Laden with gifts, the servant arrives in the country of Abraham's kinsmen toward evening. Eager for the success of his mission, he requests a sign from the Lord at the well outside the city: "I shall say to a girl, 'Please lower your jar so that I may drink'; if she answers, 'Drink, and I will water your camels also,' that will be the girl whom thou dost intend for . . . Isaac."[15]

Before his prayer is over, a beautiful young girl comes to draw water. The servant hurries toward her, and repeating the formula, asks for a drink. He receives the response he prayed for when Rebeccah lowers her water jar for him to drink, refills it, and waters all the camels. The servant thereupon presents Rebeccah with a gold nose-ring and two gold bracelets, asking if there is room for staying the night in her father's house. She replies that she is the daughter of Milcah and Bethuel, son of Abraham's brother Nahor, and runs ahead to announce the visitor.

Impressed with Rebeccah's gifts, her brother Laban goes out to greet the visitor. Abraham's servant tells Laban and Bethuel of his mission, repeating the question: "What if the woman will not come with me?" Father and brother respond that they can say nothing for or against the Lord's decree. The following morning, Rebeccah's mother and brother suggest that she remain with them another ten days. The servant, however, is eager to complete his mission. When Rebeccah is summoned for her opinion, she decides to leave at once with Abraham's servant.

As they travel through the Negev, Rebeccah sees Isaac approaching. She dismounts from her camel and veils herself. Isaac conducts her to his tent, where Rebeccah becomes his wife. ". . . and he loved her and was consoled for the death of his mother."[16]

Rebeccah's freedom of movement is clear in the biblical text, together with an awareness of her destiny, and the expression of Isaac's love for mother and wife. Like Sarah, Rebeccah is initially barren; Isaac appeals to God, and Rebeccah conceives. The quality of her pregnancy ("the children pressed hard on each other in her womb") foreshadows the rivalry of her sons and Rebeccah's initiative in determining their destiny. Unlike

Sarah, Rebeccah enters into direct discourse with Yahweh, questioning the meaning of her pregnancy. Yahweh tells her that two nations will be born of her and that the older son will be servant to the younger. She subsequently gives birth to twins.

The elder, Esau, a hunter who keeps his father supplied with venison, is Isaac's favorite, but Rebeccah prefers Jacob. When Isaac grows old, Rebeccah determines that Jacob, rather than Esau—as the custom of primogeniture would suggest—should receive his father's blessing. She acts on that determination by convincing Jacob to dress in Esau's clothes when he brings Isaac a dish of goat meat that she has prepared.

Blind in his old age, Isaac falls for the ruse. Dressed in Esau's clothes, Jacob smells and feels to the touch like his elder brother, and Isaac endows him with his blessing. When Esau returns from the hunt, he is furious at the deception and threatens to kill Jacob after Isaac dies and the period of mourning is over. Aware of the enmity between them, Rebeccah acts to save Jacob by sending him away to live with her brother Laban until Esau's anger cools.

She explains such a move to Isaac with a professed aversion for Hittite women, like those Esau has married. "If Jacob marries a Hittite woman like those who live here, my life will not be worth living." Prodded by Rebeccah, Isaac agrees that Jacob shall leave to find a wife for himself among Laban's people.

Jacob's meeting with Rachel introduces the theme of romantic love and commitment. It's love at first sight the moment Jacob glimpses Rachel tending her father's sheep. Overwhelmed with feeling, Jacob raises a heavy stone from the well, waters the flock, kisses Rachel, and is literally "moved to tears."[17] He offers Laban seven years of work for the privilege of marrying Rachel.[18]

When the seven years are over, Laban substitutes the elder Leah for her younger sister. Only on the following morning, having married and slept with Leah, does Jacob realize that he has been deceived. (They're all alike in the dark??) Laban excuses the deception by insisting that it is the custom of his country to marry the elder daughter first. If Jacob is willing to work another seven years for Laban, he may marry Rachel once the seven-day wedding feast, celebrating the union with Leah, is over. Unwilling to forego the relationship with Rachel, Jacob agrees.

The womb-against-womb motif, initially suggested by the antagonism between Sarah and Hagar, is intensified in this story of two sisters married to the same man, the elder unloved and fertile, the younger loved and barren. God's compassion for Leah's misery is reflected in the serial birth and naming of her sons: the first, Reuben (see, a son!); the second, Simeon (hearing, signifying that God has heard her); the third, Levi (union, expressing Leah's conviction that she and Jacob will be united through her capacity to produce male offspring); the fourth, Judah (praise, offered to God for that reunion that Leah presumes is imminent). Jacob, however, still prefers Rachel.

Yet Rachel, envious of Leah's fecundity, pleads with Jacob to give her a son, to which he impatiently responds: "Can I take the place of God, who has denied you children?" Like Sarah before her, Rachel gives her maidservant Bilhah to Jacob. Bilhah conceives twice and bears two sons. Leah, in turn, offers her servant Zilpah, who bears another two sons to match those born of Bilhah, acting as Rachel's proxy.

This depressing and endless rivalry over the bearing of sons is highlighted by the story of the mandrakes, in which Rachel, by far more clever, succeeds in outwitting her sister. When Leah's son Reuben brings mandrakes to his mother at harvest time, Rachel asks for them.[19] Leah refuses, still rankling over Jacob's preference for her younger sister: "Is it so small a thing to have taken away my husband, that you should take my son's mandrakes as well?" But when Rachel offers to exchange a night with Jacob for the mandrakes, Leah readily agrees.

She greets Jacob that evening with the news: "You are to sleep with me tonight; I have hired you with my son's mandrakes."[20]

Again, Leah bears two more sons, Issachar and Naphtali, followed by the birth of her daughter Dinah. Meanwhile, either God or the mandrakes have relieved Rachel's barrenness, and she bears Jacob her first son, whom she names Joseph.

While the serial bearing of sons is consonant with patriarchal ethos, it functions essentially as a literary device in the Rachel/Leah narrative to establish the common origin of the twelve tribes of Israel. The emergence of the significant son or culture hero is further highlighted by the long period of barrenness or difficulty that precedes his birth. Isaac is born of Sarah when she is ninety; Jacob and Esau struggle in Rebeccah's womb. Joseph, the most prominent of all Jacob's sons in the history of Israel, is born *not* to the fertile Leah, but to the barren Rachel.

With the birth of Joseph, Jacob's fourteen years of service to Laban come to an end. He makes appropriate arrangements with his father-in-law to settle a portion of the flocks with him. Once more, Laban deceives Jacob by promising him all spotted or brindled sheep, and turning them over, instead, to his own sons. Nonetheless, Jacob outwits Laban by crossbreeding the herds, and continues to prosper. But animosity between them grows, and Jacob determines to leave with his family for his own country.

Rachel and Leah support Jacob's decision to depart, expressing their own rancor at Laban's greed and duplicity. "We no longer have any part or lot in our father's house. Does he not look on us as foreigners, now that he has sold us and spent on himself the whole of the money paid for us? But all the wealth that God has saved from our father's clutches is ours and our children's."

To assure that rightful inheritance, Rachel takes Laban's teraphim[21] or household idols before they leave. When Laban returns to discover the departure of Jacob's household, together with the missing teraphim, he sets out in pursuit. Overtaking Jacob, camped for the night in the hill country, Laban demands the return of his idols and searches Jacob's tents for them. Rachel, meanwhile, excuses herself from rising in her father's presence because "the common lot of women" is upon her. She is, in fact, sitting on the camel bag that holds the teraphim. Unaware that Rachel has taken the teraphim and angered by Laban's accusations, Jacob vows that anyone found in possession of Laban's gods shall die for it.

After settling in Canaan, Rachel dies in childbirth, bearing her second son and Jacob's twelfth, rounding out the ancestral history of the twelve tribes. In the severity of labor, Rachel recognizes her imminent death, naming her son Ben-oni (son of my ill luck), later changed by Jacob to Benjamin (son of the right hand, or good luck).

Postbiblical commentaries on Rachel and Leah reveal changing attitudes toward women, sexuality, and the rivalry between the sisters. In keeping with the ascetic turn of the times, they are portrayed as pious goodie-goodies, desiring sex only for purposes of procreation. Since biblical text runs counter to many of these later proclamations, abundant reinterpretation was necessary to bring it into conformity with prevailing ideals of modesty and chastity for men and women. Striking among the transformation of biblical images within a six hundred-year period (200 B.C.E.–400 C.E.) are the following:

Rachel tending the flocks: While Rachel and Rebeccah clearly move about the countryside with considerable freedom in biblical text—indeed, it was customary for women to take over agricultural work in the ancient Near East—later commentaries treat such behavior as extraordinary. The Jerusalem Targum assumes that Rachel tends Laban's sheep only because he has no sons, further positing the earlier outbreak of a plague among Laban's cattle, leaving so few that they could be easily tended even by a woman. The biblical reference to Laban's sons in that sequence where he favors them over Jacob is explained away with the interpretation that they had not yet been born at the time of Rachel's meeting with Jacob.

Tears and kisses: Obviously embarrassed at Jacob's effusiveness in meeting Rachel, the rabbis provided an ingenious variety of explanations. Jacob's kiss, filial at best, created a stir among the bystanders who censured such unchaste behavior. Their censure, in turn, reduced Jacob to tears. "Scarcely had he kissed Rachel when he began to weep, for he repented of having done it."[22] Or he wept remembering that Isaac had sent Rebeccah gifts while he had none for Rachel. Or a presentiment of Rachel's death elicited his tears, et cetera.

Josephus, writing for a Greek-speaking population toward

the end of the first century of the Christian era, simply reverses Jacob's and Rachel's roles in describing their meeting at the well. In Josephus's version, Rachel runs up to greet Jacob, throws her arms around him, and bursts into tears—an expression of sisterly rather than sexual devotion.[23]

Rivalry between the sisters or chastity and childbearing: The rivalry between the sisters is somewhat ameliorated in rabbinic commentary, partly in response to emerging Christian polemic, claiming the younger Rachel as symbolic of the new Christianity. Rachel is portrayed as envious of Leah not for her fecundity, but for that piety that is rewarded by the capacity to bear children. The mandrake episode is treated as a good deed on Rachel's part (the fruit's reputed aphrodisiac attributes are ignored); Rachel offers Leah a night with Jacob in exchange for the mandrakes so that Leah may bear him more children. Yet another version castigates Rachel for her "unbecoming behavior," suggesting that she would have borne four sons rather than two had she acted with more decorum. Leah's compassion for Rachel (scarcely an issue in biblical text!) is introduced and elaborated in a midrash about the birth of her daughter Dinah, who was initially—according to the commentary—a man-child turned into a female by Leah's prayer that she not embarrass her sister with the birth of yet another son.[24]

God is moved by Rachel's tears: Most significant among the commentaries on Rachel is that midrash drawn from the text of Jeremiah after the destruction of the first Temple when the Patriarchs and Moses plead Israel's cause before God. Their pleas elicit only silence until Rachel appears and invokes God's mercy: ". . . I, a woman, a creature of flesh and blood, of dust and ashes, was not jealous of my rival." (Leah) "Thou, O God . . . why wast Thou jealous of the idols, empty vanities? Why hast Thou driven out my children, slain them with the sword, left them at the mercy of their enemies?" Then the compassion of the Supreme God was awakened, and He said: "For thy sake, O Rachel, I will lead the children of Israel back to their land."[25]

Jungian analyst Rivkah Schaerf Kluger[26] uses the figures of women in the Old Testament as a source for understanding problems of the modern female psyche, linking archaic images or archetypes with contemporary experience. While certain aspects of Dr. Kluger's thesis are questionable,[27] her delineation of the spiritual progression of the matriarchs within patriarchal context is particularly apt and provocative. In Kluger's view, the archetypal defeat of the Great Mother that preceded the emergence of monotheism resulted in woman's loss of her heavenly counterpart, that goddess who was the image of her self. This defeat corresponded with the exclusion of women from the new cult, diminishing their attachment to the new deity and eliciting a yearning for the older polytheistic beliefs in which their sense of self was more firmly grounded. The women of the Old Testament thus experienced a particularly painful transition, reflected in the conflicts and ambivalence of women today.

Sarah, in this view, remains the harem wife, passively obeying Abraham's instructions. Rebeccah, by contrast, exhibits distinct spiritual growth. In parallel incidents centered on the wife-sister motif, Abraham and Isaac present their respective wives as their sisters to foreign rulers. When Sarah is presented to the Pharaoh in the older Yahwistic version and again to Abimelech in the later Elohistic narrative, God intervenes to prevent sexual consummation between Sarah and the foreign ruler. Rebeccah, however, does not enter Abimelech's "harem." When Abimelech glimpses Isaac and Rebeccah "laughing together," he gets the idea—without intercession from God—that theirs is not a sibling relationship. The difference between the two matriarchs is further underlined by Rebeccah's sense of destiny in choosing marriage with Isaac and by the exceptional quality of her pregnancy, elaborated in a midrash where Rebeccah asks the women of the land: "Did it happen so with you?" When they respond negatively, she wonders, "Why then should it happen differently with me than with all other women?" Again, in manipulating the blessing for Jacob, Rebeccah's awareness emerges in sharp contrast to Isaac's blindness.

In the Rachel/Leah sequence, Rachel is perceived as the more distinctive personality, and, significantly, that one preferred by Jacob. The theft of the teraphim is interpreted as clinging to the old gods;[28] the departure with Jacob, entrance to new consciousness. The recurrent theme of barrenness, most poignantly experienced by Rachel, is thus viewed as necessary for the transition to another spiritual level. "Cornered by a vital interest," suggests Dr. Kluger, women "arrived at an encounter with the new God."

JEZEBEL AND ATHALIAH

jezebel: a wicked or scheming woman . . .
                    (Merriam-Webster Pocket Dictionary)

Before leaving the images of Judaism's traditionally revered women, a word about two other biblical figures—the first, infamous throughout the ages; the second, notable as the only woman monarch in the kingdoms of Israel and Judah.

Jezebel's penetration into contemporary usage as a common noun denoting a treacherous or abandoned woman is potent tribute to the vigor and vitality of the biblical image. Yet the source of those treacheries ascribed to the biblical Jezebel is often forgotten. Jezebel was a Tyrean princess married to Ahab, ruler of the Northern Kingdom of Israel. The taking of foreign brides to assure sanguine relationships between neighboring nations was a not uncommon occurrence, to which the multiple marriages of Solomon amply attest. In this instance, Jezebel quite naturally brought her gods with her—Tyre's reigning deity was the goddess Asherah. To be sure, Ahab—and Jereboam before him—were more than receptive to Baalism long before Jezebel's entrance. Yet the intensification of the conflict between the priests of Baal and the prophets of Yahweh is, perhaps with good reason, attributed to Jezebel. 1 Kings 18:13 remarks on Jezebel's having put to death more than one hundred of Yahweh's prophets. Indeed, when Ahab returns with news of Elijah's victory on Mount Carmel, Jezebel threatens Elijah with death.

While Elijah is saved from death by Yahweh, the landowner Naboth does not fare so well. The issue in Naboth's case is not deity, but property. Ahab wants Naboth's land; Naboth refuses to turn it over to him. When Jezebel notices Ahab moping about the palace and eating poorly, she asks what bothers him and he tells her. Jezebel promises Ahab that the land shall be his, fulfilling that promise by executing a ruse that results in the death of Naboth. As retribution for her treachery, Elijah predicts that Jezebel will be trampled underfoot by horses and her corpse picked apart by dogs. This prediction, too, comes to pass.

Rabbinic commentary on biblical text debated the respective guilts of Ahab and Jezebel: "Wicked as Ahab was, his wife Jezebel was incomparably worse. . . . Once Rabbi Levi expounded the Scriptural verse in which the iniquity of Ahab and the influence of his wife over him are discussed, dwelling longer on the first part. Ahab visited him in a dream and reproached him with expatiating on the first half of the verse to the exclusion of the latter half. Thereupon the rabbi took the second half of the verse as the text of his lectures for the next two months, demonstrating all the time that Jezebel was the instigator of Ahab's sins."

Yet another midrash maintains that even Jezebel had some good qualities, "hardened sinner" though she was. Sympathy with others in joy and sorrow are accredited to her, manifest by her participation in funeral corteges and wedding processions. As reward for these traces of human kindness, "the limbs and organs with which she had executed these good deeds were left intact by the horses that trampled her to death. . . ."

Exit Jezebel.

Athaliah, wife of Joram, ruler of the Southern Kingdom of Judah, was reputedly Ahab's daughter. Her ascension to the throne after the death of her husband and son is particularly remarkable since the laws of the monarchy excluded women from royal succession. Athaliah, however, took matters into her own hands after the death of her son, Ahaziah. Although she ruled over Judah for seven years, Athaliah's forceful seizure of power was considered unlawful, and rival factions eventually succeeded in terminating her reign as well as her life. (2 K.: 11)

Woman's rather gloomy economic and legal status throughout the ancient Near East is reflected in laws and customs concerning family life, marriage, divorce, adultery, and the inheritance of property. Israelite law (c. 1000 B.C.E.) has its prototypes in the Sumerian Code of Ur-Nammu (c. 2050 B.C.E.) and in the Babylonian Code of Hammurabi (c. 1700 B.C.E.), as well as certain affinities with Hittite laws dating from about 1450, and Assyrian codes—harshest in their treatment of women—from 1100 B.C.E. While the laws and customs of ancient Israel differed in some respects from those of surrounding civilizations, the similarities are far more pronounced than the divergences.

The Family

The ancient Near Eastern family of historical times is patriarchal in character and organization.[29] Some biblical scholars, most notably Robertson Smith,[30] have suggested that matriarchal organization preceded the patriarchate, pointing to vestiges of matrilocal and matrilineal origins in biblical text, among them the wife-sister motif repeated in the stories of Abraham and Isaac, the question of whether or not Isaac is to settle with Rebeccah's people, Jacob's sojourn with Laban, the father of Rachel and Leah; and the customary naming of children by the mother. Indeed, one may read the insistence with which father-son genealogies are repeatedly enumerated in the early books of the Bible as indication of the imposition or overlay of patriarchal forms on matrilineal origins. Even today, traditional Judaism counts descent from a Jewish mother essential for membership in the group. The reason for the importance of the maternal line in religious affiliation is, of course, rather obvious: Maternity has always been readily discernible, while paternity remains conjectural.

Nonetheless, assumptions about the prehistoric origins of a group are themselves conjectural at best; various arguments have been raised against the thesis of matriarchal origin;[31] written legal documents now available from the ancient Near East are overwhelmingly patriarchal in emphasis; and it is from this context that we derive our sense of woman's role in the family and the larger social group. Indeed, the power exerted by the matriarchs Rebeccah and Rachel is typical of that indirect access to influence characteristic of women under patriarchy.

In short, the husband or father is boss in the ancient Near Eastern family. The wife refers to her husband as *ba'al* (master) or *adon* (lord) in ancient Israel; the Decalogue (Ex. 20:17) lists her among her husband's possessions, along with his servants, maids, ox, and ass. While woman's humanity is legally recognized in moral and ritual circumstances,[32] her status within the family in relationship to father or husband is clearly that of a subordinate. Stronger states such as Babylonia under the Third Dynasty of Ur and later under Hammurabi succeeded in curbing the unlimited powers of the paterfamilias; weaker states, such as Assyria and Palestine during the second millennium, were less successful in limiting his power.[33] These variations are reflected in laws circumscribing marriage, divorce, adultery, and the inheritance of property.

Marriage and Divorce

The ancient Hebrews, like other peoples in the area, considered marriage a civil rather than a religious affair, characterized by contract and ceremony. Its ceremonial aspects emerge in the stories of the matriarchs: Rebeccah's veiling on meeting Isaac; again, the veiling of the bride preceding consummation of the marriage in the story of Rachel and Leah, followed by the wedding night and seven days of feasting. The contractual elements of the marriage consisted essentially of a transaction between two families, sealed by a covenant and the presentation of gifts.

Before the marriage could take place, the bridegroom was required to present the bride's father with a sum of money or its equivalent, referred to as the *mohar* in Canaan and Israel, the *tirhatu* in Babylonia and Assyria. One school of thought defines the *tirhatu-mohar* as "bride price," signifying purchase of the wife; another explains it as a "compensation gift" for the father's loss of his daughter's services as an agricultural worker.

Divorce was both notoriously easy and entirely the husband's prerogative throughout most of the ancient Near East. According to Sumerian law, a man could divorce his wife simply by pronouncing the formula "You are not my wife," together with payment of a small fee. The Hammurabi Code adopted the law with the stipulation that a sick wife could not be divorced against her will. Since a written agreement was required for marriage under Babylonian law, minimal protections for the wife could be written into the contract, among them the reversion of the *tirhatu* to the wife in the event of divorce. Some Babylonian marriage contracts stipulated that the wife could divorce the husband by paying a similar fine.

Assyrian law made no such provisions for the woman; she was literally at her husband's mercy. Similarly, a Hebrew could divorce his wife at will without making provisions for her future maintenance. Later Deuteronomic legislation placed some restrictions on divorce. The husband was required to give his wife a "bill of divorce" (24:1).[34] A man could not divorce his newly married wife on the pretext that she was not a virgin; such accusations had to be proven; if proven false, the husband had to pay a fine and could never divorce his wife (Dt. 22:19).

Woman's status in the Hebrew colony of Elephantine in Egypt (c. 400 B.C.E.) was considerably higher than that in Israel proper. Written marriage contracts from Elephantine stipulate the reversal of the *mohar* to the wife upon divorce by her husband, together with any property that she has brought into his home: "Her dowry of cash and clothing . . . he must hand over to her on one day and in a single act, and she may leave him for wherever she will. . . ."[35] Provision is also made should the woman decide to divorce her husband: "If . . . Yehoyishma should divorce her husband, Ananiah, and say to him, 'I divorce you, I will not be wife to you,' she shall become liable for divorce money. . . ." The divorce fine to be paid by the wife is itemized in the contract, together with the stipulation that she may retain those goods that she brought into the marriage and that upon dissolution of the marriage "she shall depart for her father's house."

The Elephantine marriage contracts also contain the formula pronounced at the marriage, much in the way that it is pronounced at traditional Jewish weddings today in which the wife is sanctified unto the husband while she remains silent. The Elephantine formula was pronounced by the husband: "She is my wife and I am her husband, from this day forever." The woman made no declaration.[36]

While monogamy emerges as the biblical ideal, expressed in the Adam-Eve story, the books of the prophets, and later rabbinic commentaries on biblical text, polygamy was widely practiced and accepted in ancient Israel. By the days of the late monarchy (c. 700 B.C.E.), only the Kings engaged in polygamy; unions among commoners were usually monogamous.

A similar ambivalence informs Babylonian custom, which stresses the monogamous ideal while retaining the polygamous option. Babylonian law, for example, stipulates that a man can only take a second wife under certain circumstances, among them the sterility of his first wife. Assyrian law contains no such ambiguities. Within the polygamous Assyrian family, the husband could virtually take as many wives as he pleased, whether his first wife bore him children or not.

Adultery

Adultery in the ancient Near East was in no sense an assault on woman's chastity, but rather a crime against her husband's exclusive rights to her. Adultery was only a crime when sexual intercourse took place with a betrothed or married woman. Penalties were extremely harsh for the woman involved, while not necessarily so for the man. Clearly at stake was the importance of maintaining the genealogical line and inheritance of property through the father.

The inequity of the penalties involved is most strikingly stated in the oldest legal code of all, the Sumerian laws of Ur-Nammu: "If the wife of a man, by employing her charms, followed after another man and he slept with her, they shall slay that woman, but that male shall be set free."[37]

The Hammurabi Code required that both the adulterous woman and her lover be drowned. If the husband, however, forgave his wife, the lover, too, would be pardoned by the King. If a woman is unjustly accused of adultery by her husband, she must take an oath in the name of a god and return to her husband's house. "The ordeal by waters" administered to a woman suspected of adultery in biblical and talmudic law has its source and counterpart in the Babylonian code that stipulates that a woman accused of adultery by a stranger must undergo the ordeal by water "for the sake of her husband."

An Assyrian woman who committed adultery in her lover's house was put to death; so, too, the man—provided he knew she was married. An Assyrian husband who found his wife in the act of sexual intercourse with another man was enjoined to kill them both on the spot. If he failed to do so and brought the couple before a court, the judges, upon investigating the case, would administer the same punishment to the man that the husband inflicted upon his wife.

Unlike Babylonian and Assyrian views of adultery, Old Testament law considered it an offense against the morality of the community, as well as an assault upon "the honor of the husband." Levitical injunctions against adultery (Lv. 20:10–11, 20) are contained in a passage that includes prohibitions against homosexuality, incest, and intercourse during a woman's menstrual period (Lv. 20:9–21). The penalty for adultery is death for both the man and the woman, as it is for incest with a parent and for homosexuality (which is addressed only to men). Brother-sister incest and intercourse during menstruation incur excision from the group. The community of Israel is further enjoined by Levitical law to engage in none of those practices purportedly common among their neighbors (Lv. 20:22–27). Deuteronomic law again stresses the issue of morality between the community and God, further emphasizing the penalties for adultery as a means for ridding Israel of "evil." Additional qualifications are placed upon an adulterous relationship with a betrothed woman. If the adultery takes place in town, where the woman could presumably cry out for help, both the man and the woman are to be stoned to death. If the engaged woman is "raped" in the countryside, where presumably none could hear her cries for help, only the man is put to death (Dt. 22:22–27).

Sexuality with an unmarried woman was treated far less harshly. Sumerian and Babylonian law usually required that intercourse with a virgin be followed by payment of a fine and marriage. Again the emphasis is not on the woman, but on the dishonor to her father. According to the Deuteronomic code,

"When a man comes upon a virgin who is not pledged in marriage and forces her to lie with him, and they are discovered, then the man . . . shall give the girl's father fifty pieces of silver, and she shall be his wife. . . . He is not free to divorce her all his life long" (Dt. 22:28–29).

Laws of a community more often reflect its ideals than its practices. Prohibitions against certain acts would obviously be unnecessary if proscribed behaviors did not occur. Leviticus 18:18, by way of example, forbids marriage and intercourse with two sisters; yet the story of the twelve tribes of Israel emanates from just such a union between Jacob and the sisters Rachel and Leah. The human sexual drive, subject to regulation in all communities, often finds ways of circumventing prohibitions placed upon it.

This very ingenuity accounts, in part, for divergent attitudes toward sexuality in biblical text. While sensuality is clearly celebrated in the Song of Songs, sexuality is stringently circumscribed in the legal codes. Levitical law makes no issue of virginity; later Deuteronomic legislation emphatically demands it. If a husband accuses his newly married wife of not being a virgin after he has slept with her, her parents are required to spread the proof of the bride's virginity—a blood-stained garment—before the elders of the town at the town gate. If the accusation is proved false, the man must pay a hundred pieces of silver to the girl's father, and the man forfeits his right to divorce his wife. When no proof of virginity is provided, the girl is stoned to death by the men of the town. The Deuteronomic law is depressingly explicit in detail and harsh in its denunciation of the woman: "She has committed an outrage in Israel by playing the prostitute in her father's house. . . ." (Dt. 22:13–21).

Inheritance of Property

While it was possible for wives and daughters to inherit and manage property in Babylonia and Egypt, no such provisions existed for women in ancient Israel and Assyria. Legal documents from the Old Babylonian period[38] included a suit brought by a brother against his sister for rights to their late father's estate. The sister's response is recorded: ". . . in the city of Subaruwa, I am indeed reckoned as an heir in the estate of my mother; why have you then taken the extra share of the estate? You and I must rather divide our father's house equally." Ensuing legal proceedings result in the division of the estate between brother and sister, with the brother retaining first choice over which half of the property will go to him.

The fundamental rule in Israel was that property went only to sons who could maintain the paternal name and line. The story of the daughters of Zelophehad, however, provides a precedent for inheritance by daughters when there are no sons. In Numbers 27, the five daughters of Zelophehad petition Moses for the right to their father's estate. Moses brings their case "before the Lord," who determines that their claim is just and that "when a man dies leaving no son, his patrimony shall pass to his daughter." To assure that their patrimony shall not pass to another tribe, the daughters of Zelophehad are subsequently required to marry within their father's tribe (Nb. 36). Rabbinic commentary on the Biblical ruling significantly notes that "God's love is not like the love of a mortal father; the latter prefers his sons to his daughters, but He that created the world extends His love to women as well as men."[39]

Women, nonetheless, were seldom treated with equality in the community of man. Widows had no share in their husband's estate, leaving them at the mercy of the community or in the care of their sons. If the husband died, leaving no sons, his property passed to male relatives within his clan. One notable exception to the division of a father's estate occurs in the Book of Job, where Job's three daughters share equally in the estate with his seven sons. Whether this reflects later custom or merely Job's munificence is not clear.[40] Contracts from the Jewish colony at Elephantine in which women were generally more privileged provide that a childless widow may inherit from her husband. The widow Judith, in later Apocryphal text,[41] inherited a large estate from her husband, which she disposed of quite freely before her death, indicating a liberalization of custom that paved the way for the recognition of a widow's rights, eventually sanctioned by Jewish law.

The images and legal status of women in the Bible profoundly influenced later rabbinic law and attitudes toward women that penetrate contemporary life. For some, the statements and statutes expressed in the sanctified first five books or Torah remain incontrovertible. Yet talmudic law, regarded by Orthodox and Conservative Jews today as an expression of Torah, did introduce change; and the concurrent aggadic or midrashic embellishments on biblical models convey the values and ideals of a later age.

Indeed, the Bible itself, covering a period of nearly two thousand years and composed over the course of some seven hundred years, incorporates a variety of attitudes toward women. Motherhood, of course, remains woman's noblest calling; it is her *b'rakah* (blessing). Only in motherhood does woman achieve equality with man, indicated in the command to respect both mother and father. Remaining laws are addressed primarily to men, except for those instances, reflected in the material of this chapter, that of necessity include women: family, marriage, and sex. Biblical laws for ritual purity are addressed to both men and women.

Assumptions that woman's status in Judaism was higher than that in surrounding civilizations is, of course, blatantly self-serving nonsense. Higher than some, lower than others is about all one can say in a brief comparative analysis. Babylonian and Egyptian women were clearly more privileged in the ancient Near East than the women of Israel; Assyrian women were less so. Material from the Jewish colony at Elephantine in Egypt reflects greater freedom and protection for women.

While the Bible remains a book primarily written by men for men, women appear in it with more frequency and variety than is commonly remembered. The popular vision of woman as Adam's rib, seductively handing out apples to generations of men, simply ignores those other aspects of womanhood that did emerge even within the clearly patriarchal ethos and bias of the Old Testament. Those images contained in a civilization's myth of origins, however, are particularly potent; despite attempts to reinterpret Eve's rib origin as a signal of equality and oneness with man, the suggestion of woman's subordinate status, implicit in the story, persists. The relationship between literary image and legal and social status is intricate and enduring. Throughout the ages, specific images have been retained and highlighted or embellished to reinforce prevailing attitudes.

Woman's place in Judaism was profoundly affected by the impact of exile after destruction of the second Temple, reflected in the ensuing crystallization of Jewish laws and customs. The impact of exile on the people as a whole and on their attitudes toward those women among them cannot be minimized. Some of Judaism's most virulent statements about women emerge from this period. While retaining the Torah as sacred source, commentaries invariably reflected the turbulence and misgivings of a period in which women, in a sense, suffered a second exile.

7

Woman in Exile

> When a man explicitly vows to the Lord the equiva-
> lent for a human being, the following shall apply: If
> it is a male from twenty to sixty years of age, the
> equivalent is fifty shekels of silver . . . if it is a fe-
> male, the equivalent is thirty shekels.
>
> (Lv. 27:2–4)

Twenty shekels less for a woman! While Levitical cost differen-
tials can scarcely encompass the diversity and complexity of
cultural attitudes toward women that emerged throughout centuries of Jewish life and thought, they speak to the heart of
woman's status in Judaism: Worth something, yes; but less than
a man.

("How much do you love me?" my grandparents would ask
in Yiddish, holding me in their arms as a child. "One dollar's
worth? Five?" Should I have replaced my own uneasy attempts
to settle on a sum with Levitical distinctions? Five dollars for
grandfather and three for grandmother?)

Neither individual portraits nor composites can adequately
convey the experience of Jewish women during nearly two
thousand years of Diaspora following the destruction of the
second Temple in 70 C.E. Their conditions varied from country
to country within given time periods during which individual
exceptions to general rules invariably emerged. While the stories of those few exceptional women chronicled in the annals of
Judaism significantly speak to woman's potential for expression
and action, they scarcely speak for the experience of women in
the general population. Those women, indeed, seldom spoke

for themselves. They are known through the words of their husbands, sons, brothers, and fathers—those sages and rabbis spanning generations who compiled that vast corpus of Jewish law and commentary crucial for the development and continuity of Judaism, which we know today as the Talmud.

The Talmud developed simultaneously in Palestine and Babylonia, with the center of prominence shifting to Babylonia in the fourth century C.E., after a series of uprisings and prohibitive edicts under Roman rule decimated the Palestinian population and diminished its academies of learning. Underlying the evolution of the Talmud is the unequivocal assumption of separate orders of life for male and female, buttressed by a profound ambivalence toward women—an ambivalence whose negative aspects were invariably heightened during those times of turmoil and stress that periodically assailed Judaism throughout its history.

In this context, woman's proper sphere was perceived as home and family; man's, that realm of learning and scholarly debate that has characterized Jewish life from the Rabbinic Era (c. 200 B.C.E.–500 C.E.) onward. With the onset of exile after destruction of the Temple in Jerusalem, study and exposition of the Torah assumed even greater importance. Mishnah, or oral law, derived from Torah over the preceding two centuries, was refined and explicated; midrashic elaborations of biblical text proliferated; academies of learning and synagogues sprang up in Palestine and Babylonia to replace the Temple, which had formerly served as a focal point for ritual observance; the scholar/rabbi replaced the Temple priest as leader of the religious community.

Woman's exclusion from that scholarship central to formative Judaism is reflected both in rabbinic commentaries on women and the laws governing their conduct, as well as in the very process of academic discourse from which those commentaries evolved. Among the six major orders of the Talmud, by way of example, the third order of Nashim (Hebrew for "women") is entirely devoted to the subject of women. The seven tractates contained in Nashim deal almost exclusively with regulations for marriage and divorce, the inheritance of property, the status of the Levirate and the widow, tests and penalties for the adulteress, and conditions under which a woman's vows may be annulled—suggesting the perception of women as a separate and second caste.

Stipulations in the *ketubah* (marriage contract) required that a husband support his wife, that he fulfill her sexual needs, that —in some instances—he not divorce her with undue cause, and that he provide some financial settlement for her in the event of divorce or widowhood. Divorce, nonetheless, remained the male's prerogative, despite ameliorating legislation that permitted women to petition the Jewish court of law for divorce under certain circumstances. Specific cases refer to a husband's impotence, his denial of conjugal rights, the unreasonable restriction of his wife's freedom to attend weddings and funerals, and the husband's working at a "repulsive" (!) occupation. If the wife's petition was judged valid by the court of law, it then attempted to coerce the errant husband into initiating divorce. The painful situation of the *agunah* (anchored woman), however, remains unchanged to this day. When no qualified witnesses can testify to a husband's death or disappearance, his wife becomes an *agunah* who can never remarry. In a society that values marriage for both men and women, perceiving no other viable options for the woman, the distress of the *agunah* is particularly acute. Inheritance, too, continued to proceed along male lines, with some hedges introduced so that a father or husband might set aside portions of his goods or estate for wives and daughters. Upon marriage, a woman's property reverted to her husband, who was empowered to manage or dispose of it.

Within the sphere of marriage, home, and family, women were afforded greater protections in the Rabbinic Era than in the biblical period. Their confinement to the home was also greater. Moreover, such protections as were introduced took for granted a setting that remained clearly patriarchal; and all majority opinions rendered about women assumed their proper place as home and family, rather than public or religious life. That sense of woman as a separate caste was further reinforced throughout the centuries by the evolution and disposition of laws for ritual purity, contained in the sixth order of the Talmud, Toharot. Initially applicable to both men and women, laws for ritual purity were closely interwoven with Temple rites and observance. When it became clear that the synagogue was more than a somewhat temporary replacement for the Temple in Jerusalem, the various regulations of Toharot eventually fell into disuse, except for the tractate on Niddah, which deals with seclusion and examination of the menstruant. Indeed, the laws of Niddah, mandatory for Orthodox women today, were frequently elaborated and extended with a zeal that borders on morbid fascination.

Yet it is their exclusion from that historical process through which the Talmud evolved that proves most problematic for women today. Patterns of scholarship set in the early centuries of this era, together with an underlying ambivalence toward women, continue to operate in contemporary spheres of both secular and religious academic and professional life.

"What kind of work do you do?" a podiatrist asked me recently, admiring my newly acquired beach tan.

"I'm writing a book," I answered, "about women and Judaism."

"Don't tell me," he drew back, "that you're one of those intellectual women!" Unrolling some tube gauze, he shook his head despairingly. "Intellectual women mean trouble."

Trouble is what the rabbis saw as they debated the issue of whether or not women should be taught Torah. "Teaching a daughter Torah," suggested Rabbi Eliezer ben Hyrcannus in the first century C.E., "is like teaching her lechery." His colleague Ben Azzai disagreed, maintaining that some knowledge was essential for women, while yet another sage observed that woman's learning centered on the spindle. And so the debate continued over the centuries until Eliezer's views finally gained precedence.

Can this mean that no Jewish women engaged in intellectual discourse until the modern era? Hardly. A handful of renowned female scholars—usually the daughters of learned men—is invariably displayed whenever women rankle at their exclusion from the sacred realm of learning. Indeed, the opinions of second-century female scholar Beruriah are recorded in the Talmud; yet medieval commentators attempted to discredit her person—while retaining her opinions—with trumped-up charges of sexual vulnerability.

Clearly at issue was not the question of whether or not women were capable of learning, but whether it was proper that they do so. The very structure of the academy tended to exclude them. Scholars would often travel long distances to spend months and years of study with their mentors and colleagues, while wives (of necessity?) remained at home. (How a husband could fulfill his "sexual obligations" under such circumstances remains a mystery.*) The semimonastic *ambiance* of the academy together with that climate of camaraderie in intellectual discourse essential for a real grasp of Talmud precluded the participation of women—except for rare instances—in talmudic debates and decisions. Such a setting further reinforced the views of those rabbis like Eliezer who were temperamentally inclined to regard scholarly women as trespassers on male territory. Even those less inclined to banish women exhibited a marked ambivalence toward their achievements, admiring them on the one hand while imposing limitations on the other.

Nowhere is this more evident than in the responses of those fathers—like my own—who impart a love of learning to their daughters, only to find themselves uncomfortable with the results. "Not very intelligent," my father would sourly comment after brief conversations with young women my brother introduced when those women failed to meet his A+ standards for intellectual clarity. His stringent evaluations, however, were promptly followed by the inevitable qualification: "But if she were smarter, she'd drive him crazy." (Such vacillation is almost enough to drive a daughter crazy!) Even more than the podiatrist whose professed aversion to "intellectual" women—like Eliezer's—is relatively conflict-free, my father's vacillation speaks to the heart of that ambivalence that permeates the Talmud.

* Needless to say, Torah study superseded the lesser requirement for sexual fulfillment. While such sublimation in Torah served the scholar well, one cannot help but wonder about his wife. Rabbinic tradition holds that her fulfillment consisted in helping him.

Response by daughters and wives to such conflict-laden views may well be twofold: open rebellion against those restrictions placed on women, which at its extreme may view every male/female encounter competitively as a battleground for proving oneself equal to or better than the man, while fearing the reverse is true; introjection remains the other option, in which that cultural conflict articulated by the father is absorbed into the self, resulting in the subtle sabotage of all attempts for achievement and success. Stridency or self-sabotage: How is one to choose?

Insight, if not amelioration of such debilitating conflicts, may be derived from examination of that cultural background that both generated and reinforced them. Man's traditional view of woman as compassionate helpmate and nurturer of children—that "perfect" mother/wife all of us so sorely need to meet the trials of life—clearly reflects his own needs. While those needs may occasionally coincide with woman's preferences, her preferences are usually beside the point.

"In Judaism," a renowned contemporary Orthodox scholar informed me, "woman is queen of the coop."

It is not the coop, however, but the academy that was historically accorded highest status in formative Judaism. While wives were lauded for the sacrifices they made in sending husbands and sons to the Yeshivot, it was scholarship, study of Torah, and the *obligatory* performance of positive commandments that assured the continuity of Jewish spiritual and communal life.

Moreover, ambivalence toward the intellectual achievements of women served both to limit their contributions to Jewish life and to perpetuate the kinds of academic and religious settings that militated against their participation. That separation of the sexes that filtered into Judaism at a point in time that remains difficult to determine, despite zealous attempts to fix its origins in the sacred era of the second Temple, coupled with the semi-monastic climate and relative isolation of the early academies, excluded women from those very processes vital for participation in formative Judaism. Patterns long set do not readily change; and the arguments of the past are frequently employed to support the prejudices of the present. Observant Jewish feminists today thus find themselves in a double bind. Their requests for change must invariably be addressed to those men involved in the halachic[1] process, which is presumably ongoing, while participation in that process is still denied them.

"The Talmud is unique in that no student can master it in full without taking an active part in the creative process,"[2] observes contemporary scholar Adin Steinsalz. "It is impossible to arrive at external knowledge of this work. . . . True knowledge can only be attained through spiritual communion, and the student must participate intellectually and emotionally in the talmudic debate, himself becoming, to a certain degree, a creator."[3]

That intellectual creativity required for mastery of the Talmud was historically reserved for men, while women presumably enjoyed their biological creativity as wives and mothers. To be sure, unconscious envy of that biological creativity unique to women may well have served to further reinforce traditionally distinct divisions between male and female roles. Yet it was the scholar, not the mother, who was venerated as the "aristocrat" of Jewish society. While entrance to the talmudic academy was predicated on no exclusivity (save that of ability), and the sons of poor or unlearned men often became great scholars, membership in the academy conferred elite status. That "spiritual communion" essential for a true grasp of Talmud—the pillar of Jewish life set on the cornerstone of Scripture—was clearly unattainable for nearly all women during the Rabbinic Era. How, then, did the Talmud evolve, and how did the rare female scholar like Beruriah become part of it?

Most significant in the genesis of the Talmud are the periods of the Tannaim (from the Hebrew root *tana* [one who studies]), c. 40 B.C.E.–200 C.E., followed by the Amoraim (from the verb *amar* [to speak or interpret]), c. 200–500 C.E. Tannaitic methods of scholarship, initiated by R. Hillel in Babylonia and R. Shammai in Palestine, continued to flourish for nearly three centuries. Rivalry between the houses of Shammai and Hillel is an integral part of talmudic history. Although both schools fell within the tannaitic tradition, disputes between them persisted for generations until Hillel's more liberal views finally prevailed.

Before the fall of Jerusalem, Hillel's youngest disciple, Johanan b. Zakkai, who had opposed the revolt against the Romans, received permission from Vespasian, later to become Emperor, to establish a school at Yavneh in Palestine. In 73 c.e., three years after the Judaeo-Roman wars that culminated in the ransacking and burning of the Temple, the academy at Yavneh opened.

Most prominent among R. Johanan's disciples were the conservative Eliezer b. Hyrcannus, known as "Rabbi Eliezer the Great," the congenial R. Joshua b. Hananiah, and Eliezer's brother-in-law, Rabban Gamaliel, who re-established and led the Sanhedrin.[4] These three sages taught the following generation's Tannaim at the "Yavneh vineyard"—producing, in the case of Eliezer's statements about women, some rather sour grapes.

Eliezer's views on the "obscenity" of teaching daughters Torah have been cited. Unlike his friend and rival R. Joshua, a poor man who earned his living as a blacksmith, Eliezer was the son of a wealthy family who began to study at a relatively late age, but soon advanced to the first rank of scholars. He is remembered for his outstanding abilities and charismatic personality, his phenomenal memory and autocratic temperament. Although his official mentor was R. Johanan, Eliezer leaned toward the House of Shammai in the severity and conservatism of his halachic rulings. If Eliezer was Yavneh's autocrat, R. Joshua was its diplomat. A homely man whose wit and wisdom was universally engaging, R. Joshua was often delegated to represent his people in Rome. At Yavneh, the two were often in conflict. At one time when Eliezer refused to accept a majority ruling, his colleagues were forced to excommunicate him after a dramatic struggle, during which he is portrayed as calling on the forces of Nature and the Almighty for aid, eliciting R. Joshua's response that the Torah no longer resided in heaven but was entrusted to the judgment of the majority of sages on earth. Despite such confrontations, Eliezer's rulings remained a vital foundation for mishnaic oral law. In addition to his formidable intellect, firm convictions, and sour disposition toward women, one may also infer that Eliezer was something of a

fussy eater from the talmudic note that his wife, Imma Shalom—
herself the daughter of a famous rabbi and sister to R. Gamaliel, head of the Sanhedrin—prepared as many as fifty different
dishes for Eliezer at a single meal to please his palate.

Among the following generation's Tannaim, the story of
Eliezer's pupil Akiva b. Yosef is most extraordinary. Akiva's
rise from illiteracy to pre-eminent scholarship—fame, fortune,
and martyrdom—through the goodwill and self-abnegation of
his wife, Rachel, is an exemplary moral tale of woman as self-
sacrificing enabler *par excellence*. Rachel, the daughter of one
of Jerusalem's wealthiest men, first meets Akiva when he is
tending her father's sheep.† Rachel promptly falls in love with
the illiterate but pious shepherd and determines to marry him.
On hearing of her betrothal, her father disinherits her, taking
a vow that the couple will never receive his support. They
marry in winter and live in abject poverty. With Rachel's encouragement, Akiva begins to learn to read at forty, whereupon
his unusual insight and ability quickly manifest themselves.
Again, presumably urged by Rachel, Akiva leaves Jerusalem
for the academy at Yavneh to study under the eminent scholars
R. Joshua and R. Eliezer. In the course of his years at Yavneh,
Akiva's talents are duly recognized; he moves from the position
of disciple to that of colleague. Rachel, meanwhile, in Jerusalem, is so poor that she has to shear and sell her hair to buy
bread.

Upon returning to Jerusalem after twelve years at Yavneh,
Akiva overhears a neighbor deriding Rachel: "Your father did
well to you— First, because he is your inferior, and second, because he abandoned you to widowhood all these years." To
which the self-effacing Rachel replies: "Yet were he to hear my
desires, he would be absent another twelve years." Miracle of
miracles! Although she never learns of his presence, Akiva receives his wife's sanction for yet another departure. "Seeing
that she has given me permission," observes the shepherd-
scholar, "I'll go back." Without more ado, Akiva returns to the
academy for twelve more years.

† A curious reversal of the Jacob/Rachel story.

But Rachel ultimately attains her pathetic moment of glory when Akiva returns to Jerusalem. His fame has spread throughout the land in the twenty-four years since Rachel saw her husband last, and the whole town turns out to greet him. The intervening decades have dealt less kindly with Rachel, now a haggard, aging woman. "Where do *you* think you're going?" asks the ubiquitous neighbor, appalled that so lowly a drudge should expect to be recognized by so eminent a scholar. "A righteous man knoweth the life of his beast," replies the ever-humble Rachel, quoting *Proverbs*‡ as she prepares to join the crowds awaiting Akiva. Flanked by his entourage of twenty-four thousand disciples, Akiva makes his entrance. At the sight of the shabby old woman meekly making her way through the crowd to approach their leader, the disciples hastily brush her aside. "Make way for her," Akiva gently reprimands them, "for my learning and yours are hers by rights." He further instructs them that the definition of a rich man is "he who has a wife whose deeds are worthy."

Yet Akiva's ensuing wealth encompassed more than his wife's worthy deeds. When Rachel's father heard of Akiva's magnanimity toward his daughter, he pleaded for the remission of his earlier vow. Akiva kindly annulled it for him, and Rachel's father gratefully shared his wealth with her husband. Talmudic references to Rachel fade at this point, and she recedes into oblivion. Akiva, meanwhile, travels far and wide, dispensing wisdom and collecting funds. He eventually marries a beautiful Roman proselyte,[5] the wealthy widow of Tineus Rufus, Roman governor of Judea—perhaps eliciting Akiva's later teaching that a man may divorce his wife merely on the grounds that "he finds another woman more beautiful."[6]

When Bar-Kokhba's rebellion against Rome began in 132

‡ Pr. 12:10, rendered in The New English Bible: "A righteous man cares for his beast, but a wicked man is cruel at heart." That Rachel should choose to identify herself with the "behemoth"—literally, cattle or beasts of the field—clearly conveys her sense of self, that acme of female masochism that has been lauded throughout the ages. That the rabbis took no issue with the identification of wives and cattle is equally remarkable. Rashi's commentary on the proverb: "A righteous man does not scorn his wife." From Tosephot "He knows that I was pained on his account."

C.E., Akiva not only supported the uprising, but also declared Bar-Kokhba the Messiah. Before the rebellion broke out, Akiva traveled throughout the Jewish world—from Babylonia to Egypt, through North Africa and Gaul—recruiting money and rallying political support. On returning to Palestine, he placed thousands of his disciples at Bar-Kokhba's disposal.

The struggle that ensued was one of the bloodiest in Jewish history. The Romans pursued a "scorched-earth policy" that devastated Judea. War claimed close to a million victims, including an entire generation of Akiva's disciples. Following the devastation, Hadrian placed a ban on Torah study. Akiva continued to teach publicly, despite the risks, and succeeded in training a new group of disciples before he was apprehended by Roman authorities. He died a martyr's death after being tortured, reportedly expiring with the prayer of "Shema Yisrael . . ." on his lips.

Among the next generation's sages, the extraordinary female scholar Beruriah emerges as a striking counterpoint to Akiva's self-abnegating Rachel. The only woman whose halachic teachings are rendered in the Talmud, appearing in various tractates —*not* including that of Nashim (dealing exclusively with regulations for women)—Beruriah's views are characterized by cogent argument, incisive wit, a generous yet reasoned compassion, and an educated intelligence. The daughter of Rabbi Hananyah b. Teradyon, martyred in the aftermath of the Bar-Kokhba uprising, and the wife of Rabbi Meir, one of Akiva's most brilliant younger pupils, Beruriah clearly held her own in talmudic debates. Her opinions often prevailed over those of her contemporaries.

One such debate, recorded in the Tosefta,* finds Beruriah pitted against her brother, who holds an opposing view on a technical matter about the Sabbath. Beruriah's argument wins the support of her colleagues, eliciting R. Judah b. Baba's comment, referring back to their father, "His daughter has an-

---

* Tosefta (additions) are compiled separately from the Talmud, although they date back to mishnaic times. They are generally used to elucidate abstruse or fragmentary passages of the Mishnah. The first of these references to Beruriah may be found in Kelim B. K. 4, 17; the second in Kelim B. M. 1, 6.

swered more correctly than his son." In yet another instance, Beruriah provides a solution for two rabbinical schools engaged in conflict. Again, her resolution is endorsed by the elder R. Judah with the observation, "Beruriah has spoken rightly."

Despite those tragic circumstances in which her life was framed—Beruriah's father was burned at the stake for defying Roman proscriptions against teaching Torah; her mother similarly was executed and her sister taken to a Roman brothel from which, urged by his wife, Rabbi Meir rescued her[7]—Beruriah retained remarkable fair-mindedness. Her compassion for humanity corrupted by evil and her ability to distinguish between sin and sinner are most astute in her response to Meir when she finds him praying for the death of some highwaymen who have given him inordinate trouble.

"How can you justify such a prayer?" she asks her husband in the talmudic tractate Berakhot (Blessings), illuminating the distinction between sin and sinner. "Because it is written: 'Let *hattaim* [sins] cease?' Is it written *hotim* [sinners]?" She chides him gently with the Scriptural reminder: "It is written '*hattaim*'! Further, look at the end of the verse 'and let the wicked men be no more.' Since the sins will cease, there will be no more wicked men! Rather pray they should repent," Beruriah advises her husband, and Meir accepts her counsel. "He did pray for them, and they repented."[8]

Intellect once more merges with compassion when Beruriah tells Meir the dreadful news of their sons' death. For my own part, I find the cool intelligence hard to take in this instance. Yet it is this story—from aggadic literature, rather than those from the Tosefta or Talmud—that is most frequently retold throughout the ages, conceivably because it portrays Beruriah in the traditionally more acceptable role of wife and mother, in addition to its insights on the confrontation with death and the hallowing of the Sabbath:

"When two of their sons died on the Sabbath, Beruriah did not inform Meir of their children's death upon his return from the academy in order not to grieve him on the Sabbath. Only after the Havdalah prayer (closing the Sabbath) did she broach the matter, saying, 'Some time ago a certain man came and left something in my trust; now he has called for it. Shall I return it to him or not?' Naturally Meir replied in the affirmative, whereupon Beruriah showed him their dead children. When Meir began to weep, she asked: 'Did you not tell me that we must give back what is given on trust? The Lord gave, and the Lord hath taken away.' "⁹

While Beruriah's concern for her husband's feelings has been unanimously lauded by rabbis throughout the ages, contemporary scholars have remarked upon the nonstereotypic responses ascribed to Meir and Beruriah in this midrashic tale. Contrary to talmudic assumptions of woman's "lightheadedness," as well as later allegations of emotionalism and hysteria, it is Meir who is overcome by weeping in this instance and Beruriah who keeps cool.

Notwithstanding her capacity for compassion when circumstances warranted it, Beruriah clearly did not suffer fools gladly, nor did she regard rabbinic tendencies to restrict conversation with women without rancor. She pokes fun at the absurdity of both in the following talmudic anecdote:

"Rabbi Yossi the Galilean was once on a journey when he met Beruriah. 'By what road,' he asked her, 'do we go to Lydda?' 'Foolish Galilean,' she replied. 'Did not the Sages say, "Engage not in much talk with women?"¹⁰ You should have asked, "By which to Lydda?" ' "¹¹

Beruriah's derision of rabbinic inhibitions against extended conversation with women suggests that such prohibitions were not regarded with utmost seriousness during the era of her commentaries—that the interdict against engaging in "much talk with women" operated in the realm of suggestion rather than that of mandate later ascribed to it. Evidence of Beruriah's familiarity with Torah and Mishnah, as well as her direct participation in the talmudic process, is further reinforced by the following talmudic excerpt, in which she is held up as a model for scholarship to a young rabbinical student nearly a century after her death.¹²

"Rabbi Simlai came before Rabbi Johanan and requested: 'Let the master teach me the Book of Genealogies . . . in three months.' Thereupon Rabbi Johanan took a clod of earth and threw it at him, saying: 'Beruriah, wife of Rabbi Meir and daughter of Rabbi Hananyah ben Teradyon, who studied three hundred laws from three hundred teachers in one day, could nevertheless not do her duty in three years, yet you propose to do it in three months!' "[13]

Despite the acknowledgment of Beruriah's scholarship and the retention of her judgments in the Talmud, the academic brotherhood could not long tolerate the image of woman as distinguished scholar. The reference to Beruriah's "duty" in the preceding passage clearly indicates that the obligatory period of study for accreditation as rabbi traditionally denied women may well have been incumbent upon a woman like Beruriah in the second and third centuries. Succeeding generations of rabbis, however, found her membership in the academy increasingly problematic. That predisposition against teaching daughters Torah, articulated by R. Eliezer amid considerable controversy in the first century, eventually became the norm. If teaching a woman Torah was debatable, to teach her Talmud was clearly taboo. How then did Beruriah learn? *Eavesdropping* served as the answer for later generations of rabbis to explain—or, more accurately, explain away—Beruriah's obvious familiarity with the law, as well as her participation in the talmudic process. One legend has it that Beruriah learned by overhearing her father reciting the Mishnah aloud to himself.

Yet eavesdropping remained a paltry palliative for the discomfort engendered by woman's scholarship. A far more potent resolution to the rabbinate's conflict over including a woman in their midst surfaced in the legend, rendering Beruriah *a woman, after all!*, recounted by Rashi nearly a thousand years after Beruriah's death.† Rashi's commentary endeavors to illuminate an obscure reference in the talmudic tractate *Avoda Zara* following that passage in which Beruriah calls upon Meir to rescue her sister from a Roman brothel. Although the rescue proves successful, indications of a backlash are suggested by the

---

† As the Encyclopedia Judaica puts it: "Rashi . . . quotes a legend to the effect that as a result of her pretension of being above feminine weakness she was led astray, with tragic consequences . . ."

rather murky allusion to Meir's subsequent departure: The Romans ran after him and "he then arose and ran away and came to Babylon. Some say it was because of that incident that he ran to Babylon; others say because of the incident about Beruriah" (bAvoda Zara 18a). No further information about either Meir's departure or the "incident" concerning Beruriah is provided by the Talmud until the famous medieval scholar Rashi introduces a legend of unknown origins into his elucidation of the passage:

"Beruriah once again made fun of the saying of the Sages that women are lightheaded. Then Meir said to her: 'With your life you will have to take back your words.' He sent one of his students to test her, to see if she would allow herself to be seduced. He sat by her the whole day until she surrendered herself to him. When she realized (what she had done), she strangled herself. Then Rabbi Meir ran away on account of the scandal."

Only a woman, after all! But can this be the same woman who exhibited such restraint in conveying news to her husband of the death of their sons? That same Beruriah whose crisp wit and even-handed judgments are recorded in the Talmud? Whose opinions occasionally prevailed over those of her male colleagues? Who was held up as a model for scholarship to a young rabbi a century after her death? How those extraordinary abilities, accorded recognition in the early centuries of this era, must have grated on succeeding generations of scholars to elicit the legend of Beruriah's downfall in the course of a millennium!—a downfall classically predicated, like Eve's, on that purported "weakness" of woman, inevitably linked with her sexuality. Underlying such traditional ascriptions of "weakness" to woman is fear of her strength—her intellectual and sexual potency. The unlikely story in which Meir maneuvers Beruriah's seduction by one of his students (a disservice to them both!), recounted by Rashi in the eleventh century, serves to allay that fear and discomfort engendered by the image of a potent woman. "*Only* a woman in the end!" rings the eternal moral of this paternal tale. By simply lifting Beruriah's skirts, the story manages at once to undercut her stature while blunting Beruriah's derision of rabbinic tendencies to circumscribe the behavior of women. Talmudic allegations of woman's "lightheadedness" thus remain intact with the forced rendition of the female scholar's susceptibility to seduction. Despite certain external narrative refinements, the story of Beruriah's downfall—presumably typical of her sex—conveys essentially that same underlying power struggle manifest in the act of rape: Man lords it over woman.

Tradition is clearly more comfortable with the self-effacement of Akiva's Rachel than with Beruriah's formidable scholarship. While Beruriah emerges as the far more vivid and vigorous figure in early rabbinic literature, her very vigor eventually costs Beruriah her reputation. Rachel's image, on the other hand, emerges "untarnished" throughout the centuries. What need, after all, to defame a woman who identifies herself at the outset as her husband's *behema* (beast)? To be sure, the ubiquitous notes on Rachel's "encouragement" of Akiva's scholarship may well have included some initial tutorial sessions. How else but through Rachel's teaching would the illiterate shepherd have learned to read at the age of forty, living in abject poverty with his once-wealthy wife and sleeping on straw at the outset of their marriage in winter? It was not unusual for daughters of wealthy Jewish families to receive decorative secular educations as adornments for marriage. Yet the suggestion that Rachel might have taught Akiva is carefully avoided, and she remains the unblemished model of wifely self-abnegation. The story of Rachel's sacrifices for Akiva is reiterated to young men and women in Sunday schools today, reinforcing the Judaic ideal of the self-sacrificing wife *par excellence*—the woman who gives all to enable her husband to attend the Yeshiva.‡ Beruriah's image fared less well; Sunday-school students seldom learn of her.

The striking contrast between the images of Beruriah and Rachel, as they have been transmitted throughout the ages, highlights that profound ambivalence toward women that per-

‡ Substitute medical school for Yeshiva and you have the ubiquitous modern counterpart of the rabbinic archetype.

meates human history. The fate Beruriah suffers is not a singular one for those women who move beyond the roles traditionally assigned them in Judaism. Rabbinic embellishments on biblical figures reveal similar discomfort with the images of potent women. What is viewed as admirable strength in men is all too often perceived as intolerable arrogance in women. Nowhere is this more clearly stated than in rabbinic commentaries on the biblical figures of Hulda, the prophetess, and Deborah, the judge.

"Eminence is not for women," observes one rabbi. "Two eminent women are mentioned in the Bible, Deborah and Huldah, and both proved to be of a proud disposition. . . . This unpleasant feature of their characters is indicated by their ugly names."[14]

The etymological putdown refers to the Hebrew derivation of their names: Dvorah for bee and Hulda for weasel. Indeed, the association of women's names with those of animals is not exceedingly uncommon: The biblical Leah is derived from *liatu* (wild cow); Rachel, from the word for "ewe" or "lamb." Akiva's Rachel may have been closer on the mark than one might wish in defining herself as her husband's beast! The rabbinical name game on Deborah and Hulda—like the seduction scene on Beruriah—was a popular means for diminishing the impact of those few women in Jewish history who transcended the prescribed spheres of home and hearth.

"Haughtiness does not befit women," commented yet another rabbi. "There were two haughty women, and their names are hateful, one being called hornet and the other a weasel. Of the hornet, it is written, 'And she sent and called Barak' instead of going to him. Of the weasel it is written, 'Say no to the man' instead of 'Say to the King.'"[15]

Straining to come to terms with Hulda's prophetic gifts, still other commentaries maintain that her powers of prophecy were derived from the righteousness of her husband (who figures not at all on the biblical scene). That Josiah should have sought guidance from the female Hulda rather than the male prophet Jeremiah, who was her contemporary, proved even more problematic for later exegetes. One farfetched explanation has it that Josiah knew he would receive a more compassionate pronouncement from a woman—an assumption that completely ignores the Scriptural evidence manifest in Hulda's prophecy of destruction. Oh, to what pains the sages went! What voluptuous stretches of imagination, what violations of reason and credibility—and all to discredit or diminish those few women who managed to excel in areas traditionally marked off as male domains.

Indeed, the mixed feelings and exegetical abuses inspired by such "unusual" women as Deborah, Hulda, and Beruriah very much speak for themselves. They call up that pervasive and profound ambivalence whose negative aspects are heightened during periods of turmoil and stress. They speak to the heart of that *ambiance*—the general climate of desolation and foreboding following the destruction of the second Temple and the ravages of war and exile—that wrenched itself free of its own sense of annihilation by condemning the women in its midst. It was in such a time that the prayer thanking God "for not having made me a woman" was introduced into daily liturgy. And it is in such times that the mingled fear and contempt exhibited toward women evokes in them the sense of having been subject to a second exile.

The greatest obstacles to change remain rooted in the psyche, rather than in Jewish law. While men may well find comfort in that historical pattern that distinguished sharply between male and female roles, increasing numbers of women find such distinctions frustrating and confining.

"The most formidable barrier . . . to the acceptance of women as authority figures and the equals of men," observes contemporary scholar Paula Hyman, "lies in the psychological rather than the halachic realm."[16]

Nowhere is this more evident than in the history and evolution of the edict *kol be-ishah ervah* (woman's voice is an abomination), derived from talmudic commentary after the fall of the second Temple, and exploited in subsequent centuries to sanctify the demand for her silence.

8

Blood, Breath, and Voice

> A man should ever avoid women . . . it is forbidden
> to hear the voice of a woman singer or to gaze at a
> woman's hair. . . .
>
> *(Kitzur Shulchan Aruch,* 1961)

> A silent woman is a gift from the Lord. . . .
>
> (b. Sira, c. 180 B.C.E.)

The phrase *kol be-ishah* (voice of woman) occurs repeatedly in
biblical and rabbinic literature, followed by observations that
run the gamut from contempt to idealization. Most damaging to
women is the powerful edict *kol be-ishah ervah*[1] (woman's
voice is an abomination), linked in talmudic thought with corruption preceding the destruction of the second Temple and the
period of mourning following it. *Ervah* clearly pronounces
woman temptress, luring man to commit Judaism's three unpardonable sins: adultery/incest, murder, and idolatry.

Picked up and elaborated by medieval codifiers, the *ervah* indictment effectively excluded women from significant areas of
spiritual and intellectual life. All public association with women
became suspect—a threat to spiritual purity and the fulfillment
of man's covenant with God. The ban on woman's voice and the
subsequent avoidance of all sensory stimuli perceived as emanating from her—the sight or touch of female hair and skin—are
scarcely implicit in the general moratorium on celebration and
song from which the *ervah* indictment is derived. Yet the compelling association between disaster, sin, sexuality, and woman
proved stronger than the historical context from which the ban

on singing emerged—initially advocated as an expression of
deep mourning over loss of the Second Temple.

"When the Sanhedrin ceased, song ceased from the places of
feasting. . . .

When the Temple was destroyed . . . men of faith disap-
peared from Israel."

These lines from the concluding Mishnah of the tractate Sotah ("the adulterous woman") reflect the deep note of pessimism and despair on which the tractate ends. The haunting fear
that Israel was doomed to continuing decline is expressed in
the mournful cadences of a lament decrying the spread of lawlessness and corruption that preceded the fall of the Temple
and the sense of sterility and loss that followed it:

"R. Joshua testified that from the day the Temple was destroyed, there is no day without a curse, the dew has not descended for a blessing, and the flavor has departed from the
fruits. . . ."

The ban on singing is predicated on Scriptural allusion to
Isaiah: "They shall not drink wine with a song . . ." (Is.
24:9) and echoes Isaiah's despair after the first exile:

> The new wine dries up, the vines sicken,
> and all the revelers turn to sorrow.
>> Silent the merry beat of tambourines,
>> hushed the shouts of revelry,
>> the merry harp is silent.
> No one shall drink wine to the sound of song;
> the liquour will be bitter to the man who drinks it.
>
> . . . .
>> all revelry is darkened
>> and mirth is banished from the land.[2]

Only the last line of the Mishnah suggests the subsequent association of woman and sexuality with destruction: "But the
Sages say: Immorality and witchcraft destroyed everything."

This slender suggestion is taken up in the *gemara,* which
notes that R. Huna abolished singing together with ritual sacrifice and celebration that included the purchase and use of
geese. R. Hisda subsequently came along to abolish R. Huna's
edict on geese, but *not* on woman's voice. "A woman's leg is

sexual incitement," suggests this same R. Hisda, alluding to a rather obscure line in Isaiah: "Uncover the leg, pass through the rivers," followed by "Thy nakedness shall be uncovered; thy shame shall be seen."[3]

This evocation of woman's nakedness linked with the ban on her voice elicited a spate of rabbinic endorsements. R. Joseph said: "When men sing and women join, it is licentiousness; when women sing and men join, it is like fire in tow. For what practical purpose is this mentioned? To abolish the latter before the former!" R. Isaac said: "A handsbreath exposed in a married woman constitutes sexual incitement. In which way? Shall I say if one gazes at it? But has not R. Sheshet already said '. . . to tell you that if one gazes at the little finger of a woman, it is as though he gazed at her secret place!'? No, it means in one's own wife and when he recites the Shema"* Samuel said: "A woman's voice is a sexual incitement (*kol be-ishah ervah*), as it says, 'For sweet is thy voice and thy countenance is comely' (Cant. 2:14)." Again R. Sheshet—who happened to be blind—observes that "woman's hair is a sexual incitement" by invoking *Canticles* 4:1: "Thy hair is a flock of goats."

Commenting on R. Joseph's judgments in the fourth century, Rashi in the eleventh century suggests, "A woman's singing arouses sexual passion. The latter [man's joining in song initiated by woman] is more serious because it implies a willful act on the part of the man to listen to the female voice." All of this, incidentally, is based on that verse in Song of Songs that opens with a plea to the beloved to "let me hear thy voice. . . ." It is more than curious that those Scriptural allusions from Song and Canticles that celebrate the beauty and sensuality of women are talmudically employed to advocate the avoidance of them—pinpointing the profound ambivalence that underlines rabbinic attitudes and judgments about women.

The negative aspects of that ambivalence peak in the pronouncements of Maimonides and later in the Shulchan Aruch, which applies the ban on listening to woman's voice not only to

* Reference to the dispute over whether the ban on listening to woman's voice refers to social situations or only to reciting the Shema prayer when one is in bed with one's wife and she is naked.

homes and parties but to worship services as well. Although women were permitted to be called to the Torah, according to the Talmud, and to participate in the seven obligatory readings for the Sabbath, such sanctions were abolished by Maimonides to preserve what he termed "the honor of the men." Woman's call to the Torah, in Maimonides' view, might suggest that no qualified men were available; such indignity was to be averted at all costs. The price exacted from women was their mandated silence.

Significantly, earlier sections of the tractate Sotah from which the *ervah* indictment erupts describe the "ordeal by bitter waters" used to test women accused of adultery. While the "ordeal," mentioned briefly in Numbers,[4] has its prototype in the Sumerian Code of Ur-Nammu,† the description in Sotah is the only extant source of information on the practice as it was conducted by the Hebrews before the fall of the Temple. Although the "ordeal"—banned by R. Johanan b. Zakkai—went the way of the desecrated Temple, its retention in the Talmud together with the lament over destruction, exile, and the interdict against woman's voice is not mere coincidence. The theme of harlotry is a recurrent motif in later biblical, Apocryphal, and rabbinic writing—literally denouncing the wayward wife in relationship to her husband, metaphorically castigating the wayward nation of Israel in relationship to its God. The specifics of the "ordeal" and the commentaries upon it reveal rabbinic attitudes toward adultery, illuminating both its symbolic aspect with the nation cast as harlot, as well as its more earthly counterpart, in which woman was required to submit herself to a test that she could scarcely survive.

In administering the test, the priests first try to talk the woman accused of adultery into admitting her guilt by pointing to others who have, so that God's name, which is written on a scroll and blotted out by being dipped into the bitter waters (a compound mixed with dust or ashes from the tabernacle floor until the dust rises above the water) will not be used in vain. If

----

† Like the test for witchcraft some two thousand years later, the Babylonian woman suspected of adultery was thrown into a body of water. If she floated, she was judged innocent; if she sank, guilty. (Code of Hammurabi)

the woman admits her guilt, her marriage is dissolved and she waives the marriage settlement. If she denies guilt, she is brought to the East Gate, where she is humiliated for all the town to see before being given the bitter waters to drink. A priest tears her garments until her bosom is bared, undoes her hair, and removes all ornaments from her to render her as unattractive as possible. "If clothed in white, she is dressed in black . . . to make her repulsive." Common ropes are bound about her breasts and she is held up to ridicule before the town so that "all women may be taught not to do after your lewdness." The ensuing discussion in the *gemara* underlines the need for displaying the suspected adulteress to all women "so that they may be intimidated, and she, humiliated."

God's will is invoked to justify the measure-for-measure vengeance meted out by the priestly community of men to the offending woman: "In the measure with which a man measures it is meted out to him. She adorned herself for a transgression: the Holy One, blessed be He, made her repulsive. She exposed herself for a transgression: the Holy One, blessed be He, held her up for exposure. She began the transgression with the thigh and afterward with the womb: Therefore she is punished first in the thigh and afterward in the womb, nor does all the body escape."[5]

The effects of drinking the bitter waters thus conform to the punishment presumably due a woman suspected of dishonoring her husband by turning to another man: "She beautified her face for him (the other man); therefore her face is made to turn green in color. She painted her eyes for him; therefore her eyes protrude. . . . She signaled to him with her finger; therefore her fingernails fall off. . . ."[6] No case histories exist of those whom the "ordeal by bitter waters"—presumably a test *for* adultery—proved innocent. Clearly this test, like those administered to women throughout the ages, were designed to insure guilt and offset the likelihood of future infractions.

> Immorality in a house is like a worm in the sesame plant . . . anger in a house is like a worm in the sesame plant. Both these statements refer to a woman, but in the case of a man, there is no objection. [R. Hisda]

Despite the gross double standard implicit in the "ordeal by bitter waters" and explicit in R. Hisda's preceding commentary on it, the nagging vision of woman as a powerful force persists, evoking perpetual ambivalence toward her. Just as deliverance from Egypt was rabbinically conceived as a reward for the "righteous women who lived in that generation,"[7] destruction and exile are later attributed to woman's capacity for luring man into those unspeakable acts—adultery/incest, murder, and idolatry—that sever his relationship with God. Man's susceptibility to the seductiveness of the harlot-wife-mother thus provokes the anger of the all-powerful God-father. Underlying this oedipal construct is the more deeply submerged fear (and yearning) for the all-powerful mother—that primal perception of woman as source of life and death, her fecundity and sexuality formidable forces that must be contained. The penalties for adultery provide one means of containment; the taboos on menstruation and parturition, another.

So pervasive is the unspoken fear of woman that the drive to contain and suppress both her spirit and her sexuality persisted long after R. Johanan b. Zakkai suspended the "ordeal by bitter waters," in a kind of pathological cultural denial of his reasons for doing so.

The suspension of the "ordeal" is recorded in the concluding section of Sotah that laments the general lawlessness and corruption of justice that preceded the destruction of the Temple:

"When adulterers multiplied, the ceremony of bitter waters was discontinued, and it is R. Johanan who discontinued it, saying: 'I will not punish your daughters when they commit whoredom, nor your brides when they commit adultery, for they themselves (the fathers and the husbands) go aside with the whores and the harlots.'"[8] The *gemara* goes on to point out that the water proves a man's wife only when he, himself, is free from corruption, "but when the man is not free from iniquity, the water does not prove his wife."

This relatively more even-handed disposition of adultery echoes the prophet Hosea's response in similar circumstances when he denounces the men of the land for paying homage to false gods:

Therefore your daughters play the wanton
   and your sons' brides commit adultery.
I will not punish your daughters for playing the wanton
   nor your sons' brides for their adultery
because your men resort to wanton women
   and sacrifice with temple-prostitutes.
A people without understanding comes to grief;
   they are a mother turned wanton.[9]

Hosea's identification of the errant nation with the "mother turned wanton" places the community of men in wife/harlot relationship to God. In this marital metaphor, man—and *not* woman—is accused of infidelity to God by both the biblical Hosea and the talmudic Johanan, who hold him responsible for the spread of lawlessness and the escalation of adultery that provoke God's anger and ensuing disaster. Yet the sense of man's transgression invariably fades with time; woman's remains curiously indelible. The anxiety of responsibility proves too great to bear; what is initially perceived as man's breach of his covenant with God is eventually translated as woman's incitement to sin. The route is by now familiar: Catastrophe is presumably precipitated by sin; sin eventually becomes linked with sexuality, which ultimately—in man's perception—finds its source in woman. That source, in turn, must be carefully guarded against and contained. The ban on woman's voice, presumably the source of those unpardonable transgressions that turn man away from God, places her beyond the range of hearing. Man is thus protected from temptation; and woman, not so incidentally, is removed from that most important sphere of all in Judaism—religious communal life. The metaphoric marriage between the men of Israel and God completes a male-female unit from which the women of Israel are implicitly excluded. That exclusion from the religious covenant is made explicit with the *ervah* indictment of woman's voice.

The evil inclination: The evolution of the rabbinic concept of *yetzer ha'ra* (the evil inclination or the evil imagination) is essential for an appreciation of those unwholesome attributes later attached to the ban on singing, initially advocated as an expression of mourning for loss of the Second Temple. Attempts to resolve the terrible dilemma posed by the phenomenon of evil in a world presumably created and governed by a just, reasonable, and honorable God moved in two directions. Apocalyptic thought and writing, on the one hand, introduced the theory of the Fall, elaborated in later Christian theology as the doctrine of Original Sin. Man, in this thesis, was born corrupt as a result of the first couple's intransigence. Eve's bite of the forbidden fruit had tainted her offspring forevermore. Rabbinic thought, on the other hand, developed the intriguing concept of *yetzer ha'ra,* in direct opposition to the Fall doctrine of Original Sin, as explanation for the phenomenon of evil. (To have left the phenomenon unexplained—open to that arbitrary capriciousness of the polytheistic world from which monotheism had presumably rescued mankind—would undoubtedly have provoked even greater anxiety than those troublesome attempts to resolve the dilemma.)

According to the rabbis, the capacity for evil, embodied in the *yetzer* (inclination), was injected by God to each soul at birth. The *yetzer,* in and of itself, was not necessarily evil, but rather a kind of psychic energy that might be turned to productive use. Stronger "inclinations," by way of example, reputedly resided in men of greater stature. Man's moral struggle thus emerged as paramount in the *yetzer* construct. The greater the man, the stronger his "inclination"; hence, the more significant his struggle. Man's moral worth was judged not by the weakness of his *yetzer,* but rather by his ability to overcome it—the force of his commitment to the law that stood in opposition to the temptations of man's "evil imagination."

The rabbinic concept of *yetzer ha'ra* as a potent psychic force foreshadows, in a sense, later psychoanalytic theories of libido—*sans* the rabbinic necessity for moral judgment. Although the *yetzer* itself is not necessarily sexual, it is frequently portrayed in sexually enticing terms. A typical portrayal, for example, presents Satan in the guise of an alluring woman, descending upon an unsuspecting pious husband—usually on his way home for the Sabbath—to test his moral endurance. The continuous association of the satanic with the female cannot help but have an impact on cultural attitudes toward women. While the rabbinic theory of *yetzer ha'ra* emerged in direct opposition to the Fall doctrine of Original Sin, both ultimately find the source of sin in woman. The Fall doctrine links woman with evil directly at the outset; the rabbinic concept of *yetzer* only indirectly—and possibly heretically—after years of association, reinforced by vivid presentations in aggadic literature, appealing to the popular imagination, of temptation perpetually clothed as sexual seduction. Successive (and excessive!) elaborations of the ban on woman's voice and blood render it difficult to draw the line between that potent *yetzer,* initially injected by God to each soul at birth, and subsequent assumptions that the source of evil or temptation resides in women. A dilemma, indeed! Given the belief in a just, reasonable, and omniscient God, the advent of catastrophe calls for an initiating cause, a precipitating evil. Since the evil cannot emanate from the transcendent and omnipresent God—nor dare it be arbitrary!—it is reasonably ascribed to man, and, just as unreasonably, unloaded on woman. Man's burden of responsibility and guilt grows intolerable; he lifts it from his shoulders and bestows it upon woman.

Yet there is far more to the perception of woman as source of sin than a simple transfer of responsibility. A deeper fear lurks beyond man's susceptibility to temptations of the flesh, and that is the terror of its dissolution. Sexuality is inevitably linked with death—a reminder of the vulnerable, corporeal self. The urge for transcendence asserts itself in denials of imminent death—in the suppression of all those orifices and images that evoke it. Mouth, vagina, and womb—voice, breath, and blood—all speak of the birth of life and its ultimate abandonment to death. The ubiquitous folkloric image of the *vagina dentata*—literally the vagina (mouth) with teeth—is vivid testimony to the perception of danger attendant on submergence in the female. (A hero invariably comes along, in most of these tales, to detooth the vagina. I hesitate to suggest that the rabbis similarly devoiced its facial counterpart.) The unavoidable knowledge that man enters the world through the womb, birth canal, and vaginal orifice of woman carries with it the possibility that he departs in a similar manner. The sense of woman as source of sin is a more comfortable displacement for the more terrifying possibility that she is the source of life and death—evoking the archetype of the devouring mother that inhabits the night life of the soul.

So it is that man's transgressions fade with time, while woman's remain indelible. Man's image of himself emerges from the daylight world of definition and ordered being, of regulation and law. His perception of woman as the alien and threatening other—a vision that finds its source in the archaic image of the all-powerful mother—stirs fears of absorption, of return to the chaos of beginnings. The nightmare of chaos perpetually threatens to invade man's ordered daylight world. Woman is identified with chaos, relegated to that primeval blackness that gave birth to light—the darkness of the human heart, the night side of the soul. Man's infractions are thus rendered discrete and temporal; woman's, amorphous and eternal. (Woman's tragedy, of course, is that she is just as vulnerable and temporal a creature as man; yet man's projection of the archetype of the nourishing/devouring mother upon her invariably renders her more suspect than he.)

Man's visceral discomfort with woman's sexual reminder of his mortality manifests itself in the need to guard himself against her by regulating her behavior and her sexuality. Such fears and needs are scarcely indigenous to Judaism; they span time, space, and cultural boundaries. They are reflected in the Kikuyu legends of woman's rule, in the Ona suppression of her "magic," in taboos on menstrual blood and parturition that are very nearly universal, suggesting similar universal discomfort with the sorry facts of life. When such discomfort grows intolerable, women are—more often than not—scapegoated to alleviate it. Man's inhumanity toward woman cuts across cultural boundaries; what is unique to Jewish, Christian, and Islamic versions is the invocation of God's will by way of justification. The ruse, whether conscious or not, is as old as Creation. Indeed, it is the very matter of Creation that elicits it—blood, breath, and voice, the very substance of being—elements counted everywhere as essential for the creation of the world and human life.

Judaism's addition of voice to its taboo system reflects the importance of word, breath, and voice in its own Creation myth. The biblical God calls the world into being through the words he speaks. "And God said: 'Let there be light. . . .'"

The significance of the word in initiating Creation is further emphasized in midrashic elaborations on Genesis. According to one version, God first consults the Torah about his plans, which she endorses. The Torah, in this context, is conceived as having emanated from God's wisdom (like Athena springing from Zeus's head) long before the creation of man: "In the beginning, two thousand years before the heaven and earth, seven things were created: the Torah written with black fire on white fire, lying in the lap of God. . . ." When God consults the Torah in another version, she expresses some doubts about His enterprise, concerned that the sinfulness of man will prevent him from following her precepts. God reassures her and proceeds with His plan, calling the world into being with the sound of His voice.

Again, word precedes form in the notion that the letters of the alphabet adorned God's crown: "When God was about to create the world by His word, the twenty-two letters of the alphabet descended from the terrible and august crown of God, whereon they were engraved with a pen of flaming fire. . . ." Each of the letters clamors for ascendancy, pleading with God to create the world through it. Each, for various explicit reasons, is judged unsuitable until the letter *beth* is chosen because it is the initial letter for both *baruch* (blessing) and *b'reshit* (in the beginning). Only the modest *alef* refrains from asserting its claim; God subsequently rewards it by placing *alef* first in the Decalog.

Culminating God's Creation, breath is the essential element in bringing man to life. Determining to infuse Adam's clodlike body with a soul, God, according to one midrash, breathes the soul into Adam's nostrils because "they discern the unclean and reject it . . . so the pious will shun sin and cleave to the words of Torah." Another source suggests that the soul of man was created on the first day as the spirit (literally, *ruach* [breath]) of God moving upon the waters.[10] God's breath, from the beginning, thus carries man's most important attribute: that soul or spirit that differentiates him from the rest of the animal kingdom. That the breath of God was the source not only of man's physical vitality, but also of his intelligence[11] is reiterated in the Book of Job: "Surely it is the breath that is in man and the inspiration of the Almighty that give him understanding."

Breath, understanding, voice, and word intermesh when God brings the animals before Adam to see what he will call them. Midrashic elaborations of Adam's gift for naming attribute all the world's crafts to him, as well as all its languages: "The names of the animals were not the only inheritance handed down by Adam to generations after him, for mankind owes all crafts to him, especially the art of writing, and he was the inventor of all seventy languages" (Br. 24).

Blood is notably absent from the biblical Creation story and subsequent rabbinic elaborations, except for an incidental gloss that enumerates blood, wind, and breath as three forms the soul may take. Yet many other versions of man's creation do not speak in terms of inspiration by divine breath, but rather of the infusion of rude clay by divine blood. In the *Enuma Elish,* the Babylonian epic of Creation, man is fashioned from the blood and bone of the rebellious god Kingu. Similarly in Greek legend, man sprang from the blood of the slain Titans who had rebelled against the rule of Kronos. A popular belief, cited by Emperor Julian, maintains that the human race emerged from those drops of Zeus's blood that fell after he completed the ordering of the world. The Koran recognizes Allah as having "made man out of flowing blood"; and the Maori of New Zealand believe that their creator god Tibi mixed red clay with his own blood to form man.

The prominence of blood in myths of Creation, together with a wide variety of blood rites and taboos, testify to the enormous sense of awe and numinosity surrounding it. From those archaic Aurignacian female idols, tinged with red ocher more than twenty thousand years ago, through centuries of pagan blood rites, to the Catholic sacrament of bread and wine, as the body and blood of Christ in ritual today, blood is both symbol and substance for life and death, birth and rebirth, creation and resurrection. While breath is the spirit, blood is the very essence of life.

The idea that "blood speaks" infuses biblical narrative, tribal rites and taboos, and the practice of capital punishment in modern times. When Cain slays Abel, Abel's blood "calls from the ground for vengeance," reflecting the ancient and enduring belief that the blood (or ghost) of a murdered man cries out for revenge. In the Old Testament, it is the actual blood, not the ghost of the slain, that informs references to manslaughter and retribution due the slayer. The priestly document in Numbers, stating the penalty for homicide, underscores the belief that blood spilled cries for revenge: "Blood, it polluteth the land: and no expiation can be made for the land for the blood that is shed therein, but by the blood of him that shed it." Fear of the potency of blood underlies superstition among contemporary primitive tribes that witches and workers of evil can be rendered innocuous if their blood is shed; it informs the ritual purification practiced by warriors who have killed in battle; it is consonant with levitical law that commands the hunter to cover with dust the blood of the animal that is poured on the ground and with levitical injunctions mandating seclusion and ritual purification for those who have had contact with a corpse or with menstrual blood. The blood, itself, ethnologists point out, need not actually *speak;* it may also deliver its message by refusing to be stanched.

The belief that so long as blood lies exposed to the air and has not run off or soaked into the ground, it continues to call aloud for vengeance, but that its mouth can be stopped and its voice stifled with a handful of earth, is powerfully expressed by the prophet Ezekiel in pronouncing the wrath of God on Jerusalem for all the innocent blood shed there: "Woe to the bloody city, to the caldron whose rust is therein. . . . For her blood is in the midst of her; she set it upon the bare rock; she poured it not on the ground to cover it with dust; that it might cause fury to come up to take vengeance. . . ."[12] Guilt and danger are thus exacerbated for Jerusalem because the blood shed in its midst still welters in clotted pools—like rust in a caldron—rather than being covered with dust or allowed to soak into the ground.

Apprehension is invariably stirred by the shedding of blood, whether in war, murder, or the menstrual cycle. The recurrent association of blood with the awesome mysteries of life is inescapable. The nearly universal insistence on purification rites for the warrior and the menstruant—as well as the similarity of those rites—provides enduring testimony to the numinous powers endowed blood by the human mind. In Fiji, by way of example, anyone who clubs a human being to death in war becomes consecrated or taboo. He is smeared red with turmeric, and a special hut is built for him in which he is required to pass the next three nights. Until the three nights have elapsed, he is not permitted to change his clothes, remove the turmeric, or enter a house with a woman in it. Similarities between seclusion of the warrior and the menstruant in ancient civilizations or contemporary primitive societies is obvious. Far more perplexing is the modern vulgarization of what was once consecrated or taboo: the bestowal of medals upon the warrior and the expression of revulsion at the menstruant.

> Oh! menstruating woman, thou'rt a fiend
> From whom all nature should be closely screened
> (Crawley, *The Mystic Rose,* Vol. I)

> Any community in which there is flattery is as repulsive as a menstruant woman. . . .
> (R. Eleazar, Sotah 42g)

Contempt renders fear more manageable; and man's early perception of woman as source of life and death, that alien other who—unlike him—bleeds periodically without dying, eventually translates itself into those restrictions and expressions of revulsion that keep woman at a distance. Even so, man's discomfort is scarcely alleviated; his apprehension surfaces on confrontation with those very qualities that separate her from him: the cyclical advent of her menstruation and her capacity for giving birth.

Those fears that generate elaborate rituals for menstruation and parturition enjoy crosscultural ubiquity. The Dogon of West Africa believe that the menstruant brings misfortune to everything she touches. Like the Fiji warrior, she is isolated in a hut with special eating utensils. If she is seen passing through the village, general purification must take place. The Wogeo of South Australia maintain that man's contact with a menstruant will result in death from a wasting disease, against which there is no remedy. The Bantu of Uganda believe that the menstruating woman who handles her husband's effects will bring illness upon him; if she touches his weapons, he is sure to be killed in the next battle. Capetown Bantu males similarly fear that death in battle will result from looking upon a woman ready to give birth. Natives of New Guinea believe that a man who views a menstruant will swell up and die; that if he treads in her tracks, his legs will grow sore and drop off. The Romans maintained that growing corn withered and wine turned sour at the approach of a menstruant; folk traditions in eastern Europe today hold that a menstruating woman must not bake bread, make pickles, churn butter, or spin thread, because all will go wrong; Silesian women are forbidden to plant seedlings or work in the garden. Conversely, the positive attributes of menstrual blood—its mana or "magic"—are conveyed by folk remedies advocating it as a cure for leprosy, as a love charm to be placed into a man's coffee, as a means for curing the fields of insects and pests. (If the menstruating woman strips herself naked, in this instance, worms and other pests will fall away from the ears of corn.) Again, woman's blood—like her voice—stirs profound ambivalence in the hearts and minds of men.

Jewish laws for the seclusion and purification of the menstruant through ritual immersion (the *mikvah*) find their source in levitical provisions for ritual purity. These provisions were further elaborated in mishnaic times before the fall of the Second Temple, to make sure that all those who entered the Temple area to worship or offer sacrifice were ritually pure—untainted by recent contact with mortality or death.

"When a woman has a discharge of blood, her impurity shall last for seven days; anyone who touches her shall be unclean till evening. Everything on which she lies or sits during her impurity shall be unclean (*tumeh*) till evening. Anyone who touches her bed shall wash his clothes, bathe in water, and remain unclean till evening. . . . If a man goes so far as to have intercourse with her and any of her discharge gets on to him, then he shall be unclean for seven days, and every bed on which he lies down shall be unclean."

When menstruation was prolonged, or when a discharge occurred out of the regular cycle, the same rules applied. On the eighth day, the woman was required to "obtain two turtledoves or two young pigeons and bring them to the priest at the entrance of the Tent of the Presence. The priest shall deal with one as a sin offering and with the other as a whole offering, and make for her before the Lord the expiation required by her unclean discharge."

Laws for ritual purity applied to discharges from men as well as women: "This is the law for the man who has a discharge, or who has an emission of semen and is thereby unclean, and for the woman who is suffering her menstruation—for everyone, male or female, who has a discharge, and for the man who has intercourse with a woman who is unclean."

Later in Leviticus, the penalty for intercourse with a menstruant is excision, underscored by emphasis on the differentiation between Israel's practices and those of surrounding nations: "You shall not approach a woman to have intercourse with her during her period of menstruation. . . ." Injunction against intercourse with a menstruant is followed here by bans on adultery, homosexuality, sodomy, and bestiality, culminating with the penalty of excision: "This is how the land became unclean and I punished it for its iniquity so that it spewed out its inhabitants. You, unlike them, shall keep my laws and my rules: None of you, whether natives or aliens settled among you, shall do any of these abominable things . . . for anyone who does any of these abominable things shall be cut off from his people. Observe my charge, therefore, and follow none of the abominable institutions customary before your time. . . ."

Again, parturition or childbirth conveys ritual impurity, an impurity that lasts twice as long with the birth of a female than with a male: "When a woman conceives and bears a male child, she shall be unclean for seven days. . . . On the eighth day, the child shall have the flesh of his foreskin circumcised. The woman shall wait for thirty-three days because her blood requires purification; she shall touch nothing that is holy, and shall not enter the sanctuary till her days of purification are completed. If she bears a female child, she shall be unclean for fourteen days . . . and shall wait for sixty-six days because her blood requires purification." Following the allotted period of purification for the birth of a male or female—like that after the cessation of menstrual discharge—the mother brings the sacrificial offering of a lamb and a pigeon to the Temple priest who "shall present it before the Lord and make expiation for her, and she shall be clean from the issue of her blood."

The concepts of *tumah* and *tahara,* while frequently translated as "unclean" and "clean," have nothing at all to do with contemporary notions of physical cleanliness. They emanate from the perception of ritual that distinguishes between the realms of the sacred and the profane, between timelessness and temporality. The state of *tumah,* in this context, is tainted by the profane—tinged with temporality and death; that of *tahara* aspires to the sacred and eternal. The most powerful source of *tumah,* for example, is contact with a corpse.

Medieval codes extended restrictions on the menstruant far beyond those advocated in biblical and talmudic law. The period of seclusion for the menstruant was expanded from the levitical seven days to at least fourteen—an additional seven days of "purity" tacked onto the original seven allocated to the menstrual flow before a woman was judged fit to return to normal marital contact—literally half of a fertile adult woman's life. Restrictions on contact with a woman—including unseemly conversation—during her extended period of menstrual impurity were similarly enlarged upon, culminating in a veritable pageant of avoidance.

The suggestion is popularly made today that it was women, themselves, who demanded greater restrictions placed upon them, out of concern for their ritual purity. Needless to say, this suggestion is invariably advanced when women today question the morbid elaborations of the menstrual taboo. If women, themselves, indeed demanded the escalation of their seclusion (and the evidence is questionable), one may well wonder why. The "acceptable" traditional notion that they were so overwhelmingly eager to maintain their ritual purity and avoid contaminating others with the taint of menstrual blood may well be countered with a variety of other conjectures: Might they not have wanted an extended vacation from serving their husbands and sleeping with them? Or were they, perhaps, weary of periodically presenting their menstrual stains for examination by the qualified resident sage?

"Come and hear the case of Yalta," wife of the fourth century's Rabbi Nahman, recorded in the Talmud: "She once brought some blood to Rabbah b. Bar Hana, who informed her that it was unclean. She then took it to R. Isaac, the son of R. Judah, who told her that it was clean. . . ."[13]

Yalta's round of the rabbinical circuit to gain a favorable judgment on her ritual purity casts some doubts on the seriousness with which women presumably regarded such judgments. Yet the Talmud is most concerned with the issue of disagreement among the sages and the possibility that the rabbis might have been influenced by the observations of a mere woman. The indignity of such a possibility is summarily circumvented in the following excerpt:

"But how could he act in this manner, seeing that it was taught: If a sage declared (a person or article) unclean, no other sage may declare it clean. And we explained that first he informed her indeed that it was unclean, but when she told him that on every other occasion he declared such blood as clean but on that day he had a pain in his eye, he changed his view and gave her his ruling that it was clean. Now this proves quite clearly, does it not, that a woman is believed? R. Isaac b. Judah may have relied on his own traditions and experience, not on Yalta's evidence. The reason why he at first declared the blood as unclean was merely to show his respect to Rabbah b. Bar Hana."[14]

Clearly, Yalta's ingenuity—her suggestion that impaired vision prevented the examining rabbi from rendering a clear judgment, and her cavalier round of the rabbinical circuit to gain a favorable opinion—presented problems to subsequent rabbis. The daring suggestion that Yalta's case proved that a woman might be believed elicits the preferred view that R. Isaac b. Judah did not base his opinion on anything a mere woman might have said, but rather on his own experience and authority, motivated throughout *not* by Yalta's observations, but by respect for his male colleagues. This traditional assertion of male bonding and authority is particularly problematic for women today who find that neither their voice nor blood may speak for itself—that they still cannot bear witness, even to their own experience, but must invariably be subjected to the judgments of a male hierarchy.

Ritual purification through immersion in the *mikvah* or ritual bath marks the transition from the state of *tumah* to that of *tahara*. Referred to in the Bible as *mayim hayyim* (living water), any natural gathering of waters that is at least "forty *sah* in volume"‡ constitutes a *mikvah*. Seas, lakes, rivers, and running streams may thus serve as natural baths or *mikvot* for ritual immersion. More commonly today, *mikvot* are artificially constructed to detailed specifications that fulfill the requirements for immersion in "living waters" in towns and cities. Generally, a building is constructed around a huge cistern—called a *bor*—which collects rain water. The building contains small sunken pools, each of which shares a wall with the *bor*. Each shared wall has a hole cut in it, which may be plugged or left open. The pools are "seeded" with *bor* water and filled with tap water. When the holes in the adjoining walls are unplugged, so that the waters are touching or "kissing," the pool becomes a legally valid *mikvah*.[15] The outward accouterments of buildings housing the *mikvah* may vary widely—as indeed they do—ranging from the simplest accommodations to the opulence of a *mikvah* recently constructed in Beverly Hills replete with showers, hair dryers, carpeted waiting rooms, and piped-in music.

Although men are no longer bound by laws of ritual purity,

‡ A *sah* is estimated as approximately 13,222 cubic centimeters.

some follow the custom of immersion after seminal emissions and before Torah study or prayer; others elect to use the *mikvah* before the Sabbath and holidays. Women, however, are legally obligated to use the *mikvah* as termination for the state of *niddah* after menstruation or childbirth, before marriage, and as part of the ritual of conversion. Rabbinic law permits only married women to attend the *mikvah*.[16]

The state of *niddah* today includes the duration of the menstrual flow, followed by a dormancy period of seven days during which there must be absolutely no sign of blood. Each day of dormancy is counted from sundown to sundown; a tampon is inserted each day in the morning and late afternoon to make sure that there is no blood in the vaginal passage. Finding a spot of blood obligates the woman to start counting again from the beginning. After the seventh sundown marking seven *consecutive* days that are free of bleeding, the woman goes to the *mikvah*.

Preparation for the *mikvah* includes a thorough bath or shower with hair carefully washed and combed free of snarls. Fingernails and toenails are cleaned with special care; all ornaments and foreign substances adhering to the body must be removed—rings, earrings, and jewelry; nail polish, Band-Aids, and makeup. Immersion is private; each woman enters the *mikvah* pool alone. She stands in the water, feet slightly apart, arms outstretched before her with fingers spread. Lips are loosely compressed; eyes, loosely closed. She then bends at the knees so that the entire body, including her head and all hair, is submerged. A *mikvah* attendant usually supervises immersions to make sure that they are complete. A blessing in Hebrew follows the first immersion and precedes the second:

> Blessed are You, Lord our God, King of the Universe, who has made us holy with Your commandments and commanded us concerning immersions.

Some women elect to immerse themselves two or three times before and after the blessing. Some recite an additional *kavvanah* or prayer as a meditative technique for centering themselves in the aura of the performance of the *mitzvah* of immersion. Once the woman has thus passed from the state of ritual impurity to one of purity, sexual relations between husband and wife are resumed.

For observant women, the practice of *niddah* (which at its root means "banishment") and *mikvah* is tinged with conflict. On the one hand, it is one of the three *mitzvot* required of women (the other two are lighting the Sabbath candles and baking challah); on the other hand, it is tainted with a sense of revulsion—misconceived or not—at woman's menstrual "uncleanness." A variety of rationales have been proffered to enhance the practice of *niddah*. Most convincing among them is Rachel Adler's moving conceptualization of *tumah* and *tahara* as that nexus point where life and death meet, endowing ritual immersion in the *mikvah* with a sense of periodic renewal and rebirth. Yet she observes that the point at which menstrual impurity was isolated from the general category of ritual impurity "was the point at which pathology entered halacha. At that point, *tum'at niddah* became divorced from the symbolism of death and resurrection and acquired a new significance related to its accompanying sexual prohibitions. Whereas *tum'at niddah* had been a way for women to experience death and rebirth through the cycle of their own bodies, it became distorted into a method of controlling the fearsome power of sexual desire, of disciplining a mistrusted physical drive.

"The state of *niddah* became a monthly exile from the human race, a punitive shunning of the menstruant. Women were taught disgust and shame for their bodies and for the fluid that came out of them, that good, rich, red stuff that nourished ungrateful men through nine fetal months. The *mikvah,* instead of being the primal sea in which all were made new, became the pool at which women were cleansed of their filth and thus became acceptable sexual partners once more. . . ."

Less convincing are contentions that the practice of *niddah* leads to continence in marriage (sure it does, but so what?), that it promotes more harmonious sexual relations between husband and wife, that it expresses a sense of sanctity and respect for the woman. Patently absurd is the pseudoscientific approach of the commentary in the Soncino edition of the Pentateuch, which maintains that the practice of *niddah* and *mikvah* make for an improved hygiene that renders observant Jewish women less susceptible to uterine cancer than non-Jewish women.

Like the ban on woman's voice, the escalation of restrictions on the menstruant reflects that atavistic dread of woman's sexuality—heightened during periods of struggle or despair—that seeks to contain that which is most feared and serves to exclude women from participation in public life. Literary images of woman as a source of sin, and popular folklore perceiving her as most dangerous during the menstrual state interact with laws and customs to mandate her seclusion. The exemption of women from public appearances in nearly all religious and legal matters coincides with their general cloistering. Separate quarters for women, segregation in the synagogue, veiling and the covering of hair to protect men from temptation—all were introduced in the course of centuries following the First and Second Exiles, coinciding with a literature that portrays women as increasingly dangerous.

Postexilic sections of Proverbs warn against "the alien woman . . . with her wheedling words," ". . . the smooth tongue of the woman who is a stranger." While the virtuous wife is properly lauded, the adulteress is harshly denounced, her seductiveness perceived as a betrayal leading to death: "Her house is the way to Sheol, the descents to the courts of death." The link between voice and sexuality, between absorption and dissolution through woman's mouth or through her vagina and birth canal is eminently clear in Proverbs 22:14: "The mouth of the alien woman is a deep pit, into it falls the man whom Yahweh detests."

The incipient misogyny of Proverbs was exacerbated in Apocryphal and apocalyptic literature, culminating in the diatribes against woman's seductiveness by the celibate Essenes at the turn of the millennia:

> [The harlot] utters vanities. . . .
> She seeks continually [to] sharpen [her] words. . . .
> Her beds are couches of corruption,
> . . . depths of the Pit.

. . . .
> She is the foremost of all the ways of iniquity;
>> Alas! ruin shall be to all who possess her,
> And desolation to all who take hold of her.
>> For her ways are the ways of death,
> and her paths are the roads to sin;
>> her tracks lead astray to iniquity,
> and her paths are the guilt of transgression.
>> Her gates are the gates of death,
> in the opening of her house it stalks. . . .[17]

Given such views of women, it is small wonder that they were subsequently secluded and veiled, restrained from conversations with men and from appearances in public. While customs varied from town to countryside and among different social classes, the visibility of women and their freedom of movement had clearly diminished in the Rabbinic Era. When Jewish women did go out in public, their heads and faces were generally veiled. To appear without head covering was considered sufficient grounds for divorce without the obligated payment stipulated in the *ketubah*.[18] The thoroughness with which a woman might be veiled is dramatically illustrated in the story of the administration of the ordeal by bitter waters, recorded in the talmudic tractate Pesachim: "Once there was a high priest to whose lot it fell to administer the water of bitterness. The woman was brought to him and he uncovered her head and took her hair down. Then he took the vessel to give her to drink; he looked at her and saw that it was his mother!"[19]

Variations in the degree of seclusion and veiling are suggested by medieval commentator Rashi: "Modest women who enter covered, uncover only one eye so they can see. . . . The women living in the villages do not need to be so withdrawn, for there is not so much banter and levity there . . . they do not cover their faces. . . ."

Emphasis on veiling, like seclusion of the menstruant and the ban on woman's voice, reveals the fear of confrontation with a dangerous or numinous aura—that aspect of mana associated with all objects and persons who are taboo. Ethnologist James G. Frazer notes the custom in various groups of veiling the

King when he appeared in public to protect commoners among whom he walked from the power presumably exuded by the King's breath or glance.[20] Similarly, the ark containing the Torah scrolls—the holy of holies—is veiled, as is the immanence of God. Nonetheless, the veiling of women, while initiated from similar impulses, was soon transformed into a means for inhibiting their movement and their impact on public life. One can scarcely envision Deborah, for example, dispensing justice through face veils, nor the prophetess Hulda delivering oracular pronouncements through opaque screens. Yet those occasional daughters of learned men who taught Torah to male students during the Middle Ages purportedly did so from behind a curtain.

"In separation of the sexes," suggests historian Israel Abrahams, "the synagogue only reflected their isolation in the social life outside" where they were separated, as well, at banquets and social events. The rigid separation of the sexes in prayer, according to Abrahams, "occurred no earlier than the thirteenth century."[21] It is pointless here to enter the dispute over when separate seating for women occurred. Some point to the *ezrat nashim,* the women's court of the Second Temple, as evidence of separation before the Common Era, reinforcing their dubious argument with the discussion in the talmudic tractate Succoth, which refers to the necessity to separate the men from the women at the harvest festival because of the merrymaking and hanky-panky going on. Obviously, it may be argued just as well that if separation had been mandated at that point in time, the men and the women would have not been together in the first place. The evidence at best, drawn from scant rabbinic references and ambiguous architectural details, is highly conjectural. Moreover, the trend moved toward heightened segregation of women from the early Middle Ages onward, escalating in the seventeenth and eighteenth centuries. In their own prayer meetings, women were led by female precentors, some of whom acquired considerable reputations.

Even more significant is the recent resurgence of the heightened barrier between men's and women's sections in certain Orthodox synagogues. That dimly lit balcony to which my grandmother was relegated in the old Orthodox synagogue I remember from childhood was eventually replaced by a simple aisle in more modern buildings so that men and women, although they did not sit together, sat at the same level, could see and hear equally well, and could participate in services. More recently, Rabbi Steven Riskin of the Orthodox Lincoln Square Synagogue in Manhattan "even" permitted some women in his congregation to wear tallit at services. But other segments of Orthodoxy have hardened in their response to the women's movement.

"Where once separate seating without a *mechitzah* (physical barrier) was deemed adequate," notes Anne Lerner,[22] "the current generation has established *mehizot* in congregations, new and old, or raised the height of existing *mehizot*." Thus far, the acme of technology for separation seems to have been reached by a Hasidic congregation in Brookline, Massachusetts, which recently bought a 550-pound thermopane mirror-coated one-way panel, originally intended for the new Hancock Tower in Boston, for use as a *mehizah*. This exceedingly weighty technological coup will permit the women behind it to view the services. (Whether they will also be able to hear remains moot.) The men, seated on the thermopane's mirror-coated side, will happily see only themselves—protected from the titillating vision of their mothers and wives.

Indeed, medieval veilings, Orthodox separations, ancient menstrual taboos, and talmudic bans on woman's voice intrude with surprising force on contemporary discussions of woman's role in Judaism, buttressed by fear of competition from increasingly accomplished women in religious and professional spheres.

For Dr. Mortimer Ostow, Chairman of the Department of Pastoral Psychiatry at the Jewish Theological Seminary of America (the major teaching and rabbinical institution for the Conservative movement), the vision of woman as rabbi elicits conjectures of psychological upheaval and sexual indulgence.[23] "Antinomian orgies" are predicted by him in his distortions and polemical abuse of psychoanalytic theory.

"A woman appearing as a central figure in a religious service is likely to . . . encourage erotic fantasies," argues Ostow, citing the talmudic "kol be-ishah ervah" edict with its attendant elaborations on the avoidance of woman's voice, hair, and body, lauding earlier rabbis for their "psychobiologic" insight.

Like R. Eleazar at the turn of the millennium, Ostow views "menstrual discharge . . . repulsive," updating it with the addition: "When soiled with menstrual blood, the female genitals now arouse the old revulsion against excreta." Menstrual separation, according to Ostow, functions to allay the anxiety of men who "believe unconsciously that a menstruating woman can injure them, the most common injury imagined is being rendered impotent."

Those men who indulge in coitus with a menstruant, Ostow maintains, are moved by the need for infantile sado-masochistic gratification. Those who are neither excited nor repelled by the menstruant, according to him, may suffer yet another blow to their egos by the presence of women in the pulpit:

(They) "will be awed and humiliated by the woman whose competence in religious matters clearly exceeds their own . . . their self esteem within the community in which they live will be shaken, as will their confidence in their own virility."

Like the medieval Maimonides, Dr. Ostow urges the silence of women to preserve the "honor" of men, conceding that "women will naturally ask why their self-esteem must be sacrificed in deference to those of shaky men. It seems unjust to recommend such a sacrifice," he piously continues, "yet the society whose men have little self-respect and who are unreliable sexual partners is one which holds little gratification for women."

Despite an avowed absence of "documentation," the assumption is advanced for man's impotence in the face of woman's competence. Woman is thus warned that if she steps out of line, she may have to forgo that sexual gratification presumably central to her life.

Men, meanwhile, are to be shielded from sexual arousal in the synagogue, inevitably introduced, in this highly questionable view, by the visibility of women in positions of authority. Suppression, I would suggest, is a poor substitute for transcendence —the necessity of the human spirit to move beyond the limits of the physical and temporal world, integral to religious feeling and expression for both men and women. Denial of the flesh is a sorry replacement for the appreciation of its temporal pleasures and limitations; and sanctimoniousness bears little relationship to sanctity.

Yet the sanctimoniousness with which women are enjoined to maintain a low profile in the sacred realms of worship and liturgy at no less an august body than the Rabbinical Assembly of America, reminds one of the story, apocryphal or not, of Golda Meir's response to a suggestion from the Knesset that a curfew be imposed on women to avoid the incidence of rape. "Since it is men rather than women who commit rape," she retorted, "it would be far more sensible and proper to impose the curfew on them." Interest in the curfew promptly diminished.

The ordeal by bitter waters was banned nearly two thousand years ago. Yet the sexual humiliation of the suspected (or potential) adulteress, as well as the female scholar like Beruriah, has scarcely abated. The ban on woman's voice, introduced as an expression of mourning over destruction of the Second Temple, was inflated and conflated with escalated menstrual taboos over the course of centuries, until *kol* (the voice) *be-ishah ervah* (of woman is an abomination) virtually became *kāl* (*all*) *be-ishah ervah*. The dynamics underlying this sequence of interpretations, as well as the attitudes generated by it, serve to mandate woman's exclusion from significant areas of spiritual and intellectual life, denying her that very essence or "breath" of human being: the recognition of her soul, the expression of her spirit.

Blood, breath, and voice of woman: *kol be-ishah ervah.* Is it not time to discard the mantle of mourning, to move beyond assumptions of abomination and idolatry, celebrating woman's re-entry into the human community where her voice may at last be heard in all its fullness?

9

Unveilings

"What does a woman want?" Freud discreetly inquired of Princess Marie Bonaparte nearly fifty years ago.

"EVERYTHING!" was the loud, sustained reply from his literary heirs in the New World some thirty years later.

Castrating, nagging, devouring, and complaining: such were the women who populated American literature and thought in the fifties and sixties. The submerged murder of the mother, ritualized in Marduk's slaying of Tiammat, erupted in the inflamed fears, fantasies, and expectations of sons and husbands some three thousand years later. What had been an archetype became a stereotype; group ritual gave way to personal bewilderment; the communal purging of the vision of the devouring mother-dragon was replaced by the isolated *Angst* of the individual male writer, castigating the women in his life for their failure to meet his needs. Philip Wylie's *A Generation of Vipers* attacked the cult of momism on the general American scene: Mom was not all sweetness and apple pie (and why, oh why, ever should she be?); and popular magazines similarly devoted themselves to the portrait of the American woman as an aggressive, castrating bitch. Less than a decade later, Jewish women were singled out by their sons and consorts for those failures and flaws that only a Jewish son can know! Stereotypes proliferated: the Jewish American Princess, Portnoy's mother, the ashtray emptying Balabosta and the housewife's revenge, that pushy Hadassah woman (the Jewish establishment's rib), and the non-Jew's view of "the Jewess" as erotic exotic.

Oh how the Jewish prince despaired of his nagging, guilt-provoking, *latke*-pushing mother, to say nothing of her narcissistic, demanding, sexually withholding daughter, the JAP. Roth and Bellow, Greenburg, Malamud, and Mailer—all had their say. While Jewish men—gifted writers, scruffy Catskill comedians, and egomaniacal movie producers—viewed their women as loudmouthed, sexually repressed slobs (set against the equally unreal image of the blond, restrained *shiksa* with upturned nose), the non-Jew valued the "Jewess" as dark, pulsating, and deeply sensual. None of it had much to do with what women were really about, and no one seemed particularly to care. Woman's *geshrai* remained restricted to kitchen or psychiatric ward (the two occasionally indistinguishable); and what passed for portraits of women in the literature of the time was the outpouring of male fantasy, that concatenation of yearning and despair, exacerbated by a profound inability to differentiate between the dream and the dreamer, the wish and the actuality.

Yet those acid caricatures of JAP and Jewish mother touched a nerve in the general population; the response was immediate, overwhelming, and to some extent enduring. Not only did the stereotype infuse the fifties and sixties, it filtered into the seventies as well. One recent, sweltering summer evening, I found myself wedged between two male colleagues at a local watering place for journalists.

"So you're writing a book," said one. "What's it about?"

"Jewish women."

"The JAP," snorted his buddy, "she's writing a book about Jewish American Princesses!"

"My mother," mourned the first, cataloguing a litany of familiar complaints: too much chicken soup, too much guilt, too much insistence on wearing galoshes.

What makes for such abiding attachment to such outdated clichés? I wondered. Why the persistence and drawing power of the stereotype? Must forty-year-old men forever lament mothers who presumably mandated galoshes when their sons were six? A vision of generations paraded before me and behind me: Middle-aged men, slogging along in galoshes in the heat of August, metaphorically trapped in the footwear of childhood, seemingly unwilling or unable to emerge of their own accord. "Giving up the galosh," I have come to suspect, is tantamount to relinquishing one's childhood with its attendant protections, pleasures, and frustrations. Can it be that the Jewish prince *needs* his vision of the princess consort, as well as his wicked *latke*-pushing Queen Mother?

For the stereotype serves to simplify the complexities of human behavior, restoring the fabulous fictions of childhood. The awful realization that *no one* gives a hoot whether you wear your galoshes may be far more disconcerting than blaming someone who supposedly does. It is this clandestine clinging to childhood—inwardly maintaining its fictions while outwardly protesting them—that further perpetuates the stereotype and reveals the ambivalence underlying it.

Yet despite the durability of the stereotype and its infiltration into the hip late sixties and seventies, another phenomenon marked the onset of change. Women began to question the accusations leveled against them. Their responses introduced a new dimension into age-old conjectures about what women really wanted. Pauline Bart addressed the plight of Portnoy's mother in her essay on women and menopausal depression; Charlotte Baum, Paula Hyman, and Sonya Michel undermined stereotypes of JAP and Jewish mother in their history of the Jewish woman in America. Commenting on the evolution of attitudes toward the Jewish woman that shifted from "veneration" at the turn of the century to "vituperation" at its midpoint, the authors note that the Jewish woman found herself profoundly dislocated in the process of "Americanization." At the turn of the century, she was admired for her strength and endurance, qualities necessary for survival in immigrant life. Balabosta and businesswoman, her hours were long and arduous; she worked in kitchen and sweatshop, factory and office, serving more often than not, as the economic mainstay of her family as well as its central cohesive force. That central role was displaced by a peripheral one in the process of "Americanization." Jewish men were eager, once they were able, to adopt the prevailing American attitude of the time: Women do not belong in business. The villainess was now the loud, meddlesome wife; the heroine, modest, quiet, culturally accomplished—as genteel and Gentile as possible. By World War II, many immigrant families had "established" themselves, and the robust and energetic main-stay of the family found herself relegated to the sidelines to serve as an adornment for her newly successful husband. Many were unable to accommodate so great a transformation. The stereotype emerging from their failure was that of the *nouveau riche* wife, vulgar, useless, pretentious, and trivial—predecessor to those acidly embellished caricatures of Portnoy's mother and the JAP.

"I knew I was getting somewhere," exclaimed a young doc-toral candidate at a Jewish women's conference early in the seventies, "when the rabbis stopped laughing at me and started screaming."

Laughter proved increasingly inappropriate as the decade unfolded. For the first time in recorded history, Jewish women publicly proclaimed their determination to depart from inequi-ties of the past. Indeed, the decade the seventies marked a turn-ing point for women in major Western religions: the onset of change at a unique moment in history when renascent feminism and a resurgence of spiritual life converged to promise a future radically different from the past.

Describing herself as "latently Orthodox," an "ignorant Jew" excluded from all-male domains of Yeshiva learning because she "flunked the physical," the tall, dark-haired doctoral candi-date in Renaissance drama articulated a growing feeling among Jewish women today that diverges sharply from responses in the past. Traditionally, women in the major Western religions either submitted to religious dogma or fled the faith. Unwilling to accept submission, tokenism, or apostasy, women in the seventies—like this one—began to demand profound revi-sions within established bodies of traditional law and practice.

While Jewish women in the dim and recent past eloquently catalogued their dissatisfaction with biblical archetypes (docile helpmate and mother of sons) and popular stereotypes (Port-noy's mother and the JAP, imperfect consort to Roth's perfect

Prince), action commonly ended with its verbal expression or with havoc privately wreaked in personal and family life.

Despite the idealization and contempt heaped upon them in equal abundance, Jewish women of other generations stopped short of entering male sanctuaries of authority and power. Not so today. The traditional reluctance to publicly assert their claims has vanished. Illuminated by feminist insight, increasing numbers of Jewish women are arguing their case with a sweetly reasoned militance that can no longer go unheard.

The tenor of their argument was clearly voiced early in the seventies when Sandy Eisenberg Sasso, Reconstructionist Judaism's first female rabbi, addressed an all-male panel of Orthodox rabbis (most resistant to change, as a group). "As Reconstructionists," observed the young woman rabbi, "we believe the past has a vote, but *not* a veto."

Indeed, it was Mordecai Kaplan, founder of the Reconstructionist movement, who called attention to the unequal status of Jewish women thirty years ago: "Few aspects of Jewish thought and life illustrate so strikingly the need of reconstructing Jewish law as the traditional status of the Jewish woman," wrote Kaplan. "In Jewish tradition, her status is unquestionably that of inferiority to the man. If the Jewish woman is to contribute her share to the regeneration of Jewish life, and if in turn Jewish life is to bring out the powers for good that are in her, this status must be changed. She must attain in Jewish law and practice a position of religious, civic, and juridical equality with the man, and this attainment must come about through her own efforts and initiative."[1]

Whether or not he intended it, Kaplan spoke in the prophetic vein. While unusual women made their mark on Jewish life throughout history, nothing before matched the kind of mass movement that coalesced in the seventies. Punctuated at its outset by the proliferation of consciousness-raising sessions (offshoots of the larger feminist movement) and the formation of political action groups, the decade bore witness to the initiation of change in all areas of secular and religious life, beginning with the ordination of women as rabbis in Reform and Reconstructionist branches of Judaism and culminating with the uneasy formation of a two-year study committee at the austere Rabbinic Assembly of 1977, which would render its recommendations on the admission of women to the Conservative rabbinate in 1979. Such a study would have been unheard of less than a decade ago. While the queasiness with which it was undertaken remains appalling, the fact that the Conservative movement—America's largest Jewish rabbinical group—was at last impelled to seriously confront the feminist impetus for change, provides ample testimony to the quality and intensity of women's efforts in the seventies.

What distinguished the Jewish women's movement of the seventies was its diversity, determination, and the broad range of its concerns. A variety of groups emerged under the loose rubric of Jewish feminism, representing women of all ages, backgrounds, and religious affiliations—Reform, Reconstructionist, Conservative, and Orthodox, as well as the nonaffiliated who perceived the profound impact of religious inequity on secular life. They joined forces to initiate change in liturgy, ritual, ceremony, and community organization; and their voices were heard both within and without the "establishment."

On the countercultural scene, a kind of Jewish "underground press" emerged—some sixty newspapers with names like *Chutzpah, Rock of Ages,* and *Genesis II,* containing articles critical of the Jewish establishment and advocating communal life, world peace, gay liberation, and feminism. Some, like *Lilith's Rib* and *Off Our Backs,* specifically addressed feminist issues. In February of 1971, the first issue of the *Brooklyn Bridge,* identifying itself as a "revolutionary Jewish newspaper," presented its view of the oppression of Jewish women:

> Jewish daughters are thus caught in a double bind: We are expected to grow up assimilating the American image of "femininity"—soft, dependent, self-effacing, blond, straight-haired, slim, long-legged—and at the same time be the "womanly" bulwark of our people against the destruction of our culture. Now we suffer the oppression of Women of both cultures and are torn by the contradictions between the two. These contradictions take some curious

forms. Jewish men demand that their Women be intellectual sex-objects. So Jewish families push their daughters to get a good education. The real purpose is not to be forgotten, however. While Ph.D.'s do make Jewish parents proud of their daughters, the universities are recognized as hunting grounds for making a "good marriage." Grandchildren assure the race.

We've been called "Jewish princess" and "castrating bitch" by the rest of the world and by our own men loud and clear. We've been defined as a "Jewess" and been the object of rape. As Jewish Women we are strong, but always the force *behind* our men. We were strong in order to survive, and kept things together for our families and our culture, and for this we are now attacked as being "Jewish mother," ridiculous and disgusting as that has come to be.[2]

While some women protested their cultural and social assignments, others addressed themselves to the position of Jewish women in religious life.

Ezrat Nashim

In September of 1971, a group of thirteen young women from Conservative and Orthodox backgrounds who had met in consciousness-raising groups, formed a study group called Ezrat Nashim, the Hebrew name for the women's court in the ancient temple. While their background varied, all were well educated in both Jewish and secular areas, and all were committed to Judaism, providing what would soon emerge as a significant "loyal opposition" from within.

After meeting for several months at the New York Havura, the group felt itself increasingly drawn toward translating its perceptions into political action, and extending its impact to other women with similar concerns. Working from the premise that "while Jewish tradition regarding women was once far ahead of other cultures, it has now fallen behind in failing to come to terms with developments of the past century," Ezrat

Nashim determined to press for change within the traditional framework of religious practice.

"We are deeply committed to Judaism," they concurred at the outset, "but cannot find adequate expression for our total needs and concerns in existing women's social and charitable organizations, such as Sisterhood, Hadassah, etc. Furthermore, the single woman—a new reality in Jewish life—is almost totally excluded from the organized Jewish community, which views women solely as daughters, wives, and mothers. The educational institutions of the Conservative movement have helped women recognize their intellectual, social, and spiritual potential. If the movement then denies women opportunities to demonstrate these capacities as adults, it will force them to turn from the synagogue and to find fulfillment elsewhere."

In March of 1972, Ezrat Nashim presented its manifesto to the Rabbinical Assembly, calling for "an end to the second-class status of women in Jewish life." (Although they had been refused permission to address the convention formally, presumably because they had not applied early enough, the group attended the Assembly "uninvited" to argue their case, receiving considerable support from some of the rabbis at the convention, as well as many of their wives.) Specifics of the manifesto requested that:

- women be granted membership in synagogues
- women be counted in the *minyan* (quorum of ten required for worship)
- women be allowed full participation in religious observances (including *aliyah*—being called to read the Torah)
- women be recognized as witnesses before Jewish law
- women be allowed to initiate divorce
- women be permitted and encouraged to attend rabbinical and cantorial schools, and to perform rabbinical and cantorial functions in synagogues
- women be encouraged to join decision-making bodies, and to assume professional leadership roles in synagogues and in the general Jewish community

· women be considered as bound to fulfill all *mitzvot* equally
with men.

No official stand was taken on the issues by the Rabbinical
Assembly that year, but some Conservative synagogues began
including women in the *minyan.* Orthodoxy remained aloof
from feminist requests. Chancellor Gerson Cohen of the Jewish
Theological Seminary, America's leading Conservative rabbinical school, expressed sympathy with Ezrat Nashim's manifesto. Yet when two young women applied for admission to the
seminary's rabbinical school the following autumn, their applications were rejected by the majority decision of an all-male
panel. The issue, however, had indisputably been raised; and
momentum for its support gathered as the decade unfolded.
Early in 1973, the Conservative rabbinate officially endorsed
the inclusion of women in the *minyan,* as well as their participation in *aliyah.* Orthodoxy expressed dismay.

Kol Isha

Meanwhile, Ezrat Nashim continued to press for changes in
ritual and ceremony, providing speakers on those issues and
contributing source material and support to various Jewish feminist groups that proliferated during the decade.

In 1972, a small group of Orthodox women in their early
twenties began to meet to study *halacha* (Jewish law) in order
to approach leading Orthodox rabbis with suggestions for
change. Significantly, the group called itself Kol Isha, counter-
pointing the talmudic interdict banning woman's voice with
their determination to be heard. One of the problems for Orthodox women, commented a former member, is the inadequate
education they receive in many Orthodox schools. Most of
those schools do not teach *gemara* (commentary on the Talmud) to women, depriving them of tools necessary for changing
halacha or Jewish law. Since men and women do not study together in Orthodox schools, women's classes traditionally omit-
ted intensive study of talmudic commentary, subscribing to the
view that women should not learn Talmud.

Although Kol Isha was rather short-lived as a group (meeting for not much longer than a year), it distinguished itself as the first organized group of Orthodox women pressuring for change. During its life span, it approached several rabbis, among them Rabbi Saul Berman of Yeshiva's Stern College for Women and Rabbi Steven Riskin of the Lincoln Square Synagogue in New York. Both subsequently addressed themselves to the women's issue in synagogue practice (moderate as that address was) and in education. Rabbi Berman contributed an important essay on the status of women in halachic Judaism to *The Jewish Woman: New Perspectives,* published by Schocken Books in 1976. More recently (1978), Yeshiva University's Stern College for Women added a course in Talmud that parallels the method and intensity universally used in similar courses for men. At the same time, half the enrollment for the entering class of Yeshiva University's Law School is female, a rise of 10 per cent over the preceding year, suggesting the steady, if slow, penetration of woman's voice into Orthodox spheres. If women can scarcely yet aspire to the Orthodox rabbinate, they *can* study law, and increasing numbers are evidently taking advantage of that option.

Some of Kol Isha's members remained within the Orthodox movement; others left it. All participated in the first national Jewish Women's Liberation Conference of 1973 and in the formation of the Jewish Feminist Organization the following year.

National Jewish Women's Conference

During a summer meeting of the North American Jewish Students' Network in 1972, a caucus of women splintered off from the larger group to discuss their roles in Judaism and the New Left. Plans for the National Jewish Women's Conference were initiated at that meeting.

Defying archetype and stereotype, more than five hundred women of varying ages, lifestyles, and religious and geographical backgrounds flocked to the Conference, held in New York City in February of 1973. Wearing blue jeans and pants suits, long skirts and short skirts, wild-haired and hatted, women ranging in age from sixteen to sixty-five (some of them mothers and their daughters) crowded meeting rooms and corridors to press issues that had been simmering for more than three thousand years: their status as women in a tradition that venerates the patriarchal norms of the Old Testament.

Consciousness-raising sessions, film showings, panel discussions, and small workshops on a variety of subjects, including halacha, gay Jewish women, mysticism, marriage and divorce, menopausal depression, problems of the aged, and volunteerism highlighted the conference. Groups of women met late into the night, infused with a growing spirit of elation and that intriguing blend of tradition, counterculture, and carefully reasoned militance that would characterize the Jewish feminist movement of the seventies.

A women's *minyan* and "traditional services" led by young women in *tallit* (prayer shawls) and *tefillen* (phylacteries), customarily worn by men, greeted the Sabbath, followed by discussion of woman's exclusion from spiritual Judaism. For women at the Conference, that exclusion exacerbated a growing sense of isolation, an increasing tension between membership in the feminist community with its commitment to equality and autonomy for women and the position of women in Jewish life, and of disappointment at the discrepancy between the theoretical equality of Judaism's promise and the inequity of its practice.

"Women," observed theology lecturer Judith Plaskow Goldenberg, "have had our power of naming stolen from us. From the time God brought the animals to Adam in the Garden of Eden to see what he would call them, it has been through the words of men that we have known and addressed the world. Although we do not know in advance that their words are not our words, neither do we know that they are . . . for there are times when the male power of naming oppresses and excludes us."

Speaking to that sense of oppression, women throughout the conference called upon both the history of their people and their own experience to explore attitudes and conditions that confounded them in daily life.

"As an Orthodox Jew," exclaimed an attractive young woman in maroon velour pants suit during a consciousness-raising session, "I really need a movement like this to pull things together." Having achieved "the American dream"—a high-paying career as an economist with a prestigious Wall Street firm—she told the group, "I had to start seeing a psychiatrist. It was frightening to me. I knew I was professionally able, but I didn't feel I belonged.

"There are certain very positive feelings we all have about Judaism," averred the economist, "but what we may be negative about—my quandary—is what our role is as a woman in this circle."

As the conference drew to a close, its participants overwhelmingly felt the need to continue, to translate their aspirations into action. Several projects were initiated, among them a speakers' bureau, a newsletter, and the compilation of source material about Jewish women, including both their role in history and the revival and initiation of women's ritual: ceremonies to celebrate the birth and naming of daughters, to mark the life cycle of women, and the advent of the new moon—the Rosh Chodesh ceremony, a woman's ritual from biblical times that had fallen into disuse. Throughout the following year, groups continued to meet on a local level in New England, New York, New Jersey, Pennsylvania, Washington, D.C., Illinois, and California.

A second conference, in April 1974, was considerably different in both scope and response. Discussing "Changing Sex Roles: Implications for the Future of Jewish Life," the conference was open to men and women, who met in separate sessions—a rather paradoxical arrangement that lacked the cohesion of the preceding year. Yet it was at the 1974 conference that the Jewish Feminist Organization, conceived in 1973, was formally born.

Jewish Feminist Organization, 1974–76

Designed to serve as an umbrella organization for a wide variety of local groups, as well as for individual women throughout the country who sought its aid, the JFO set up regional offices in New York, Toronto, Chicago, and Los Angeles.

"We Jewish feminists have joined together here in strength and joy," reads the introduction to its statement of purpose, "to struggle for the liberation of the Jewish woman. Jewish women of all ages, political, cultural, and religious outlooks and sexual preferences, are all sisters. We are committed to the development of our full human potential and to the survival and enhancement of Jewish life. We seek nothing else than the full, direct, and equal participation of women at all levels of Jewish life—communal, religious, educational, and political. We shall be a force for such creative change in the Jewish community."

Among its activities, the JFO continued to sponsor conferences, retreats, workshops, and seminars; it established and maintained a Jewish feminist speakers' bureau, lent its support to local groups pressuring for change in synagogue and community, and sought to develop links with the feminist movement in Israel and to serve as liaison with the larger feminist movement in the United States. Marking its first anniversary, the New York chapter ran an all-day conference on "Women: Myth and Reality" in the spring of 1975. By now, the JFO received substantial coverage from the general press, and once more, hundreds of women gathered to examine the impact of feminism on their personal and communal lives. A cautionary note was introduced by Judith Hauptman, the first woman to teach Talmud at the Conservative Jewish Theological Seminary and a founding member of Ezrat Nashim.

Referring to a "neochauvinist backlash," evident in the tendency among some of the seminary's professors to outwardly proclaim themselves allied with feminist concerns while undercutting that alliance with jokes about women, as well as in the long-standing failure to introduce change into the profound and often tragic inequities of Jewish marital law, Hauptman urged that the abundance of energy in initiating changes be maintained to sustain those changes.

"We haven't won the revolution yet!" Congresswoman Bella Abzug concurred. (Both Congresswomen Abzug and Elizabeth Holtzman had been keynote speakers at the first National Jewish Women's Conference in 1973, and attended each of the conferences in subsequent years.) Addressing her "original sisters" this year, Abzug continued: "One Israeli Prime Minister is not a revolution; one telephone repair operator is not a revolution; one lieutenant governor is not a revolution; and one right in a million is not a revolution!"

Indeed, the revolution has scarcely begun. Given Judaism's proclivity for cautious evolution, many more decades may pass before it is on its way. Yet the feminist ferment of the seventies had a wide-ranging and unalterable impact on Jewish institutions. Changes were often initially introduced on the periphery of organized religion—in campus groups and *havura* (fellowship) communities where services and communal life are generally egalitarian. Women's *minyans* sprang up in various cities; the New York Jewish Women's Center has been conducting them since its inception several years ago. At Brown University, a women's *minyan* meets every Sabbath, using the feminine pronoun for the Deity. Journals carried articles on the role of women in Judaism, as well as rituals to mark their life cycles.

Among community organizations, the American Jewish Congress provided quarters for the Jewish Feminist Organization and ran seminars of its own on the position of women in Jewish life. In 1973, Jacqueline K. Levine, then president of the American Jewish Congress's Women's Division, addressed the General Assembly of the Council of Jewish Federations and Welfare Funds, urging greater participation of women in policy decisions and leadership levels. "While the Jewish community structure is more open than it was a few years ago," she observed, "real change hasn't happened here yet."

In similar vein, the prestigious American Jewish Committee addressed itself to the initiation of change in Jewish life. Sabbath morning services at its annual convention in May of 1972 were conducted by a woman rabbinical student and a female cantor. Using her analysis of the Book of Ruth to illustrate woman's unequal status in Jewish law, rabbinical candidate Sandy Eisenberg Sasso led a discussion that encompassed inequities on all levels of Jewish life. In 1974, the committee organized a Task Force on Women to study the changing roles of women in contemporary American society. The task force conducted extensive surveys, testified in favor of the Equal Rights Amendment, supported antidiscrimination actions in employment, and joined in interfaith efforts to encourage greater participation by women in religious and communal life. In 1975, the Committee's Institute on Pluralism and Group Identity, working with the Women's Action Alliance, sponsored a major conference exploring the impact of the women's movement on women of diverse ethnic, economic, and social backgrounds. In 1977, the American Jewish Committee published and publicized *"Who Hast Not Made Me a Man,"* Anne Lapidus Lerner's study of the equal rights movement for women in American Jewry, one of the most concise and comprehensive reports to date.

"The chance to be a mother in Israel," maintained a panelist at the National Jewish Women's Conference in 1973, "is not enough. If I don't also have the chance to be a saint and scholar, I don't belong in Israel."

The determination to move beyond the limitations of traditional roles characterized the decade of the seventies. Women in all the major Western religions challenged long-standing prejudices that sought to exclude them from leadership and recognition. That challenge generated a response from both clergy and laity among Episcopalians, Catholics, and Jews. While the response was not always congratulatory, significant inroads were made in the course of the decade. Clearly, the time was ripe for change.

Ordination of Women

In 1972, Sally Preisand was ordained as America's first woman rabbi in the Reform movement. That same year, Pope

Paul VI sought to "modernize" the Catholic Church by abolishing the tonsure, reaffirming rules for priestly celibacy, and denying women formal investiture in duties they presently performed (the title of deacon).

Responding to the Pope on the op ed page of the New York *Times,* Teresa D. Marciano, professor of sociology at Fairleigh Dickinson University, pointed to the ordination of Sally Preisand and concomitant attempts in Judaism to create just relationships among its people as a model that the Pope might well consider.

"If God loves women as much as men," she poignantly observed, "how does the Church defend the preservation of its highest honors and mysteries for one sex only?"

That the late Pope was not readily convinced is evident in his responses to pressure within and without the Catholic Church three and four years later. Pleas for change in the Church's attitude toward women priests from various organizations of nuns and lay women within the Roman Catholic Church received an emphatic "No!" from the Vatican. A touchy correspondence with the archbishop of Canterbury in 1975–76 conveyed the Pope's "regret" at the "obstacle to unity" between Roman Catholic and Anglican Church, posed by the Anglican trend toward introducing women priests. (At the time of the correspondence, the Canadian Anglican Church had already sanctioned the ordination of women; America's branch of Anglicanism—the Episcopalian Church of America—had not yet resolved the issue.) Reiterating his "sadness" at this "menace" to unity, Pope Paul VI urged the Church's adherence to Christ's example in choosing only men as apostles.

The stormy issue of the ordination of women as priests was introduced to the Episcopalian Church of America early in the seventies. In 1970, the General Convention voted to recognize women as deacons, an order below priesthood that enabled women to perform pastoral but not sacramental services. In 1972, the House of Bishops, one of the major groups of the bicameral convention, voted in principle at an interim meeting that the priesthood should be open to women. The following year, at the convention of 1973, the House of Deputies defeated the resolution to accept women as priests. Many felt the defeat was a function of the voting procedure rather than a majority of numbers, since votes are cast not by individuals but by diocesan units.

Within the next two years, fifteen women were ordained as Episcopal priests, in defiance of the decision at 1973's triennial convention. Eleven were ordained by four bishops in a controversial ceremony in Philadelphia in 1974; another four were ordained in Washington in 1975. The women ranged in age from twenty-seven to seventy-nine; the eldest, the Reverend Jeannette R. Picard, seventy-nine-year-old widow of balloonist Jacques Picard, had literally waited nearly all her life to realize her ambition to enter the priesthood. Both the women and the bishops who ordained them unquestionably faced rancor and disciplinary actions from the national Church body. Delivering a sermon at the Philadelphia ordination, Dr. Charles V. Willie, a prominent black Episcopal layman, compared the discrimination experienced by women to that suffered by blacks. "We stand ready," he declared, "to endure the hardship and the personal sacrifice necessary to pull the Episcopal Church from its mistaken way of refusing to acknowledge the full personhood of women. We believe it a Christian duty to disobey unjust laws."

Predictably, a series of actions was initiated to censure the four bishops and eleven deacons who had participated in the ordinations of the women and to deny their validity. When the House of Bishops, meeting in Chicago in 1974, voted 128 to 9 to declare the ordinations invalid, Dr. Willie denounced the action as "male arrogance." Together with several others, he subsequently resigned from the Church's executive Council and from his position as vice president of the House of Deputies. During the heated discussion preceding the vote, the Right Reverend Paul Moore, Jr., bishop of New York, urged his colleagues not to deny the validity of the ordinations, pointing to the group's 1972 statement of principle advocating the eligibility of women for the priesthood.

The intensity of antagonism toward women in clerical roles reached a curious peak at New York's Riverside Church in

1974, when a young priest, in more than a manner of speaking, bit the hand that extended the communion wafer. The Reverend Carter Heyward, then an Episcopal deacon distributing communion, held out the chalice of wine to the young priest kneeling at the altar before her. While sipping the communion wine, the young man drew his fingernails across Dr. Heyward's hand on the chalice until blood flowed. This curious excursion into sacramental violence culminated with the young man's Christian sentiments for his female colleague's future: "I hope you burn in hell" is how he put it.

While hell hath no fury like a young priest scorned, the triennial convention of the Episcopal Church of America, meeting in 1976, voted in favor of the ordination of women as priests and bishops. Not unexpectedly, the historic decision was cheered in some quarters and lamented in others. "It's a great day!" commented Sister Kathleen Keating, who sent the convention a congratulatory telegram as national chairman of a thirty-five-hundred-member group of Catholic women promoting the ordination of women as priests in the Roman Catholic Church. At the convention itself, groups who favored the decision called for reconciliation and cautioned that the "struggle against sexism" was not yet over. A faction opposed to ordination for women labeled the convention's action "null and void" and urged a boycott of services conducted by women priests. A formal schism, however, was temporarily averted.

By 1977, some sixty women had been ordained as Episcopal priests. Forces strongly opposed to such ordinations, meanwhile, met in St. Louis in September of 1977 to formally announce their secession from the Episcopal Church, pledging themselves to the formation of a new provisional body called the Anglican Church of North America.

As an added note, an American Episcopal priest recently (in 1977) became the first woman to administer holy communion at a public service in Britain, to the embarrassment of the archbishops of Canterbury and York. While both are reputed to favor the ordination of women, they are reluctant to incur the displeasure of the Vatican. Although the Anglican Church has formally stated "no fundamental objection" to women priests, its House of Bishops ruled in 1976 that women ordained abroad may not officiate in the Church of England. The Reverend Alison Palmer, ordained in the United States in 1975, had been invited to officiate at communion in Manchester and Newcastle by the Church council, which suggested that "natural justice" in this issue had priority over obedience to authority. On August 10, 1978, the Lambeth Conference with an overwhelming vote recommended that the Church of England accept women as priests. Nonetheless, the Anglican Church voted down a proposal for immediate ordination of women the following November. (A majority vote by each of the three houses that make up the General Synod was needed. The bishops said yes to women by a vote of 32 to 17, the laity by a vote of 120 to 106. But the clergy opposed the ordination of women by 149 to 94.) This could mean no women priests in England for another ten years. One argument against them from Bishop Graham Leonard of Truro had a familiar ring: "I want women to be women."

While Conservative Judaism can scarcely look to Christ's example in choosing only male apostles, attitudes underlying the assumption that relationship with the divinity is reserved solely for men—heretical as that assumption is—are often masked by expressed concerns over the "psychological" impact of women in the pulpit and its "sociological implications"—its effect upon the family and the possibility of divisiveness among the laity at so radical a departure from traditional images of the religious leader—if not the Deity—as male. The contention among some Episcopalians and Roman Catholics that only a male priest can administer the sacraments—specious as that argument may be— simply has no analogue in Judaism. In no way is the rabbi invested with a special relationship to the divine; he—or she—is primarily a scholar and religious leader. Nonetheless, the recent minority secession in the Episcopal Church over the ordination of women tends to have a chilling effect on other religious groups, reinforcing the cautiousness of some Conservative Jewish leaders. That chilling effect is somewhat ameliorated, in terms of ecumenical comparison, by the long-time service of women in Protestant ministries, as well as the more recent admission of women as rabbis in Reconstructionist and Reform branches of Judaism itself.

After germinating for several years, a proposal to admit women to the Conservative rabbinate was placed before the Rabbinical Assembly of America (of which more than eleven hundred rabbis are members) in the spring of 1977. The issue was initially introduced by Rabbi Judah Nadich, president of the RA in 1974, and supported by its executive vice president, Rabbi Wolfe Kelman. Opinion appeared evenly divided among the six hundred rabbis who attended the meeting in 1977. Those opposed to the admission of women rabbis in the Conservative movement (with which more than half of America's Jews are affiliated) claim that their opposition is not based solely on adherence to traditional patterns. Calling on the forces of "physiology," Rabbi David M. Feldman, who has advocated liberalization of divorce laws and birth control, maintained that the absence of women in Conservative pulpits reflected a "rational sex-role division." "Some women have the 'devil theory' that men kept women from power," he argued. "It happened for physiological reasons. If only 50 per cent of us can give birth and raise families, then the other 50 per cent must do something else." (Given the reputed importance of the family in Jewish life, one can only wonder why men are not counted more significant as fathers and husbands.)

A vote on the issue was subsequently tabled for two years with the formation of an interim study commission to report its findings to the group in 1978, with final recommendations to be made before the Rabbinical Assembly in 1979. Dr. Gerson D. Cohen, Chancellor of the Jewish Theological Seminary of America, which trains 80 per cent of all Conservative rabbis in the United States, agreed to form the study group and to abide by its findings on the condition that "all activity is suspended for two years, so that our faculty will not explode."

"Natural differences" notwithstanding, a commission for the study of the ordination of women as rabbis was appointed by Dr. Gerson D. Cohen, who served as its chairman. Two distinct but closely related issues were under consideration. First, was the admission of women to the Rabbinical Assembly (currently, a male Reconstructionist or Reform rabbi may become a member of the RA if he has served in a Conservative pulpit for two consecutive years and shares the movement's ideology and practices). Second was the admission of women to the Jewish Theological Seminary's Rabbinical School on an equal basis with men.

The eleven men and three women serving on the Commission were drawn from a wide variety of disciplines, including Jewish scholarship, the rabbinate (seven of the men are rabbis), and community leadership. Over the course of the following year, they heard testimony from hundreds of individuals and groups throughout the United States and Canada. The overwhelming consensus of that testimony favored the ordination of women. Arguments from opponents rested largely on fears of fragmenting the movement or diminishing its credibility (which is virtually non-existent) with Orthodox Judaism.

In its final report to the Rabbinical Assembly convention of 1979, the Commission (by a majority of eleven to three) strongly endorsed the ordination of women in the Conservative movement, emphasizing the necessity and urgency for a revision of admission standards to include women at the Jewish Theological Seminary's Rabbinical School (the only routine means of entering the Conservative rabbinate). The Commission further recommended that the Seminary accomplish its revisions with sufficient dispatch to allow for applications from women for the academic year beginning in September 1979.[3]

But the Seminary proved reluctant, despite the advocacy of its Chancellor, who declared himself "a passionate advocate of ordination of women" in his address before the Rabbinical Assembly. Rather than pressuring JTS by adopting a strongly worded endorsement of the Commission's report, the RA passed a rather weak, noncommittal resolution delaying action until the faculty of JTS arrived at its decision.

That decision has subsequently suffered predictable delays. Originally slated for May of 1979, it was officially postponed for the following December, thereby averting the possibility of women applicants for another academic year. The "unofficial" word is that the Seminary would like to sit on its decision as long as possible, preferring to delay it indefinitely.

"Meanwhile," comments one Conservative rabbi, referring to the admission of women as rabbis, "it's the hottest subject in town. The idea is to keep it out of the press while it's being discussed internally among laity, rabbinate, and faculty groups. Eventually," he conjectures, "the answer is going to have to be 'yes.' I don't see how they can avoid it." One need scarcely fear, however, a "rush to judgment" from Conservative quarters.

Some Conservative leaders at the Rabbinical Assembly felt the issue could not be held down for another two years. "It's going to come up annually," predicted Anne Lapidus Lerner, an instructor at the seminary. "The women's movement is here to stay. There is no cogent argument that bans women from the rabbinate."

Many rabbis agreed, welcoming the introduction of women to the Conservative rabbinate. "We should be profoundly grateful," suggested Rabbi Alex Shapiro at an open meeting, "that some young women are so moved by the Almighty that they want to act in what they consider the highest service. There are such women. God willing, they should multiply among us."

At the same meeting, another rabbi—I. Usher Kirschblum of Kew Gardens in New York City—declared that he would be forced to resign from the Assembly if women were ordained. "When you speak to God as a person," he confided to a reporter later, "God is more strengthening if it is a 'he' rather than a 'she.'" Others dredged up the tired contention that the presence of a woman in the pulpit might be sexually distracting. When the argument is reversed by suggesting that female congregants might find a male rabbi distracting, it is invariably discounted with assertions that men and women are different by "nature."

Late in 1977, a female student at the Reconstructionist Rabbinical School received unanimous approval from the Rabbinical Assembly's delegation to the Commission on Jewish Chaplaincy that would enable her to begin training in the

Army's seminarian program. Thus far, three women chaplains—none of them Jewish—serve in the U.S. military. At the completion of the two- or three-year seminarian program, Jewish chaplains must receive endorsement from the Jewish Welfare Board's Commission on Jewish Chaplaincy, which is composed of twenty-one rabbis, seven each from Reform, Conservative, and Orthodox Judaism. All endorsements, thus far, have been unanimous. If the female seminarian student applies for endorsement within the next three years, Orthodox rabbis will be confronted for the first time with the issue of ordaining a woman Jewish chaplain.

In 1978, the Union of American Hebrew Congregations, representing 720 Reform synagogues with 1.1 million members in the United States and Canada, predicted that by 1979, 1 out of every 3 newly ordained rabbis would be a woman. Increasing numbers of women have enrolled at Reconstructionist and Reform rabbinical schools since the ordination of America's first woman rabbi in 1972. Out of 45 students at Philadelphia's Reconstructionist seminary in 1977, 12 were female; among 208 students in the Reform movement that same year, 48 were women.

By 1979, eighteen women were ordained in the Reform movement, sixteen of them in the United States and two in Britain. At the same time, Reconstructionist Judaism graduated six women rabbis, one of whom, interestingly enough, is serving at a Conservative synagogue. By 1980, Sandy Eisenberg Sasso, Reconstructionist Judaism's first woman rabbi, will have served in a Conservative pulpit for more than two consecutive years, rendering her eligible to apply for membership to the Rabbinical Assembly of America. Nothing in the Assembly's constitution stipulates that an applicant be male. Its study commission advocated the admission of women to its ranks in 1979, urging the Jewish Theological Seminary's Rabbinical school to open its portals to female applicants. The Seminary postponed decision. If Rabbi Sasso should decide to submit her application for membership, how would the Assembly respond? A provocative speculation.

Yet another woman, trained in the Conservative movement,

awaits confirmation as a rabbi. Lynn Gottlieb, who has completed graduate work at the Jewish Theological Seminary, has served as rabbi for more than four years at a congregation of the deaf. Several Conservative rabbis, impressed with her achievements and ability, have offered to ordain her privately. Will such private ordination be necessary after 1980?

Whether one names it revolution or evolution, the decade of the seventies clearly bears witness to a profound transformation in the images of woman. The flat, watery wash of Akiva's self-sacrificing Rachel has at last given way to the fuller tones and dimension of the Talmud's Beruriah. Masochism can no longer be counted a prerequisite for femininity. Far more significant than the polemics and speculation surrounding it is the substance of the transformation itself: the emergence of woman as scholar and rabbi.

WOMAN AS RABBI

"The last bastion of manhood is gone!" exclaimed the pilot at a small airport in Maine, laughing as we boarded his twin-engined plane.

"A what?" he had asked minutes earlier, staring at the slender, dark-haired young woman in blue jeans and white pullover in the airport's waiting room. "You're going to be a *what?*"

"A rabbi," responded Sandy Eisenberg Sasso softly, eyes clear gray, face flushed crimson, a long, deep dimple punctuating her response.

August of 1972. I had just spent the week interviewing Sandy for what I then thought would be a magazine story. In September, Sandy and her husband, Dennis, would enter their final year of study at Philadelphia's Reconstructionist Rabbinical School; they were working at a children's camp in northwestern Maine for the summer. Within the year, Sandy, at twenty-seven, would become Reconstructionist Judaism's first woman rabbi. Moved by the clarity and warmth of her address to the American Jewish Committee the preceding May, as well as by the novelty of her career, I was eager to learn more about her. In Maine, Sandy moved easily from scholarly work on sages of the past to discussion groups with young men and women in the present, with a luminosity at once immediate and transcendent.

"For me," she told a group discussing forms of worship, her gray eyes alight with sun and laughter, "communication is a form of prayer."

"Why do women always have to prove themselves?" senior girls at the camp asked her during a rap session. "Like it's such a big deal, a woman being a rabbi. Just the fact that someone's writing an article about you. Would someone write an article about Dennis?"

"I'm the first man to be married to a rabbi," Dennis responded easily.

"What will you do about getting a congregation?" the girls asked Sandy.

"We'll see what the options are," she answered.

"For *you,*" they suggested, "there won't be many!"

"That depends," Sandy laughed. "You seem so positive. . . ."

"A woman rabbi," the pilot said, shaking his head. "You must be the first one."

"The second," Sandy replied, smiling. (American Reform Judaism ordained its first woman—Rabbi Sally Preisand—in June of 1972.)

"The world's second woman rabbi," the pilot finally managed.

"Actually, the third," Sandy replied, smile widening. (The first, of whom few are aware, was Regina Jonas, who completed her studies at Berlin's Reform Seminary before World War II. Her thesis question: "Can a Woman Be a Rabbi?" received a flat "No!" from the Talmud professor who refused to sign her diploma. Dismayed but undaunted, Frau Jonas received private ordination from a liberal Reform leader in Offenbach and served as rabbi in a home for the aged until 1940, when she was taken to the concentration camps, from which she never returned.)

The plane was ready for takeoff. The pilot smiled as the bastions crumbled.

"Lady," he turned to Sandy, "you're a shoo-in for 'What's My Line?'" (Some two years later, Sandy and Dennis actually found themselves on the program.)

"You've got the end for your story, now," Dennis suggested, laughing, as we exchanged temporary farewells.

Not the end, I thought, but the beginning.

Indeed, for me, the journey had just begun. Plane trips from Maine to Boston to New York took less than three hours. My own venture into time extended much further into the past and future than I had initially anticipated. During the course of that journey, I met many of the women who would occupy the pulpits and lecterns of the future, as well as those who might have in the past, had history been ready for them. Each was unique, yet all had a quality in common: a kind of incandescence, that inner radiance of the visionary who moves beyond all models and expectations of the past. Moving beyond the model introduced intimations of the future, emergence from the stereotypes and pomposities of codified behavior. For Judaism, that emergence carried the rich promise of transformation, both in its images of women and of the rabbinate.

More than a century ago, Reform Judaism in Germany had confronted the issue of women in religious life. At Frankfurt in 1845, the Conference of Rabbis declared that women shared obligations with men in public services and that "the custom not to include women" in the *minyan* or quorum necessary for public worship "had no religious basis."

At the Breslau Rabbinical Conference a year later, the call for equality was underscored. By the end of the century, various discriminatory practices had been abandoned or reformed; among them, separate seating in the synagogue, the acceptance of civil death certificates for missing husbands so that the *agunah* (the chained wife) could remarry, and eligibility of women for "full membership with all the privileges of voting and holding office in our congregations."

Yet paper proclamations failed to obliterate cultural biases for more than a century. In 1922, Reform Judaism's Central Conference of American Rabbis judged that women could not "justly be denied the privileges of ordination." That same year, however, those privileges were denied Martha Neumark, one of Hebrew Union's most promising students, because she was a woman.

Martha Neumark entered Hebrew Union College at the age of fourteen. The daughter of David Neumark, a prominent professor at the college, her earlier years—if that can be imagined— as well as those spent at the school, were enriched by theological discussions with her father.

"To be a pupil to one whom one has always called 'Daddy'!" she later remarked, commenting on an initial feeling of estrangement in his classes, a blend of amusement and discomfort. "That man with the magnetic soul and the philosophic mien, sitting on the rostrum, seemed someone else than the wonderful father I knew at home." In time, she grew as accustomed to his classes as to his individual tutoring at home. "How rigorous he was," she recalls, "how insistent upon the mastery of every detail. Questions that no other professor would have dreamed of asking, my father coached me in thoroughly. But we were also spiritual companions. Often we would spend the evenings discussing a religious problem. Sometimes I might break in with the remark that Stirner had said so and so, and my father would smilingly rejoin; I had read him [Stirner] when I was eight years old, and even then I realized his stupidity. . . ."

Like Sandy Eisenberg Sasso and other women drawn to the rabbinate, Martha Neumark was particularly stirred by reading from the Torah at her confirmation. "The recitation of those ancient words," she observed, "crystallized a vague restlessness of mine into a desire to serve my people. The doubt never entered my mind as to whether I, a girl, would be ordained. I wanted to serve Judaism and Jews. What other requisite was necessary?"

Such exquisite simplicity soon met with ridicule and disparagement. "At first, everyone laughed at me," she reported; "indeed, perhaps they have never stopped!" Eventually, laughter subsided, replaced by a growing respect for her seriousness of purpose. During that difficult first year, however, unhappy and unanticipated circumstances strengthened her resolve. A friend, who was one of the school's best students, died during an influenza epidemic in his senior year. "It was the first time," she recalled, "that anyone with whom I had been intimately associated had died. I vowed to myself that I would try to take his place in the world of Jewish scholarship; I would carry on the work that had been torn from his hands." When that year's laughter and discouragement threatened to diminish her energies, the memory of that vow made at the loss of her friend replenished them.

In 1921, newspapers began running features on Martha Neumark with pictures declaring her destined to be "the first and only" woman in the rabbinate. A flood of love letters and proposals descended on her. "Interesting paradox," she commented in a series of articles for the *Jewish Tribune* in 1925. "At a time when I was preparing for my own subsistence, someone was offering to provide it for me."

At the same time, a sprinkling of other women began applying to rabbinical schools. Their applications received identical replies. Women might enter the college and take all the work, but under no conditions would they be granted regular scholarships; the school's bylaws stipulated that these were available only to male students. The faculty finally took action, suggesting to the school's authoritative Board of Governors that women rabbinical candidates receive the same privileges as males. The board, in turn, transferred that hot potato to the Central Conference of American Rabbis. In the summer of 1922, the Central Conference of American Rabbis debated the issue, declaring itself in favor of the ordination of women at the conclusion of its sessions.

The Board of Governors, however, proved reluctant to follow rabbinical recommendations, denying women ordination by a majority vote of its lay membership. A quorum of two rabbis and six laymen participated in that decisive vote; the rabbis opted for the ordination of women; the laymen, against it.

"The admission of women as rabbis," concluded Martha Neumark more than fifty years ago, "is merely another phase of the woman question. Despite the fact that so many have achieved eminence in their chosen fields, a struggle ensues each time that a woman threatens to break up man's monopoly upon any industrial, political, or social province."

If Martha Neumark was ahead of her time in her calling for the rabbinate, she was equally ahead of it in her perceptions of the significance of ritual, in her concept of Deity, and in her recognition of the benefits that would accrue to Judaism with the inclusion of women in its ranks. That vision expressed itself in the series of articles she wrote for the *Jewish Tribune* in 1925. Commenting on Reform Judaism's departure from ancient ceremony, she observed: "Reform Judaism is for the rational . . . but in some ways it impresses me as too academic. . . . With Santayana, I hold that religion can be made into beauty, and that true religion always is. The ritual and ceremony were what I missed." In time, Reform Judaism caught up with Martha Neumark, reintroducing more Hebrew into its liturgy, and ritual into its practice.

The evolution of her concept of Deity is particularly striking today, when popular assumptions far too readily anthropomorphize God into male or female. Crediting her father's influence, she wrote: "It was he who converted me from a belief in God as a being, anthropomorphic or attributeless, into a belief in God as a process. Every individual is born with a minimum consciousness or soul. . . . The growth of the individual increases that consciousness. . . . My father's most characteristic résumé of the problem was this: If you believe in anything else than that God is a process—that is, if you think of Him in any sort of material way, then you might as well conceive of Him as a piece of cotton or a piece of cheese."

On women as rabbis: "My work at the Hebrew Union College, my gradually enlarging acquaintance with Jewish lore, philosophy, and history has made more firm my conviction that in no manner are women incapable of entering the ministry, either by reason of tradition, or because of their inherent incapacity. Women would add new blood to the ranks of the ministry, a thing much needed at the present."

The present was not yet ready for such revitalization. Half a century later, Martha Neumark wrote Dr. Ira Eisenstein, congratulating him on the admission of women to rabbinical programs in Philadelphia's Reconstructionist College. Her attention had been caught by Sandy Sasso's article in an issue of the Reconstructionist magazine. "I had left the HUC after 6½ years of study," Neumark wrote in 1971, "with my B.H. degree and my Sunday school superintendent diploma destined to lie more or less fallow during most of the intervening decades while I raised my family (current count of grandchildren: seven!)."

"The moment I saw the purple ink and green stationery," responded Dr. Eisenstein, a sophomore at Columbia when Martha Neumark's articles appeared in 1925, "I knew that I was back in touch with my old friend."

That vigorous purple script celebrated the recognition long overdue women in Judaism. "May the ladies flourish both there and at my alma mater," she wrote warmly, "from which one is slated to graduate this year."

Yet another woman of considerably different temperament and extraordinary energy determined to become a rabbi in Germany before the outbreak of World War II, struggling to maintain that position in the turbulent years that followed, and culminated with her death at Auschwitz in 1944. Born in Berlin in 1902, Regina Jonas attended Berlin's Reform ·Rabbinical Seminary,* where she distinguished herself as an excellent student and dynamic speaker. Upon graduation, the faculty granted her accreditation as a preacher and teacher of religion, but the institute's professor of Talmud, Chanoth Albeik, the only member of the faculty authorized to grant rabbinical status, refused to sign Frau Jonas's rabbinical diploma. She eventually received private ordination at Offenbach from Max Dienemann, one of Germany's leading liberal rabbis. There was some question at the time about whether such private ordination would lead to government recognition for employment as a rabbi. All of this was, of course, soon tragically beside the point.

Nonetheless, Frau Jonas served as rabbi in a home for the aged, paid hospital calls, and until the very end—when all

* Lehranstalt für die Wisenschaft des Judentum.

synagogues were closed in 1941—she continued to deliver sermons. In November of 1942, Regina Jonas was deported from Berlin to Theresienstadt; from there, she was sent to Auschwitz barely two years later in October 1944.

Of those who once knew Regina Jonas, few remain: a handful of rabbis and scholars dispersed across the globe; among them, Günter Friedländer in Bogotá, Colombia; Emil Fackenheim in Toronto, Canada; Wolfgang Hamburger in Houston, Texas; and Alfred Jospe in Washington, D.C. It is they who have provided me with both facts and some sense of the emotional fabric of Regina Jonas's life.

In New York, Dr. Herbert Strauss, director of the Association of German Jewish Immigrants, recalls that she was essentially realistic about the popular response to a woman rabbi in her time. When making hospital calls, she would habitually introduce herself with the brisk announcement: "My name is Frau Regina Jonas. I am not the wife of a rabbi, but a rabbi. What can I do for you?"

Wolfgang Hamburger adds that one bedridden congregant at the Jewish hospital irritably responded by telling her she could mend his socks! (Perhaps nothing has changed so very much, after all! Only several summers ago in Maine, a sprightly young male camper of seven directed Rabbi Sandy Eisenberg Sasso to clear the table and carry its dishes into the kitchen. "Dishes," he informed her, "are woman's work.")

Courage, intelligence, energy, and a certain single-mindedness are the qualities that emerge from the pastiche of memories evoked by Regina Jonas. "Pugnacious" is the word that Alfred Jospe uses. Dr. Jospe was rabbi of a synagogue in Berlin whose services Regina Jonas attended. Some years her senior, he did not know her as a student, but would see her occasionally when she came to speak with him after services. His own words acutely evoke that experience:

"I want to add in all frankness," he writes in a letter to me in 1978 after several paragraphs of valuable but rather general and impersonal information about Regina Jonas, "that the few personal encounters and contacts I had with her were not always very pleasant. For reasons which I understand and appreciate today far better than most of us did at that time, she was very pugnacious—the mark, I guess, of most people who try to break through long-established barriers—and in her eagerness and desire to be fully recognized and 'accepted' in the role she had chosen for herself there was virtually nothing I ever found possible to discuss with her than the problems of acceptance or nonacceptance of a woman as a rabbi by the Jewish establishment and her rather sharp challenges, often in the most personal terms, of any doubt one might have about this development at that time."

Indeed, Regina Jonas emerges as the militant feminist *par excellence*, born ahead of her time: determined, challenging, and, no doubt, somewhat single-minded—qualities that suggest the tension between personal temperament and historical circumstance. Valor is yet another of her attributes repeatedly evoked by those remaining few who once knew Regina Jonas.

"A very valiant woman who deserves not to be forgotten," writes Günter Friedländer from Bogotá.

And from Dr. Jospe, to whom she would talk of little else but her challenge to the Jewish establishment in Berlin more than forty years ago: "I am pleased you are including her in your work. She was a valiant person (though sometimes a bit hard to take), and this memorial will do her and you honor."

The struggle of which both Martha Neumark and Regina Jonas spoke is not yet over. But so many more women are now engaged in it that it becomes happily more difficult to single them out: those scholars and students of the ministry who have multiplied in schools and seminaries throughout the world. Each is unique in herself; yet it becomes increasingly difficult to mention each by name. One begins to fall back upon "firsts":

Sally Preisand, the first woman rabbi ordained by Reform Judaism in America in 1972; Sandy Eisenberg Sasso, Reconstructionist Judaism's first female rabbi, ordained the following year. Sandy, incidentally, was undoubtedly the world's first pregnant rabbi in a pulpit during the spring of 1976, continuing in that office after the birth of her son—by no means an easy juggling of both pleasure and responsibility. Laura Geller, ordained at Hebrew Union College in New York in 1975, became the first woman rabbi to serve as Hillel director at the University of Southern California in Los Angeles. Lynn Gottlieb is the first to await Conservative certification with some other "firsts" to her credit: her remarkable work in introducing new sign language into liturgy and rituals for the deaf, incorporating that language into the series of theater and dance pieces on biblical women—a form of "modern" *midrash*—performed by the traveling Bat Kol group that she has organized.

Thirty years ago, Mordecai Kaplan called attention to the necessity for woman's attainment of equal status with men in Judaism, an attainment that he emphasized must come about "through her own efforts and initiative."

Twenty years earlier, Martha Neumark's efforts had failed. A unique talent had not met its moment in time. "Even had a position been assigned me," she wrote in 1925, "I doubt whether any congregation would have accepted a woman to officiate at high holiday services."

And even today, many are reluctant to accord the woman rabbi the kind of recognition she has earned. More and more congregations, particularly in Reform and Reconstructionist movements, accept the idea of woman as rabbi intellectually, Sandy Sasso and others have observed, but have not yet fully endorsed that acceptance emotionally. The Jewish Theological Seminary's reluctance to act on the recommendations of the Rabbinical Assembly's Study Commission for the admission of women to its rabbinical school further underscores that resistance.

Nonetheless, more than half a century after Martha Neumark so poignantly recorded so total a resistance to the acceptance of a woman officiating at high holidays, women rabbis delivered the Kol Nidre sermon (a high point of high holiday services) to congregations in New York and Cincinnati and California.

The beginning.

Notes and Sources

Introduction

1. From "The Politics of Rape: A Selected History" by Roslyn Lacks. Reprinted by permission of *The Village Voice*. Copyright © The Village Voice, Inc., 1971.

1. Glimpses and Revelations

1. Moses Maimonides, *Guide to the Perplexed* (Chicago: University of Chicago Press, 1963).

2. The *Shulchan Aruch*, Code of Jewish Law: four-volume edition by Joseph Karo with glosses by Moses Isserlies: available only in Hebrew.

3. Direct quotes are from Code of Jewish Law, *Kitzur* (abridged) *Shulchan Aruch* by Solomon Ganzfried, trans. Hyman E. Goldin (New York: Hebrew Publishing Company, 1961).

4. *Even ha-Ezer* 25:2, as quoted by Louis Jacobs, *What Does Judaism Say About?* (New York: Quadrangle Books, 1973).

5. *The Woman's Bible* by Elizabeth Cady Stanton, originally published by European Publishing Company, New York, 1898. Reissued by the Seattle Coalition Task Force on Women and Religion, Seattle, 1974.

6. *The Woman's Bible*, Editor's Preface, p. vi.

2. Origins

1. Commentary by S. R. Driver in *Pentateuch and Haftorah*, ed. by Dr. J. H. Hertz (London: Soncino Press), pp. 9, 21 ff.

2. Louis Ginzberg, *The Legends of the Jews* (Philadelphia: Jewish Publication Society of America, 1925), Vol. 5, p. 115.

3. J.b. Sirach, Si. 25:24, Apocrypha.

4. Kikuyu legends have been recorded by Jomo Kenyatta in *Facing Mt. Kenya: The Tribal Life of Kikuyu* (New York: Vintage Press, Paperback, 1976) and in *My People of Kikuyu* (London: Oxford University Press, 1966).

5. For stories of the Ona Indians and Ona demonology, see Joseph Campbell, *The Masks of God: Primitive Mythology* (New York: Viking Compass Ed., 1970), pp. 245–50, 315–17.

6. For background on the Dogon of West Africa, see Marcel Griaule, *Conversations with Ogotomelli: An Introduction to Dogon Religious Ideas* (New York: Oxford University Press, 1965).

7. Samuel Noah Kramer, *Mythologies of the Ancient World* (Garden City, N.Y.: Doubleday & Company/Anchor Books, 1961), p. 103.

8. *Sumerian Paradise Myth of Enki and Ninhursag*. ANET (Ancient Near Eastern Texts), ed. J. B. Pritchard (Princeton, N.J.: Princeton University Press, 1955; 1969, 2nd rev. ed. with Supplement).

9. Theodore H. Gaster, *Myth, Legend, and Custom in the Old Testament*, with chapters from Sir James Frazier (New York: Harper & Row, 1975), Vol. 1, p. 21.

3. Eve

1. See Raphael Patai, *Sex and Family in the Bible and the Middle East* (Garden City, N.Y.: Doubleday & Company, 1959), p. 155.

2. For Midrashic sources, see Louis Ginzberg, Vol. 1, pp. 65–87.

3. Gaster, op. cit., Vol. 1, pp. 51–55.

4. Ginzberg, op. cit., Vol. 1, p. 67. See also Vol. 5, p. 89 for a contrary view that man's intelligence matures more quickly because he has the opportunity denied woman to develop his mind in school.

5. Robert Graves and Raphael Patai, *Hebrew Myths: The Book of Genesis* (New York: McGraw-Hill, 1963), p. 69.

6. Disparities between Genesis I and Genesis II have been widely discussed in a variety of sources. In addition to those mentioned above, see also E. A. Speiser, Genesis, *The Anchor Bible* (Garden City, N.Y.: Doubleday & Company, 1964).

7. Graves and Patai, op. cit., p. 66.

8. "Better death than that green slobber!" from *The Bride of Frankenstein*, in Edward Fields' *Variety Photoplays* (New York: Grove Press, 1967), pp. 22–24.

9. Ginzberg, op. cit., Vol. 1, p. 68.

10. Nechama Liebowitz, Sidra B'reshit 5716: *Studies in the Weekly Sidra*, trans. Aryeh Newman, Jerusalem.

4. The Demon Lilith

1. Theodore H. Gaster, *A Canaanite Magical Text*, ORIENTALIA, Vol. 11, pp. 41–79.

2. In the third century this story seems to have been known in a somewhat different form, without the demonic Lilith. This version speaks of a "first Eve," created independently of Adam and unrelated to Cain and Abel, who quarreled for possession of her, whereupon God turned her back into dust. (From Gen. Rab. XXII, 7 as cited in Gerson Scholem's *On the Kabbalah and Its Symbolism* [New York: Schocken Books, 1965]).

3. Gershon Scholem, *On the Kabbalah and Its Symbolism*.

4. For material on Wachnacht and medieval practices to ward off Lilith, see Joshua Trachtenberg, *Jewish Magic and Superstition* (Philadelphia; Meridian Books and the Jewish Publication Society of America, 1961).

5. Together with divinity student Karen Bloomquist, Professor of Theology Sister Margaret Early, and feminist Catholic theologian Elizabeth Farians, in *Religion and Sexism*, ed. Rosemary R. Ruether (New York: Simon and Schuster, 1974).

5. The Suppressed Goddess

1. Alexander Heidel, *The Babylonian Genesis* (Chicago: University of Chicago Press, 1942), pp. 16–36.
2. Pritchard, *Anet*, 3rd ed., 1969: Tablet VI, p. 503.
3. *Nergal and Ereshkigal*, pp. 509–12. Also, Kramer, op. cit., pp. 124–25.
4. From available texts, it is not clear whether Nergal repeats his visit to the netherworld on two different occasions—the second following the insult to Namtar—or whether Nergal's appearance, disappearance, and reappearance occur during the course of one descent.
5. Note the biblical plural of *el*ohim to designate the early Israelite god.

6. Woman in the Bible

1. Ex. 15:21.
2. Jg. 5:7.
3. Jg. 4:16.
4. Jg. 4:9.
5. Ginzberg, op. cit., Vol. 4, pp. 34–39.
6. Gn. 2:17–18.
7. "Or to touch" is Eve's elaboration on God's decree.
8. Gn. 3:14–15. The newly declared enmity between the snake and woman decreed by Yahweh suggests an earlier relationship or mythology in which the snake is linked to the woman or goddess. (See preceding chapter.)
9. The cleavage between mind and body reached its culmination in the monumental works of the medieval Maimonides, who clearly associated the higher spheres of mind and intellect with man, while reserving the baser realms of flesh and matter for women. (See pp. 1–4.)
10. From "Testament of Reuben," in the *Testaments of the Twelve Patriarchs;* the Watchers are the B'nai Elohim (c. 100 B.C.E.—date is problematic).
11. See Pauline epistles, letters from Timothy, Ezra's Apocalypse, writings of Clement, etc. Also Midrashim on Eve, Chap. 3.
12. Phyllis Trible, "Depatriarchalizing in Biblical Interpretation," *The Jewish Woman, New Perspectives*, ed. Elizabeth Koltun (New York: Schocken Books, 1976). See also Trible's comments on earlier sections of Genesis (the Creation story) and its relationship to Song of Songs, as well as the ascription of maternal attributes to the Hebrew deity.
13. Phyllis Bird, "Images of Women in the Old Testament," *Religion and Sexism*, ed. Rosemary R. Ruether (New York: Simon and Schuster, 1974).

14. Gn. 17:15–16.
15. Gn. 24:11–14.
16. Gn. 24:67.
17. Gn. 29:11–12.
18. Gn. 29:18–19. Here Jacob's seven years of work evidently substitute for the traditional bride-price or *mohar* paid to the father of the bride.
19. The mandrake is almost universally credited with magic powers as an aphrodisiac and antidote to barrenness. The Hebrew word comes from a verbal root meaning "to love"; its English counterpart, the "love apple."
20. Later commentaries attempt to ameliorate the rivalry between the sisters, as well as the directness with which sexuality is expressed in the biblical text. (See pp. 105–6.)
21. The theft of the teraphim has given rise to wild speculation over the centuries. One view has it that Rachel could not part from her association with polytheistic belief; another piously claims that Rachel stole the gods so that Laban would not be tempted by them, that Jacob smashed them to pieces, etc. The point of the theft—consistent with the biblical text and recent archaeological scholarship—has at last been clarified by a cuneiform text from the Mesopotamian city of Nuzu, dated c. 1400 B.C. According to local usage, a man laying claim to a portion of an estate had to be in possession of that estate's household gods. Rachel's purpose in taking the teraphim, consonant with the flow of the narrative, is to secure that right for Jacob. See Gaster, op. cit., p. 200.
22. Ginzberg, op. cit., Vol. 1, pp. 354–61.
23. Antiquities, Book I, pp. 285–355.
24. Ginzberg, op. cit.
25. Ginzberg, op. cit., Vol. 4, pp. 307–10.
26. Rivkah Schaerf Kluger, *Women in the Old Testament* (1958), Jung Library, from lectures in Los Angeles (1955). Also lectures for Jung Society, New York (1976).
27. Some of my particular arguments with Kluger's thesis center on its assumption that all progress inevitably leads to growth—that optimistic evolutionary *Zeitgeist* of the nineteenth century that runs counter to the nuclear pessimism of the twentieth—as well as the romanticization of "mother religions," a certain patriarchal bias, the fact that the thesis is particularly forced in the analysis of Miriam and does not at all account for Deborah.
28. Again, the teraphim are an otiose survival of polytheistic practice, no longer informed by belief.
29. Isaac Mendelsohn, "The Family in the Ancient Near East," *The Biblical Archaeologist, Reader 3* (Garden City, N.Y.: Doubleday & Company/Anchor Books, 1970).
30. W. Robertson Smith, *Kinship and Marriage in Early Arabia.*
31. Roland de Vaux, *Ancient Israel* (New York: McGraw-Hill Book Company, 1965), pp. 19–20. Needless to say, patriarchal assumptions about prehistorical organization are as easily open to cultural or temperamental bias as are matriarchal ones.
32. The same penalty is imposed if an ox gores man, woman, or child (Ex. 21:28–31); just as the same verdict of death is executed upon man

and woman guilty of adultery (Lv. 20:10). Equal respect is commanded for both mother and father, etc.

33. Mendelsohn, op. cit.

34. Also Is. 50:1; Jr. 3:8. See Mendelsohn, op. cit.

35. J. B. Pritchard, Anet; *Aramaic Papyri from Elephantine,* Marriage Contract (427 B.C.E.).

36. De Vaux, op. cit., p. 27.

37. *Laws of Ur-Nammu.* Anet, 1969.

38. *Mesopotamian Legal Documents.* Anet, pp. 543, 545–46.

39. Ginzberg, op. cit., Vol. 3, p. 391.

40. Jb. 42:13–15.

41. Jdt. 8:7; 16:24.

7. Woman in Exile

1. *Halacha,* usually interpreted as "way of life," comes from the Hebrew root *halach* (to go or follow), referring to those talmudic principles that guide one's behavior. Despite the concept of movement embodied in the very word itself, some suggest that the dynamic aspect of *halacha* has been sorely neglected in the Modern Era—that *halacha,* in fact, seems to have come to a halt, rendering it particularly difficult at this point in time, so crucial to women, to introduce change.

2. Adin Steinsalz, *The Essential Talmud* (New York: Basic Books, 1976), p. 264.

3. Ibid., p. 9.

4. The supreme legislative and judicial authority of the Jewish people, the Sanhedrin, was abolished by the Roman general Gammus in the middle of the first century B.C.E., reinstituted, and once again banned in 71 C.E. following the fall of Jerusalem. Reorganized once more by R. Gamaliel of Yavneh, the Sanhedrin flourished until the age of the Exilarchs, about the sixth century C.E.

5. Ned. 50 (b): "How did Akiva get rich?" . . . In addition to the wealth he shares with Rachel's father, Akiva receives a loan from a wealthy matron. When he is unable to repay the debt, the matron, moved by Akiva's spiritual force, forgoes payment and bestows more gifts upon him. Yet more wealth comes his way when he marries the "wife of Turnusrufus," identified in the footnote: "Tineus Rufus, a Roman governor of Judea. After her husband's death she became a convert and married Akiva, bringing him in much wealth." See also AZ 20 (a), in which the gemara on a mishnah referring to Palestinian agricultural customs elicits the following: "Likewise when R. Akiva saw the wife of the Wicked Tyranus Rufus, he spat, then laughed, then wept . . . 'laughed,' because he foresaw that she would become a proselyte and that he would take her to wife . . ."

6. Git. 9, 10.

7. AZ 18 (b): "Said she to her husband: 'I am ashamed to have my sister placed in a brothel.'" Meir poses as a customer; the sister puts him off by claiming menstruation, then further deflects him, "There are here many, many prettier than I . . ." Assured of her purity, Meir secures her release.

8. Ber. 10 (a).

9. Midrash on Proverbs 31:1.

10. The interdict against speaking with women is recorded in Ab. I, 5.

11. bEruvin 53a.

12. Circumstantially or not, Beruriah is lauded for her scholarship in the third century during a period of relative calm in Jewish history, coinciding with Judah ha Nasi's observation, "Woman's intelligence is greater than man's."

13. bPesachim 62b.

14. Ginzberg, op. cit., Vol. 6, p. 377.

15. B. Megillah 14b.

16. Paula Hyman, "The Other Half," *The Jewish Woman: New Perspectives,* ed. Elizabeth Koltun (New York: Schocken Books, 1976).

8. Blood, Breath, and Voice

1. Talmud Sotah 48a, Ketubah 70a.

2. Is. 24:7–13.

3. Is. 47:2, 3.

4. Nb. 5:12: "If any man's wife go aside (*sisteh*) . . ." The woman (*sotah,* derived from the verb *satah*) suspected by her husband of infidelity has to submit to the ordeal of drinking the bitter water to establish her innocence.

5. Sotah 7a, 15b, 7a, 9a.

6. Ibid.

7. Those women in Exodus who refused to follow the example of the men in worshiping the golden calf.

8. Sotah 47a.

9. Ho. 4:13–15.

10. Ginzberg, op. cit.

11. Theodor H. Gaster, op. cit., p. 20.

12. Ezk. 24:6–8.

13. Niddah 20b.

14. Ibid.

15. *The First Jewish Catalogue,* p. 170.

16. Ibid.

17. Dead Sea Scrolls, Qumran, Cave IV.

18. pSotah 1, 16b, 28. See also Babylonian Talmud, bBer. 24a: "A woman's hair is an immoral thing."

19. Besiq. R 26 (129b).

20. James G. Frazer, *THE GOLDEN BOUGH: Creation and Evolution in Primitive Cosmogonies* (London: Macmillan, 1935).

21. Israel Abrahams, *Jewish Life in the Middle Ages* (Philadelphia: Jewish Publication Society of America, 1958), pp. 15–34.

22. Anne Lapidus Lerner, "Who Hast Not Made Me a Man," *The Movement for Equal Rights for Women in American Jewry* (New York: American Jewish Committee Publications, 1977).

23. For Dr. Ostow's paper, as well as the comments of other psychiatrists and scholars—some of whom disagree with him—see "Women and Change in Jewish Law," *Conservative Judaism,* Fall 1974.

9. Unveilings

1. Mordecai Kaplan, "The Status of the Woman in Jewish Law," *Future of the American Jew* (New York: Macmillan, 1948).

2. As quoted by Anne Lapidus Lerner in "Who Hast Not Made Me a Man."

3. See *Final Report of the Commission for the Study of the Ordination of Women as Rabbis,* January 30, 1979 (available from the Rabbinical Assembly). The report also includes minority opinion. See also discussion of the issue in *Moment* magazine, May 1979, and The New York *Times,* January 31, 1979.

Bibliography

Albright, William Foxwell. *From the Stone Age to Christianity*. Garden City, N.Y.: Doubleday/Anchor Press, 1957.

——. *Yahweh and the Gods of Canaan*. Garden City, N.Y.: Doubleday & Company, 1968.

Bachofen, J. J. *Myth, Religion and Mother Right: Selected Writings*. Princeton, N.J.: Bollingen Series, Princeton University Press, 1967.

Brandon, S. G. F. *Creation Legends of the Ancient Near East*. London: Hodder & Stoughton, Ltd., 1963.

Briffault, Robert. *Mothers: A Study of the Origins of Sentiments and Institutions*, 3 vols. New York: Johnson, 1969.

Buttrick, George, ed. *Interpreter's Dictionary of the Bible*, Vol. 1, *Creation*. New York: Abingdon Press, 1962.

Campbell, Joseph. *The Masks of God. Primitive Mythology*. New York: Viking Press, 1959.

——. *The Masks of God. Oriental Mythology*. New York: Viking Press, 1962.

——. *The Masks of God. Occidental Mythology*. New York: Viking Press, 1964.

——. *Hero with a Thousand Faces*. New York: Meridian, 1956.

Cassuto, Umberto. *The Goddess Anath*. Jerusalem: Hebrew University Press, 1971.

Conybeare, F. C. (trans.). "The Testament of Solomon," *Jewish Quarterly Review*, Vol. XI, 1899. New York: Ktav Publishing House, 1966.

Eliade, Mircea. *Myth and Reality*. New York: Harper and Row, 1963.

——. *Myths, Dreams and Mysteries: The Encounter Between Contemporary Faiths and Archaic Realities*. New York: Harper and Row, 1960.

——. *Patterns in Comparative Religion*. New York: Signet/NAL, 1977. Encyclopedia Judaica.

France, Anatole. "The Daughter of Lilith," *Balthazar*. London: John Lane Co., 1909.

Frankfort, Henri. *Ancient Egyptian Religion*. New York: Columbia University Press, 1948.

Frazer, James G. *The Golden Bough.* London: Macmillan, 1935.
——. *Creation and Evolution in Primitive Cosmogonies and Other Pieces.* London: Macmillan, 1936.
Gaster, Theodor H. "A Canaanite Magical Text," *Orientalia,* Vol. 11, 1942, pp. 41–79.
——. *Myth, Legend and Custom in the Old Testament,* Vol. 2. New York: Harper and Row, 1969.
——. *The Oldest Stories in the World.* New York: Beacon Press, 1958.
——. *Thespis.* New York: Schuman, 1950.
Ginzberg, Louis. *The Legends of the Jews.* Vols. I and V. Philadelphia: The Jewish Publication Society of America, 1925.
Gordon, Cyrus. *Before the Bible.* New York: Books for Libraries Essay Reprint Series, 1973. Reprint of 1962 edition.
Gourmont, Remy de. *Lilith* (A Play), trans. from the French by John Heard. Boston: John W. Luce, 1946.
Graves, Robert. *The White Goddess: A Historical Grammar of Poetic Myth.* New York: Farrar, Strauss & Giroux, 1966.
Graves, Robert, and Patai, Raphael. *Hebrew Myths.* New York: McGraw-Hill, 1963.
Gray, John. *Near Eastern Mythology.* London: Hamlyn, 1969.
Griaule, Marcel. *Conversations with Ogotomelli: An Introduction to Dogon Religious Ideas.* New York: Oxford University Press, 1965.
Gunkel, Hermann. *The Legends of Genesis: The Biblical Saga and History.* New York: Schocken Books, 1966.
Gurney, O. R. *The Hittites.* New York: Penguin, 1961.
Harding, M. Esther. *The Parental Image: Its Injury and Reconstruction.* New York: G. P. Putnam's Sons, 1965.
——. *The Way of All Women.* New York: G. P. Putnam's Sons, 1970.
——. *Women's Mysteries, Ancient and Modern.* New York: G. P. Putnam's Sons, 1972.
Heidel, Alexander. *The Babylonian Genesis.* Chicago: University of Chicago Press, 1942.
——. *The Gilgamesh Epic and Old Testament Parallels.* Chicago: University of Chicago Press, 1949.
James, Edwin. *The Cult of the Mother Goddess, An Archaeological and Documentary Study.* London: Thames & Hudson, 1959.
Kenyatta, Jomo. *Facing Mount Kenya: The Tribal Life of Gikuyu.* New York: Vintage Press Paperback, 1976.
——. *My People of Kikuyu.* London: Oxford University Press, 1966.
Kramer, Samuel Noah. *History Begins at Sumer: Twenty-seven*

Firsts in Man's Recorded History. Garden City, N.Y.: Doubleday/Anchor Press, 1959.

——. *Mythologies of the Ancient World*. Garden City, N.Y.: Doubleday/Anchor Press, 1961.

——. *The Sacred Marriage Rite*. Bloomington: Indiana University Press, 1969.

——. *The Sumerians: Their History, Culture and Character*. Chicago: University of Chicago Press, 1963.

Langdon, Stephen H. *Semitic Mythology* (Mythology of All Races Series: Vol. 5). Reprint of 1932 ed. New York: Cooper Square Press, 1970.

MacDonald, George. *Lilith*. Orig. pub. 1858. New York: Ballantine Books, 1969.

Maimonides, Moses. *Guide to the Perplexed*. Chicago: University of Chicago Press, 1963.

Malinowski, Bronislaw. *Sex, Culture and Myth*. New York: Harcourt, Brace & World, 1962.

——. *Magic, Science and Religion*. Garden City, N.Y.: Doubleday/Anchor Press, 1954.

Mead, Margaret. *Male and Female: A Study of the Sexes in a Changing World*. New York: Greenwood, 1977.

Neumann, Erich. *The Great Mother*. Princeton, N.J.: Bollingen Series, Princeton University Press, 1963.

——. *The Origins and History of Consciousness*. Princeton, N.J.: Bollingen Series, Princeton University Press, 1970.

Neusner, Jacob. *Understanding Rabbinic Judaism*. New York: Ktav Publishing House, 1974.

Patai, Raphael. *The Hebrew Goddess*. New York: Ktav Publishing House, 1967.

——. *Myth and Modern Man*. New York: Prentice-Hall, 1972.

Pomeroy, Sarah B. *Goddesses, Whores, Wives and Slaves*. New York: Schocken Books, 1975.

Pritchard, James B., ed. *Ancient Near Eastern Texts Relating to the Old Testament with Supplement*. 3rd ed. Princeton, N.J.: Princeton University Press, 1969.

——. *Palestinian Figurines in Relation to Certain Goddesses Known Through Literature*. American Oriental Society, 1943.

Rank, Otto. *The Myth of the Birth of the Hero and Other Essays*. New York: Random House, 1959.

Rappoport, A. S. *Myth and Legend in Ancient Israel*. Vol. 1. New York: Ktav Publishing House, 1966.

Reik, Theodore. *The Creation of Woman*. New York: McGraw-Hill, 1960.

——. *Myth and Guilt*. New York: Braziller, 1957.

——. *Pagan Rites in Judaism*. New York: Farrar, Strauss, 1964.

Rubenstein, Richard L. *The Religious Imagination.* New York: Bobbs Merrill, 1968.

Scharf-Kluger, Rivkah: *Psyche and Bible: Three Old Testament Themes.* ed. James Hillon. New York: Spring Publications, 1973.

———. *Women in the Old Testament.* Unpublished manuscript.

Schauss, Hayyim. *The Lifetime of a Jew.* Cincinnati: Union of American Hebrew Congregations, 1950.

Scholem, Gershom G. *On the Kabbalah and Its Symbolism.* New York: Schocken Books, 1965.

Siegel, R., and M. & S. Strassfeld, ed. *The First Jewish Catalog.* Philadelphia: Jewish Publication Society of America, 1973.

Singer, Isidor, ed. *The Jewish Encyclopedia.* New York: Ktav Publishing House, 1964.

Smith, Robertson W. *The Religion of the Semites: The Fundamental Institutions.* New York: Schocken Books, 1972.

———. *Kinship and Marriage in Early Arabia.* New York: Beacon Press, 1971.

Soncino Hebrew-English Talmud. New York: Bloch Publishing Company, Inc.

Trachtenberg, Joshua. *Jewish Magic and Superstition.* Philadelphia: Meridian Books and Jewish Publication Society of America, 1961.

Von Franz, Marie. *Creation Myths.* New York: Spring Publications, 1972.

Woolley, C. Leonard. *The Sumerians.* New York: Norton, 1965.

Index